A Lifetime
of Peace

A Lifetime
of Peace

*Essential Writings by and
about Thich Nhat Hanh*

EDITED BY JENNIFER SCHWAMM WILLIS

Marlowe & Company

A LIFETIME OF PEACE: *Essential Writings by and about Thich Nhat Hanh*

Compilation copyright © 2003 by Jennifer Schwamm Willis
Introductions copyright © 2003 by Jennifer Schwamm Willis

Published by
Marlowe & Company
An Imprint of Avalon Publishing Group Incorporated
161 William Street, 16th Floor
New York, NY 10038

Book Design: Michael Walters

Illustration by Cole Wheeler

Library of Congress Control Number: 2003110020

ISBN: 1-56924-441-3

Printed in the United States of America

Distributed by Publishers Group West

For Judy Mello Schwamm
A true bodhisattva whose love and
compassion light my way

CONTENTS

Introduction

> The source of a true smile is an awak-
> ened mind.
> —Thich Nhat Hanh

*T*hich Nhat Hanh has spent a lifetime working for peace. His work for peace begins very simply, with mindfulness and a smile. He was born in 1926 in central Vietnam, and became a monk at the age of 16. By age 30 he had written many books and articles, edited several journals, and founded the An Quang Buddhist Institute, an important center for Buddhist studies in South Vietnam. He also had begun to practice what he called "engaged Buddhism" applying Buddhist teachings to social problems.

Thich Nhat Hanh went to the United States in 1960. He stayed for three years studying at Princeton University and teaching at Columbia University. He returned to Vietnam in 1963 to join other Buddhist monks in their non-violent efforts to stop the war in their country. He created the School of Youth for Social Service to train young monks, nuns, and lay students to assist rural communities in the building of schools and clinics. The School later helped rural Vietnamese to rebuild their war-ravaged villages. Thich Nhat Hanh during this period also founded a publishing house, Van Hanh Buddhist University and The Order of Interbeing, based upon his fourteen precepts of engaged Buddhism.

Invited by the Fellowship of Reconciliation, he returned to the United States in 1966 to advocate for a unilateral cease-fire and withdrawal of all U.S. troops from Vietnam. Following this visit, the South Vietnamese government denounced his activism on behalf of peace and refused him re-entry to his native land. Shortly thereafter he was granted asylum by France. Martin Luther King, Jr., nominated him for the Nobel Peace Prize in 1967, and in 1969 Thich Nhat Hanh organized the Buddhist Delegation to the Paris Peace Talks. Thich Nhat Hanh in 1982 founded Plum Village, a Buddhist retreat center in southern France where thousands of people from around the world have spent time in study and meditation.

A small, gentle man, Thich Nhat Hanh has been a source of inspiration to other men and women who have worked for peace and justice. They include Catholic priest and writer Thomas Merton, who wrote of Thich Nhat Hahn that "he is more my brother than many who are nearer to me in race and nationality, because he and I see things the same way." Martin Luther King, Jr., nominating Thich Nhat Hahn for the 1967 Nobel Peace Prize, wrote that "I know Thich Nhat Hanh and am privileged to call him my friend. . . . He is a holy man, for he is humble and devout. He is a scholar of immense capacity. . . . He is also a poet of superb clarity and human compassion." Father Daniel Berrigan, an important anti-war activist during and after the Vietnam War, wrote about the several weeks he spent with Thich Nhat Hanh in Paris during the mid-seventies: "Every evening we prayed together in silence, for the space of a candle, at Nhat Hanh's gentle leading." More recently, Neta Golan, a young Israeli peace activist said ". . . when I met Thay [Thich Nhat Hanh] I thought about going to study with him because of the peace he radiated. I'd never seen that in a human being before, only read about it in books. And I appreciate the fact that he's a peace activist. Being in the world, I admire that. He's not closing his eyes."

Here is a brief passage from Thich Nhat Hanh's 1988 book, *The Heart of Understanding.*

> If you are a poet you will see clearly that there is a cloud floating in this sheet of paper. Without a cloud, there will be no rain; without rain, the trees cannot grow; and without trees, we cannot make paper. The cloud is essential for the paper to exist. If the cloud is not here, the sheet of paper cannot be here either. So we can say that the cloud and the paper inter-are. . . . You cannot point out one thing that is not here [in this sheet of paper]—time, space, the earth, the rain, the minerals in the soil, the sunshine, the cloud, the river, the heat. Everything coexists with this sheet of paper. . . . This sheet of paper is, because everything else is.

Engaged Buddhism flows out of a belief in the web

of Interbeing between all nature's elements. Interbeing provides the foundation for non-violent social
action by revealing our connections to others and to
the natural world. If we wound others, we wound ourselves. If we deny others freedom, we lose our freedom.
If we work to bring them peace and joy, we will have
peace and joy.

How can we live mindfully amid the routines of our
daily lives, while acting responsibly toward the world
community? How do we integrate local action with
global action? Thich Nhat Hanh would say that such work
begins with a breath and a smile. If we can breathe and be
here now, we can discover the truth that we already know,
including the truth of Interbeing. The decisions we
make from this place, a place without fear, a place of
love, will lead us in the direction of peace.

Thich Nhat Hanh writes,

> Our true home is the present moment. To
> live in the present moment is a miracle. The
> miracle is not to walk on water. The miracle is
> to walk on the green earth, in the present
> moment, to appreciate the peace and beauty
> that are available now. Peace is all around us—
> in the world and in nature—and within us—in
> our bodies and in our spirits. Once we learn
> to touch this peace we will be healed and
> transformed. It's not a matter of faith; it's a
> matter of practice.

We don't need to be Buddhists to follow the teachings of Thich Nhat Hanh—or at least we don't have to

stop being Jews or Christians or Muslims or atheists. He is the first to acknowledge that there are many roads:

> Buddhism is more of a way of life than a religion. It is like a fruit. You may like a number of fruits, like bananas, oranges, mandarins, and so on. You are committed to eating these fruits. But then someone tells you that there is a fruit called mango and it would be wonderful for you to try that fruit. It will be a pity if you don't know what a mango is. But eating a mango does not require you to abandon your habit of eating oranges. Why not try it? You may like it a lot. Buddhism is a kind of mango, you see—a way of life, an experience that is worth trying. It is open for everyone. You can continue to be a Jew or a Catholic while enjoying Buddhism. I think that's a wonderful thing.

Thich Nhat Hanh's message can help us to see the world and our place in it with clarity. He can help us to stop seeing the world as a place against which we must defend ourselves. We can begin to understand that we depend upon each other for our being. His words help us to find our home here, in this world and this moment, among each other.

—*Jennifer Willis*

from Fragrant Palm Leaves:

JOURNALS 1962–1966

by *Thich Nhat Hanh*

Thich Nhat Hanh studied and taught comparative religion at Princeton and Columbia during the early 1960's,
while the war in his native Vietnam was escalating. This
passage is from the journal he kept during that difficult
period.

23 December 1962
Princeton, New Jersey

*T*oday I received more than thirty letters, for-
warded from New York. The only ones from
Vietnam were a card from Hue Duong and a
letter from Phuong. The others were Christmas cards
from American friends. In America, people spend a fair
amount of money sending Christmas cards. Each family
keeps a list of friends, and then buys hundreds of cards,
signs each one, places them all in envelopes, and

addresses and stamps each one. If you send cards to only ten friends, you have time to select a special card for each person. You even have time to write ten short notes. But when your list includes hundreds of friends and acquaintances, you have to buy large boxes of identical cards and sign and address them assembly-line style. What is most important, apparently, is not to forget anyone. The list changes over the years—one friend dies and another behaves poorly, so that "diplomatic relations" are severed. And new friends are added to the list. Some Americans assume I must be sad, spending the holidays alone at Princeton. But I'm not sad at all. In fact, I had to refuse several invitations to visit friends' families so I could cherish this time for myself. It is very peaceful and comfortable here. I think about those people who are homeless and without heat, people who have little reason to celebrate.

In Vietnam, the war is escalating. Our people are caught between a hammer and an anvil. We've lost so much already. The country has been divided in two and engulfed in flames. Even Phuong Boi is fading into the fog. But as long as we have each other, we can never be truly alone. We want to stand with those who have been abandoned. I want others, at least occasionally, to turn their thoughts to those who suffer—to think about them but not pity them. Those who suffer do not want pity. They want love and respect.

During the Christmas season in America, many organizations make donations to those in need. People send contributions for orphans, widows, and the poor without ever seeing their faces. But a direct encounter is necessary to understand another's suffering. Only understanding leads to love. Huge sums of money and material goods are distributed to the poor during this season, but these gifts are largely the fruit of pity and not love. One organization distributes several thousand pairs of shoes to poor children. Among those who donate a few dollars to pay for a pair of shoes, I doubt that many actually envision the happiness on the face of the child when she receives the shoes, or even envision the shoes they are buying for her.

Last year at this time, I went shopping with Kenji, a young Japanese student. On Christmas Eve, the stores were packed with last-minute shoppers, everyone rushing about, anxious to get home on time for Christmas get-togethers. Kenji and I had to buy enough food to last a week, since the stores here are closed from Christmas until the first of the year. The sight of two young Asians grocery-shopping on Christmas Eve moved several people to pity. One woman asked if there was something she could do to help us. We thanked her and wished her a Merry Christmas. The checkout girl, bright and cheery, looked at us warmly and wished us a Merry Christmas. Everyone assumed we were lonely. It was Christmas, and we were so far from home. But since neither of us are Christian, we didn't have warm memories of past Christmases to make us feel lonely. In Saigon, pine boughs, Christmas cards, gold ribbons, and other Christmas trappings do announce the season. Even at Phuong Boi we celebrated Christmas Eve by staying up late decorating a Christmas tree. But we didn't experience the deep feelings our Christian friends have. Perhaps it is because we respect Christ as a great teacher but don't look on him as God. The same is true of Buddha. We respect him as a great teacher, but we don't

worship him as a god. The holiday we feel most enthu-
siastic about in Vietnam is Têt.

Still, when Christmas Eve arrived in Princeton, we
noticed how desolate Brown Hall felt. It was cold but
not snowing, so we decided to walk into town. We
strolled along the empty streets. All the houses and
stores were closed tight. Somehow, it evoked in me the
feeling of New Year's Eve back home and made me feel
homesick. We returned to Campus Center a bit melancholy, drank some tea, talked, and then watched TV.
It's funny how much our surroundings influence our
emotions. Our joys and sorrows, likes and dislikes are
colored by our environment so much that often we just
let our surroundings dictate our course. We go along
with "public" feelings until we no longer even know
our own true aspirations. We become a stranger to
ourselves, molded entirely by society. Our friends at
Phuong Boi always stood up to social conformity and
resisted society's molds. Naturally, we met with opposition, both internal and external. Sometimes I feel
caught between two opposing selves—the "false self"
imposed by society and what I would call my "true self."
How often we confuse the two and assume society's
mold to be our true self. Battles between our two selves
rarely result in a peaceful reconciliation. Our mind
becomes a battlefield on which the Five Aggregates—the
form, feelings, perceptions, mental formations, and
consciousness of our being—are strewn about like
debris in a hurricane. Trees topple, branches snap,
houses crash. These are our loneliest moments. Yet
every time we survive such a storm, we grow a little.
Without storms like these, I would not be who I am
today. But I rarely hear such a storm coming until it is

already upon me. It seems to appear without warning, as though treading silently on silk slippers. I know it must have been brewing a long time, simmering in my own thoughts and mental formations, but when such a frenzied hurricane strikes, nothing outside can help. I am battered and torn apart, and I am also saved.

I passed through such a storm this past autumn. It began in October. At first it seemed like a passing cloud. But after several hours, I began to feel my body turning to smoke and floating away. I became a faint wisp of a cloud. I had always thought of myself as a solid entity, and suddenly I saw that I'm not solid at all. This wasn't philosophical or even an enlightenment experience. It was just an ordinary impression, completely ordinary. I saw that the entity I had taken to be "me" was really a fabrication. My true nature, I realized, was much more real, both uglier and more beautiful than I could have imagined.

The feeling began shortly before eleven o'clock at night on October first. I was browsing on the eleventh floor of Butler Library. I knew the library was about to close, and I saw a book that concerned the area of my research. I slid it off the shelf and held it in my two hands. It was large and heavy. I read that it had been published in 1892, and it was donated to the Columbia Library the same year. On the back cover was a slip of paper that recorded the names of borrowers and the dates they took it out of the library. The first time it had been borrowed was in 1915, the second time was in 1932. I would be the third. Can you imagine? I was only the third borrower, on October 1, 1962. For seventy years, only two other people had stood in the same spot I now stood, pulled the book from the shelf, and decided to check it out. I was overcome with the wish to meet those two people. I don't know why, but I wanted to hug them. But they had vanished, and I, too, I will soon disappear. Two points on the same straight line will never meet. I was able to encounter two people in space, but not in time.

I stood quietly for a few minutes, holding the book in my hands. Then I remembered what Anton Cerbu had said the day before, when we were discussing how to research Vietnamese Buddhism. He told me that I was still young. I didn't believe him. I feel as though I've lived a long time and have seen so much of life. I'm almost thirty-six, which is not young. But that night, while standing among the stacks at Butler Library, I saw that I am neither young nor old, existent nor nonexistent. My friends know I can be as playful and mischievous as a child. I love to kid around and enter fully into the game of life. I also know what it is to get angry. And I know the pleasure of being praised. I am often on the verge of tears or laughter. But beneath all of these emotions, what else is there? How can I touch it? If there isn't anything, why would I be so certain that there is?

Still holding the book, I felt a glimmer of insight. I understood that I am empty of ideals, hopes, viewpoints, or allegiances. I have no promises to keep with others. In that moment, the sense of myself as an entity among other entities disappeared. I knew that this insight did not arise from disappointment, despair, fear, desire, or ignorance. A veil lifted silently and effortlessly. That is all. If you beat me, stone me, or even shoot me, everything that is considered to be "me" will disintegrate. Then, what is actually there will reveal itself—faint as smoke, elusive as emptiness, and yet neither smoke nor emptiness; neither ugly, nor not ugly; beautiful, yet not beautiful. It is like a shadow on a screen. At that moment, I had the deep feeling that I had *returned.* My clothes, my shoes, even the essence of my being had vanished, and I was carefree as a grasshopper pausing on a blade of grass. Like the grasshopper, I had no thoughts of the divine. The grasshopper's gods perceive form, sound, smell, taste, touch, and objects of mind. They know increasing and decreasing, defiled and immaculate, production and destruction. When a grasshopper sits on a blade of grass, he has no thought of separation, resistance, or blame. Human children prefer dragonflies whose wings and bellies are as red as chili peppers. But the green grasshopper blends completely with the green grass, and children rarely notice it. It neither retreats nor beckons. It knows nothing of philosophy or ideals. It is simply grateful for its ordinary life. Dash across the meadow, my dear friend, and greet yesterday's child. When you can't see me, you yourself will return. Even when your heart is filled with despair, you will find the same grasshopper on the same blade of grass.

Steve had left to spend a few days in Boston, and I was alone in our apartment. I left the bedroom door wide open day and night, like a prayer. What I was undergoing was neither happy nor sad. Some life dilemmas cannot be solved by study or rational thought. We just live with them, struggle with them, and become one with them. Such dilemmas are not in the realm of the intellect. They come from our feelings and our will, and they penetrate our subconscious and our body, down to the marrow of our bones. I became

a battlefield. I couldn't know until the storm was over
if I would survive, not in the sense of my physical life,
but in the deeper sense of my core self. I experienced
destruction upon destruction, and felt a tremendous
longing for the presence of those I love, even though I
knew that if they were present, I would have to chase
them away or run away myself.

When the storm finally passed, layers of inner
mortar lay crumbled. On the now deserted battlefield,
a few sunbeams peeked through the horizon, too weak
to offer any warmth to my weary soul. I was full of
wounds, yet experienced an almost thrilling sense of
aloneness. No one would recognize me in my new
manifestation. No one close to me would know it was I.
Friends want you to appear in the familiar form they
know. They want you to remain intact, the same. But
that isn't possible. How could we continue to live if
we were changeless? To live, we must die every
instant. We must perish again and again in the storms
that make life possible. It would be better, I thought,
if everyone cast me from their thoughts. I cannot be
a human being and, at the same time, be an
unchanging object of love or hatred, annoyance or
devotion. I must continue to grow. As a child, I always
outgrew the clothes my mother sewed for me. I can
preserve those garments, fragrant with childish inno-
cence and my mother's love, in a trunk for memory's
sake. But I must have new, and different clothes now to
fit who I have become. We must sew our own clothes
and not just accept society's ready-made suit. The
clothes I make for myself may not be stylish or even
accepted. But it is more than a matter of clothes. It is a
question of who I am as a person. I reject the yardstick

others use to measure me. I have a yardstick of my own, one I've discovered myself, even if I find myself in opposition to public opinion. I must be who I am. I cannot force myself back into the shell I've just broken out of. This is a source of great loneliness for me. Perhaps I could persuade my dearest friends to accompany me on my voyage through space, but it might be dizzying for them, and might even incite feelings of hatred or resentment. Would they force me to return to earth, back to the illusory plane of old hopes, desires, and values, all in the name of friendship? What good would that be for any of us?

That is why I want to burn down the huts where my friends dwell. I want to incite chaos to help them break through the shells that confine them. I want to smash the chains that bind them and topple the gods that restrain them. For us to grow, petty amusements or even sorrows must not dominate us. A free person neither adheres to nor violates life's rules. The most glorious moment in life is to witness a friend's *return*, not exactly a return, but an infinitely exquisite moment when he emerges from the chaos caused by the annihilation of his last refuge. There he is, liberated from the hard shells of a thousand lifetimes, standing nobly in the brilliant light cast by his burning refuge. In that moment, he will lose every thing, but in the same moment, he possesses everything. Beginning at that moment, we are truly present for each other.

During my struggle I was unable to converse, even after Steve returned. I could only manage manual chores. Steve recognized that I was undergoing something unusual and took great care not to disturb me. When I think of how sensitive he was during that time, great affection wells up in me. He didn't try to draw me into conversation. He only communicated what was essential. From time to time, I was aware that he was watching me, his eyes filled with concern. He spent time in the bedroom so I could have the front room to myself. He was so understanding. One Sunday morning I suggested we take a walk down to the river. We sat on the grass until early afternoon and then walked home. We didn't exchange a word the whole time. Back at the apartment, Steve asked, in a soft voice, "Are you tired, Thây?" I answered that I wasn't and thanked him.

Youth is a time for seeking truth. Years ago I wrote in my journal that even if it destroys you, you must hold to the truth. I knew early on that finding truth is not the same as finding happiness. You aspire to see the truth, but once you have seen it, you cannot avoid suffering. Otherwise, you've seen nothing at all. You are still hostage to arbitrary conventions set up by others. People judge themselves and each other based on standards that are not their own. In fact, such standards are mere wishful thinking, borrowed from public opinion and common viewpoints. One thing is judged as good and another as bad, one thing virtuous and another evil, one thing true and another false. But when the criteria used to arrive at such judgments are not your own, they are not the truth. Truth cannot be borrowed. It can only be experienced directly. The fruit of exploration, suffering, and the direct encounter between one's own spirit and reality—the reality of the present moment and the reality of ten thousand lifetimes. For each person, it is different. And it is different today than it was yesterday.

When we discover something to be true today through our own direct experience, we will see that our previous assumptions were wrong, or at least incomplete. Our new way of looking transcends yesterday's desire, prejudices, narrow-mindedness, and habits. We see that to use the golden molds and emerald yardsticks of yesterday's understanding is nothing less than slavery or imprisonment. When we attain a new understanding of reality, it is impossible to accept things we know to be false. Our actions will be based on our own understanding, and we will follow only those rules we have tested through our own direct experience. We will discard false rules and conventions of the current social order. But we have to expect that society will turn on us with a vengeance. Human history is filled with the tragedies caused by that vengeance. History teaches that we die if we oppose the system, yet many individuals continue to challenge the darkness, despite the danger in doing so. Those who pursue the truth are members of the community of truth seekers and reformers throughout time and space. They do not resign themselves to a collective fate that offers no laurels. The faint beams of light that appear after the desolation of the storm made me feel even more alone and abandoned. I felt the unbearable pain of a woman who is about to give birth to a child she already knows will be sentenced to death. She is consumed by despair, inconsolable and humiliated. She knows that she is with child, but a child who is already condemned to die. And she knows she will have to witness her child's death. There is no way to avoid her fate. Why couldn't she give birth to a healthy, sweet child like other mothers, a child who would give her hope, pride, and joy, a child who would earn her the praises of others? But we have to stand up for the truth. We cannot just gather moss like an old stone or assume a false self, once we see the truth.

There was a poor, young woman who dreamed of living in luxury, surrounded by jewels and silks. Then she met and married a wealthy widower, and her dream came true. She did not even mind that her husband had not married her for love. In fact, he married her because she looked exactly like his first wife. She agreed to dress, act, and speak like his first wife. At first, it wasn't a problem, but gradually it became quite oppressive. She was herself, yet she had to act like his first wife—to wear the colors she liked to wear, read the books she liked to read, and eat the foods she liked to eat. The young woman couldn't continue. It was suffocating. She was no more than a mannequin on which her husband hung his first wife's clothes and personality. But she didn't have the courage to give up the luxury she had become accustomed to. She was trapped by her own desires.

Anyone reading this story will want her to muster the strength needed to leave her husband and return to a simple country life where she can reclaim her true self. We think, "If I were in her place, that is what I would do." But we are only outside observers for whom the solution seems easy. If we were actually in her place, we would suffer the same confusion and indecision. Who among us would not? We already do the same thing. We feel forced to comply with the dehumanizing demands of society, and we bow our heads and obey. We eat, speak, think, and act according to society's dictates. We are not free to be ourselves, just as she was not free to be herself. We become cogs in the system, merchandise, not human beings. Our individuality is undermined, yet we comply because we lack the courage to refuse society's demands. We are no better than the wife of that man. We, too, have become so accustomed to our way of life with its conveniences and comforts that we allow ourselves to be colonized.

One day, she discovers that his first wife had been unfaithful to her husband. She takes this information to her husband in hopes he will come to his senses and let her be herself. But he tells her he knew about his first wife's infidelity, and because of that, he'd killed her. Her death, however, did not extinguish his anger. When he saw how closely she resembled his first wife, he married her and insisted she dress and act exactly like her. Now at last, she had become his first wife, and he could kill her again. He lunged at her, and she fought for her life.

I do not know whether she died or not. I leave the story unfinished. If she didn't, she certainly came close to the edge, like so many of us now. I hope humanity will awake in time and not wait, as she did, until the last moment to resist.

One morning I felt the sky brighten a little. I received a birthday card from home, which arrived exactly on my birthday. That was the day I felt myself reborn. In the card, Tue had copied three lines of a poem by Vu Tru:

Walking in the desolate desert
a bear attacks me by surprise.
I simply look him in the eye.

Yes, I thought. I have looked the beast straight in the eye, and seen it for what it is. I am like someone just recovered from a near-fatal illness who has stared death in the face. I got dressed, walked outside, and strolled along Broadway, thirsty for the morning sun after so many days of darkness. The winds of the storm had finally dispersed.

24–25 December 1962
Princeton, New Jersey

Two days after my birthday, I went to a Buddhist temple to pray for my mother. It was the full moon day of October, which is the anniversary of my mother's death. It was also the first day of a three-day celebration the temple had organized to commemorate the seventieth anniversary of Buddhism in the United States. About two hundred people were gathered, representing many countries, although most were from Japan. It isn't a large temple—the sanctuary is about the size of the one in the An Quang Pagoda's Buddha Hall—but it bears the illustrious name "American Buddhist Academy." Courses in Buddhist philosophy and practice are offered, as well as classes in Japanese, tea ceremony, and flower arranging. The temple belongs to the Japanese Pure Land Sect and is overseen by Hozen Seki, the senior priest, and a Dr. Phillips, who used to be a professor at the University of Delaware.

There are about eighty thousand Buddhists in the United States, mostly Chinese and Japanese. The Pure Land Headquarters is in Washington, D.C. About seventy recently ordained Pure Land ministers,

all Japanese, live throughout the United States. Some
of them also teach Japanese language and literature at
American universities. Altogether there are fifty-four
Pure Land temples, large and small. The one in New
York is smaller than the one in Washington. At the cer-
emony, I met two Theravada monks in saffron robes.
Venerable Anuruddha from Connecticut and Venerable
Vinita from Massachusetts. The Sri Lankan ambassador,
Mr. Susantha de Fonseka, was also there.

I strolled the five blocks from my apartment to the
temple at 331 Riverside Drive, and arrived just in
time for the sermon. I have to admit I didn't find the
sermon very inspiring. Such sermons will hardly be
effective in sowing seeds of Buddhism in America.
The Pure Land sect emphasizes seeking salvation from
what appears to be an external source. This approach is
familiar to Europeans and Americans, who have plenty
of seminaries and eloquent ministers to spread the
word of Christian salvation. The Pure Land sect's
efforts to look like Western churches seem to me to
reflect their lack of understanding of the true American needs. Americans place a high value on independence. Their children are encouraged to be
self-sufficient and self-reliant. A Buddhist approach
that emphasizes self-effort and self-realization, like
Zen, to build, develop, and awaken the individual,
seems to be better suited to the American spirit. Christianity and Pure Land Buddhism have the appearance
of considering that humans are too weak to achieve salvation without divine intervention. In fact, Zen is generating a lot of interest here. Professor D. T. Suzuki's
voice has struck a chord across the country. People who
live in a frenetic society, exhausted by interminable

plans and thoughts, thirst for the serenity and self-contentment that a path like Zen offers.

Americans like to eat Japanese food, listen to koto music, attend tea ceremonies, and arrange flowers. After the sermon, there was a koto concert. To me, the koto player more than made up for the lackluster sermon. I sat between two Americans who looked rather distracted during the sermon, but obviously enjoyed the music. I, too, enjoyed the music. The musician's name was Kimioto Eto, a young, around thirty-year-old man with a kind and open face. Dressed in a black kimono, he slowly mounted the stage, led by a young man gently guiding his arm. I wondered if he had poor eyesight. After Reverend Seki introduced him, Eto slowly sat down and smiled quietly. I was deeply touched by his presence. He never looked at the audience but settled his gaze on the podium that was draped with a white cloth. His smile was calm and composed. I never imagined a smile like that was possible in this country.

He said he wished to dedicate his playing to Kanzeon, the Bodhisattva of Compassion, to commemorate the seventieth anniversary of Buddhism in America. He explained that the number seven held deep personal significance for him. His father had died seven years ago, and his mother died seven months ago. His eyes filled with tears, and his quiet face was intense with feeling. I detected elements of faith, memory, and sorrow in his face. He played songs he had composed himself. The first was called "Song of Hope." Though the melody was tinged with sadness and yearning, it also expressed endurance and the will to move forward. The second piece, "Autumn

Wind," was scented with the memory of loved ones, and the third, "Language of Faith," expressed his devotion to the Way of Compassion. Each piece was followed by a long pause during which I had the impression the audience stopped breathing and simply gazed at the young musician with the serene smile. At the end of the third piece, he mentioned that he was blind. Everyone seemed moved, and indeed, my whole being was touched. No one had guessed that he was blind.

I wanted to weep. I stood up and left, even though he had several more pieces to play. Three beautiful pieces were enough for me. I walked slowly along Riverside Drive, feeling rather melancholy. I could still see Kimioto's smile in my mind, so wondrously serene. No one could smile like that unless they had passed through great suffering. I understood why his smile had stirred me so deeply the moment I saw him.

Riverside Drive was abandoned, and I remembered the warnings of friends never to walk alone at night on an empty street. Like every city on earth, New York has its share of crime. I crossed 108th Street back to Broadway, and as I did, the moon came into view, as round as the Buddha's lotus-face. It appeared like magic in a sliver of sky, framed by the towering skyscrapers. It seemed as though the moon and I were traveling in the same direction.

The full moon of October. My mother was with me. No doubt she had followed me to the temple as the moon was first peeking over the horizon. As I listened to the sermon and then to Kimioto's music, the moon shone on the temple roof, and it followed me home. My mother died six years ago on the full moon day of

October. The midnight moon is as gentle and wondrous as a mother's love. For the first four years after
she died, I felt like an orphan. Then one night she
came to me in a dream, and from that moment on, I
no longer felt her death as a loss. I understood that she
had never died, that my sorrow was based on illusion.
She appeared in my dream on an April night when I
was still living in the central highlands of Vietnam. She
looked the same as always, and I spoke to her quite naturally, without a tinge of grief. I had dreamed about
her many times before, but those dreams did not have
the same impact on me as that night.

When I woke up my mind was at peace. I realized that
my mother's birth and death were concepts, not truth.
The reality of my mother was beyond birth or death.
She did not exist because of birth, nor cease to exist
because of death. I saw that being and nonbeing are not
separate. Being can exist only in relation to nonbeing,
and nonbeing can exist only in relation to being.
Nothing can cease to be. Something cannot arise from
nothing. This is not philosophy. I am only speaking
the truth.

That night at about one a.m. I awoke, and my grief
was gone. I saw that the idea that I had lost my mother
was only an idea. Being able to see my mother in my
dream, I realized that I could see my mother everywhere. When I stepped out into the garden flooded
with soft moonlight, I experienced the light as my
mother's presence. It was not just a thought. I could
really see my mother everywhere, all the time.

In August, when I was still at Pomona, I wrote a small
book entitled *A Rose for Your Pocket,* to help the young
people back home appreciate the miracle of having a

mother. As I wrote, the birds were singing in the forest. Only after I'd sent it off to Nhien did I realize that I had been writing from this new way of seeing. It was the way I described in my letter to Thây Thanh Tu. Whenever I teach Vietnamese literature, I always mention this couplet by Ly Dynasty Zen Master Thich Man Giac:

> *Do not say that when spring is gone,*
> *that there are no flowers left.*
> *Just last night, in the front yard,*
> *a plum branch bloomed in the middle of winter.*

I always admired the feeling of this poem, but I never fully understood Venerable Man Giac's meaning until that night when I began to see the true wonder of things, like perceiving a flowering plum branch on a dark winter's night.

In our time, the struggle between old and new will reach its crescendo. It's not over yet, and we carry scars of this struggle in our hearts. Questions raised by contemporary philosophers make us feel lost and anxious. Confused minds suggest that existence is meaningless, even absurd, and this adds another coat of black to our darkened hearts. "Existence is foul. Humans are loathsome. No one can hope to be good. There is no way to beautify life." Even while adopting such mindsets, people cling to the illusion that we are free to be who we want. Yet most of the time we are merely reacting to the wounds engraved on our hearts or acting out of our collective karma. Almost no one listens to his or her true self. But when we are not ourselves, any freedom we think we have is illusory. Sometimes we reject freedom because we fear it. Our true selves are buried beneath layers of moss and brick. We have to break through those layers and be liberated, but we are afraid it may break us, also. We have to remind ourselves over and over again that the layers of moss and brick are not our true selves.

When you realize that, you'll see every phenomenon, every dharma, with new eyes. Begin by looking deeply at yourself and seeing how miraculous your body is. There is never any reason to look at your physical body with contempt or disregard. Don't ignore the very things that lie within your grasp. We don't value them. We even curse them. Consider your eyes. How can we take something as wonderful as our eyes for granted? Yet we do. We don't look deeply at these wonders. We ignore them, and, as a result, we lose them. It's as though our eyes don't exist. Only when we are struck blind do we realize how precious our eyes were, and then it's too late. A blind person who regains her sight understands the preciousness of her eyes. She has the capacity to live happily right here on earth. The world of form and color is a miracle that offers blissful joys every day. After we have this realization, we cannot look at the blue sky and the white clouds without smiling. The world constantly reveals its freshness and splendor. A blind person who regains her sight knows that paradise is right here, but before long she too will start to take it for granted again. Paradise comes to seem commonplace, and, in a matter of weeks or months, she'll lose the realization that she is in paradise. But when our "spiritual eyes" are opened, we never lose the ability to see the wonder of all dharmas, all things.

When I was a young monk I was taught that the greatest sufferings were birth, sickness, old age, death, unfulfilled dreams, separation from loved ones, and contact with those we despise. But the real suffering of humankind lies in the way we look at reality. Look, and you will see that birth, old age, sickness, death, unfulfilled hopes, separation from loved ones, and contact with those we despise are also wonders in themselves. They are all precious aspects of existence. Without them, existence would not be possible. Most important is knowing how to ride the waves of impermanence, smiling as one who knows he has never been born and will never die.

The Buddha told this story: "A man threw a stone at a dog. Crazed with pain, the dog barked at the stone, not understanding that the cause of his pain was the man, not the stone." In the same way, we think that forms, sounds, smells, tastes, and objects of touch are the sources of our suffering, and that to overcome suffering, form, sound, smell, taste, and touch must all be destroyed. We don't realize that our suffering lies in the way we see and use form, sound, smell, taste, and touch, because we view reality through the dark curtains of our narrow views and selfish desires.

Here in America, I feel an intense longing for the familiar sound of Vietnamese. There are times I think, If I could only hear a familiar voice for two minutes, I could be happy all day long. One morning Phuong telephoned. It seemed completely natural to be talking to him. Though we didn't talk long, I was in good spirits the rest of the day.

Since then, whenever I talk with a friend, I listen with all my attention to their words and the tone of their voice. As a result, I hear their worries, dreams, and hopes. It is not easy to listen so deeply that you understand everything the other person is trying to tell you. But every one of us can cultivate the capacity of listening deeply. I am no longer indifferent to phenomena that pass before my senses. A leaf, a child's voice—these are the treasures of life. I look and listen deeply in order to receive the messages these miracles convey. Separation from loved ones, disappointments, impatience with unpleasant things—all these are also constructive and wonderful. Who we are is, in part, a result of our unpleasant experiences. Deep looking allows us to see the wondrous elements contained in the weaknesses of others and ourselves, and these flowers of insight will never wilt. With insight, we see that the world of birth and death and the world of nirvana are the same. One night while practicing sitting meditation I felt the urge to shout, "The work of all the Buddhas has been completely fulfilled!"

It is not possible to judge any event as simply fortunate or unfortunate, good or bad. It is like the old story about the farmer and the horse.* You must travel throughout all of time and space to know the true impact of any event. Every success contains some difficulties, and every failure contributes to increased

---

* One day a farmer went to the field and found that his horse had run away. The people in the village told the farmer it was, "Bad luck!" The next day the horse returned and the village people said, "That is good luck!" Then the farmer's son fell off the horse and broke his leg. The villagers told the farmer that this was bad luck. Soon after, a war broke out and young men from the village were being drafted. But because the farmer's son had a broken leg, he was not drafted. Now the village people told the farmer that his son's broken leg was really "good luck."

wisdom or future success. Every event is both fortunate and unfortunate. Fortunate and unfortunate, good and bad, exist only in our perceptions.

People think it is impossible to establish a system of ethics without referring to good or evil. But clouds float, flowers bloom, and wind blows. What need have they for a distinction between good and evil? There are people who live like clouds, flowers, and wind, who don't think about morals, yet many people point to their actions and words as religious and ethical models, and they praise them as saints. These saints simply smile. If they revealed that they do not know what is good and what is evil, people would think they were crazy.

Who is the real poet? The sweet dew that a real poet drinks every day might poison others. For someone who has seen into the nature of things, knowledge gives rise to action. For those who have truly seen, there is no philosophy of action needed. There is no knowledge, attainment, or object of attainment. Life is lived just as the wind blows, clouds drift, and flowers bloom. When you know how to fly you don't need a street map. Your language is the language of clouds, wind, and flowers. If asked a philosophical question, you might answer with a poem, or ask, "Have you had your breakfast? Then please wash your bowl." Or point to the mountain forest.

> *If you don't believe me, look and see.*
> *Autumn has arrived.*
> *Scattered leaves of many colors flood the mountain forest!*

If they still cannot see, you might pick up a stick and threaten to strike them in order to get them to stop using concepts to try to understand the truth. If there had been a poet like that living in Phuong Boi, the mountain forest would have been even more radiant.

In Buddhist sutras, there is a term that is translated as "adornment." I'm reminded of the time King Hue Tong of the Ly Dynasty invited Zen Master Hien Quang to leave his meditation hut to come dwell in the palace. Hien Quang refused, saying that the talented and virtuous Zen masters already living in the capital had more than "adorned" the palace. The presence of a realized person beautifies life by their path of non-action. What does a path of non-action have to do with plans and programs?

In fifteen minutes, it will be midnight. Christmas is almost here. I am awake in this sacred hour writing in my journal. My thoughts flow, and it feels wonderful to pour them onto paper. I've written about the spiritual experience that revealed to me how to look and listen with full attention. Such moments might only come once in a lifetime. They appear as ambassadors of truth, messengers from reality. If we're not mindful, they may pass unnoticed. The secret of Zen masters is discovering the path of return to such moments, and knowing how to pave the way for such moments to arise. The masters know how to use the dazzling light of those moments to illuminate the journey of return, the journey that begins from nowhere and has no destination. Quach Thoai's poem describes the appearance of a dahlia:

> Standing quietly by the fence,
> you smile your wondrous smile.
> I am speechless, and my senses are filled

by the sounds of your beautiful song,
beginningless and endless.
I bow deeply to you.

Do you see? The moment appeared. The curtain was drawn back for a second, and the poet could see. The dahlia is so commonplace that most people do not truly see it. When you can hear its eternal song and see its miraculous smile, it is no longer an ordinary flower. It is an ambassador from the cosmos.

Tru Vu wrote:

The petal of a flower is made only of four elements,
but it emits a spiritual perfume.
Your eyes are made only of the four elements,
but they radiate the energy of love.

Tru Vu was expressing his sudden surprise. The moment arrived in a flash of light, and then it vanished. Being able to see just once in a lifetime is no small accomplishment. If you've seen once, you can see forever. The question is whether you have the determination and diligence. Many young people today feel trapped in prisons of discouragement and self-hatred. They regard reality as meaningless, and they treat themselves as despicable beings. My heart opens to them. Caught in despair, they seek liberation through destructive means. It would be wonderful if we could identify and dissolve the sources of such a dark view of life.

If you tarnish your perceptions by holding on to suffering that isn't really there, you create even greater misunderstanding. Reality is neither pleasant nor unpleasant in and of itself. It is only pleasant or

unpleasant as experienced by us, through our perceptions. This is not to deny that earthquakes, plagues,
wars, old age, sickness, and death exist. But their nature
is not suffering. We can limit the impact of these
tragedies but never do away with them completely. That
would be like wanting to have light without darkness,
tallness without shortness, birth without death, one
without many. One-sided perceptions like these create
our world of suffering. We are like an artist who is
frightened by his own drawing of a ghost. Our creations
become real to us and even haunt us.

The night of November 2nd is one I will never
forget. It was a moonless, cloudless night, and the sky
was filled with stars, each as bright as a child's eyes. In
fact, that was the sky in my mind. The actual night was
windy and rainy. The windows in my room were shut
tight, and I was unable to sleep. I had been reading
Bonhoeffer's account of his final days, and I was awakened to the starry sky that dwells in each of us. I felt a
surge of joy, accompanied by the faith that I could
endure even greater suffering than I had thought possible. Bonhoeffer was the drop that made my cup over-
flow, the last link in a long chain, the breeze that
nudged the ripened fruit to fall. After experiencing
such a night, I will never complain about life again. My
heart was overflowing with love. Courage and strength
swelled in me, and I saw my mind and heart as flowers.
All feelings, passions, and sufferings revealed themselves as wonders, yet I remained grounded in my
body. Some people might call such an experience
"religious," but what I felt was totally and utterly
human. I knew in that moment that there was no
enlightenment outside of my own mind and the cells of

my body. Life is miraculous, even in its suffering. Without suffering, life would not be possible. There is nothing permanent, and there is no separate self. Neither is there impermanence or no-self. When we see life deeply, there is no death. Therefore, it isn't necessary to say "everlasting life."

For the next month I meditated on the bodhisattvas described in the *Lotus* and other *Prajñaparamita Sutras.* These beings are so beautiful, it is easy to understand how their presence beautifies the many Buddha Lands. But why confine their beauty to Buddha Lands? How about right here on earth? The presence of bodhisattvas is enough to transform the earth into a Buddha Land. Who can say that this earth is not a Buddha Land? The pole that we raise every year at Tết expresses the realization that this very earth is a Buddha Land.

Sometimes healthy, energetic bodhisattvas, like Never-Disparaging Bodhisattva and Earth-Holding Bodhisattva, wear ragged clothes. Earth-Holding devotes himself to rebuilding roads and bridges in order to restore communication and contact. In today's world, there are countless broken bridges and innumerable Earth-Holdings devoting their bodies and minds to rebuilding bridges of communication and understanding among individuals, nations, and cultures. Wherever Never-Disparaging Bodhisattva goes, he offers words of encouragement: "You have the strength to go forward. Believe in yourself. Don't succumb to low self-esteem or passivity. You will become a Buddha." His message is one of confidence and self-determination. I think about the peasants in the countryside of all the poor countries of the world. Do they have someone to encourage them to believe in their own abilities so they can build a future that they, as much as anyone else, have a right to? Our world needs millions more bodhisattvas like Never-Disparaging.

We can rejoice that our world does have many bodhisattvas who can be found on every path of return, sowing seeds of faith, resolve, and confidence. Kwan Yin, for example, always finds ways to be with those who are suffering. She fears nothing, and uses whatever means are appropriate to the circumstance. She takes on whatever form is needed—monk, politician, merchant, scholar, woman, child, god, or demon. Can we listen deeply like Kwan Yin? Using every form and means possible, in the spirit of Kwan Yin, we will bring help to our world. The wholehearted spirits of bodhisattvas like Never-Disparaging and Earth-Holding will rebuild our world. Let us not forget Kshitigarbha, the Earth-Store Bodhisattva. He makes the vow to be with those who are in the places of greatest suffering. As long as any being remains in hell, Kshitigarbha will be there. His spirit is irrepressible. Wherever such persons are found, flowers blossom, even in the depths of hell.

Bodhisattvas are frequently shown wearing beautiful garments. Shining gems adorn their heads, arms, and necks. Monks, on the other hand, are never portrayed in fancy dress. The bodhisattva image is meant to symbolize how bodhisattvas beautify and adorn life. Their presence makes life beautiful. Artists portray them in clothes as colorful as children's New Year's outfits, as bright as an early spring day. No one sees the existence of suffering more deeply than a bodhisattva, yet no one maintains as refreshing and unwavering a smile. I can hear the bodhisattvas saying, "We are not here to weep and wail, we are here to make life beautiful." We must thank these friends and we should wear our finest clothes, too, to help them adorn life. They will delight to hear us calling them our friends. We needn't think of them as remote beings on pedestals. We can recognize their presence every day among those we see. It is not arrogance that allows us to approach them as friends. It is freedom from the rigid ideas that have encased us. O Oriole, though your throat is tiny, sing out, and let your song praise life's wonders! Kwan Yin's necklace of jewels is sparkling, and so is your song. Let the morning sun roll down the hills like a golden stream, and let all the flowers bloom as one until they cover the meadows, welcoming the miracle of mindfulness.

That wondrous night my mind and heart opened like a flower, and I perceived all the bodhisattvas as dear friends helping us right here and now in this very life, and not just as remote deities. This same insight is expressed in a daily gatha:

> When the lotus blooms,
> we see the Buddha immediately
> and touch the reality of no-birth and no-death.
> All bodhisattvas become our companions.

Once our minds and hearts have opened like flowers, they will never fade. They will be like the lotus flowers in the Pure Land. The light shed by lotus blossoms will show us where to find our friends along the path.

At midnight, while the snow was quietly drifting down, I put on a warm coat and walked to the Campus Center. I sat down beside Ralph Nelson who was watching a Christmas special on TV. Ralph's family

lives in the South, and it is too far for him to travel for
a holiday visit. I had the distinct feeling he was homesick. He'd driven to Pennsylvania the day before yesterday to visit a friend, and on the drive back to
Princeton he got caught in a blizzard and had to pull
his car over to the side of the road and sleep right
there. It can be dangerous to be caught in such a situation. The temperatures can drop so severely that even
someone inside a closed car could freeze to death.
Luckily Ralph survived the ordeal and made it back
safely to campus. I asked him, "Are you sad to be apart
from your family on Christmas Eve?"

He answered, "I'm used to living alone. It's no
big deal."

I detected some sadness in his eyes. Just then a funny
movie came on, and Ralph and I laughed together until
1:30. When we left the Campus Center, the snow was
up to our knees. I bade Ralph good night and turned
toward Brown Hall. When I got back to my room, I
changed into a dry pair of socks and warmed my feet by
the heater.

Last year I spent Christmas Day in the countryside,
where I experienced the warm spirit of American families celebrating the holiday. Christmas here is very
much like Têt. Young and old all give and receive lots
of presents.

I was asked by a young boy, "Do Buddhists celebrate
Christmas?"

I replied, "Yes. In my country, Buddhists celebrate
Christmas on the full moon day of the fourth month.
We call it 'Buddha-mas.' "

As I was warming my feet, I thought about the young
campers at Cherokee Village, and I slept very soundly.

from Call Me By My True Names:

THE COLLECTED POEMS OF THICH NHAT HANH

by *Thich Nhat Hanh*

Thich Nhat Hanh—or Thay ("teacher") as he is called by his followers—is a poet as well as an activist, monk, scholar, and teacher. He wrote these poems during the Vietnam War.

Condemnation

Listen to this:
yesterday six Vietcong came through my village.
Because of this my village was bombed—completely
　　destroyed.
Every soul was killed.
When I come back to the village, now, the day after,
there is nothing to see but clouds of dust and the river,
　　still flowing.
The pagoda has neither roof nor altar.
Only the foundations of houses are left.
The bamboo thickets have been burned away.

Here in the presence of the undisturbed stars,
in the invisible presence of all the people still alive on
earth,
let me raise my voice to denounce this filthy war,
this murder of brothers by brothers!
I have a question: Who pushed us into this killing of
one another?

Whoever is listening, be my witness!
I cannot accept this war.
I never could, I never shall.
I must say this a thousand times before I am killed.

I feel I am like that bird which dies for the sake of its mate,
dripping blood from its broken beak and crying out:
Beware! Turn around to face your real enemies—
ambition, violence, hatred, greed.

Men cannot be our enemies—even men called "Vietcong!"
If we kill men, what brothers will we have left?
With whom shall we live then?

Let Me Give Back to Our Motherland

Last night four of my brothers died:
One was Tho
One was Tuan
One was Hy
One was Lanh.
Let this be known to you,
Brothers, sisters, my people, my motherland.

Four young workers, young men,
heard my appeal,
went out to the hamlets,
worked two years
sowing trust and love
that peace might reappear.

Their flesh is mine.
Their blood is mine.
My flesh is crushed.
My blood is dried.
At midnight they were dragged
barefoot, bareheaded
to the riverside,
pushed to their knees and shot.
(And I was shot down on the riverbank.)

In your presence, O compatriots,
O brothers and sisters,
let me return the flesh of my brothers to our motherland.
Let me return the blood of my brothers to our
     motherland,
this chaste blood and pure flesh which never soiled
     our name.

And their hands—
let me return these to humanity
and let me give back their hearts to humanity
because their hands did not destroy,
because their hearts bore no hatred.

As for the skin of their bodies,
let me give this back to you, O compatriots,
the skin of four who never cooked an animal's flesh in
    its own skin.

Use, please use, the skin of my brothers
to mend those open wounds in our people's flesh,
that immense body
which swoons in agony.

The Witness Remains
Flarebombs bloom on the dark sky,
a child claps his hands;
he laughs.
I hear the sound of guns
and the laugh dies.

But the witness
remains.

Those That Have Not Exploded

I don't know why,
I don't know what made my countrymen
hurl grenades
at my brothers and sisters.

Why wish to kill
those boys with still pure brows
those girls from school with ink-stained hands?

What crime was theirs?
To hear the voice of compassion?
To do this:
Live in the hamlet
Help the villagers
Teach the children
Work in the paddies.

Last night
when those grenades burst
twelve students fell
with mangled bodies and burst skin.
One girl's flesh took sixty metal bits.

This morning, two are buried
and each one waits for dawn again
within his motherland.
Each waits for peace within his motherland
and reincarnation as a butterfly.

And so we have accepted death and sorrow.
But hear me, O sisters and brothers,
those grenades have burst and ripped apart the sky now,

those boys and girls have gone,
trailing their blood.

But there are more grenades
than those which burst last night.
But there are more grenades
and these are caught in the heart of life.
Do you hear me?
There are more, and they have not burst.

They remain
still
in the heart of Man.
Unknown, the time of their detonation.
Unknown, when they will desecrate our land.
Unknown, the time they will annihilate our people.
And still,
we beg you to believe
there is no hatred in our hearts
and in our souls no rancor,
because
what the world needs,
what our country needs
is love.

Come.
Hear me.
For time grows short
and danger is everywhere.
Let us take those grenades
out of our hearts,
our motherland,

Mankind.
Let us stand
Let us stand
Side by side.

Flesh and Skin, Bricks and Tiles

The bombers are gone,
and beneath a still sun,
the dying light of noon,
our ancient land stirs again.

The curved temple roof
is burnt out, crumpled,
but Lord Buddha sits,
his gilt all smeared,
and smiles ineffably at bricks and stones.

The quiet dusk
sends up a flute song
as from my soul;
our school children sought shelter
in that temple
where clouds now hover.

Now they are gone,
gone, like those with heads of black and shiny hair,
for they took the wounded away
and the dead will be buried tomorrow
in our cemetery
at the road's end.

O homeland,
O sisters and brothers,
your teeth are clenched.
Still today
you bear your pains in silence,
for
what else can you do?
Where else can you go?
Even the sea is too shallow
for your sorrow.

O sisters and brothers,
what will you do
with these bullets,
that steel, broken and burst in you?
O flesh and skin,
O bricks and tiles.

Our past is here
in the twentieth century,
remember, remember—
Is it true that this child
raised on potatoes and manioc
roots of our poor land,
that this child
born after Geneva,
this child
whose laughter once resounded
across spring fields
whenever the evening bell was struck in the temple,
this child,
is it true
this child had forfeited his right
to become a man?

Religion in the World
from *The Raft Is Not the Shore:*

CONVERSATIONS TOWARD A BUDDHIST
CHRISTIAN AWARENESS

by *Daniel Berrigan and Thich Nhat Hanh*

Father Daniel Berrigan and Thich Nhat Hanh encountered each other in Paris during the mid-1970's. Berrigan, an American Catholic priest, was recovering from a prison term he had served in America for anti-war activities. Hanh had been forced into exile from Vietnam due to his own anti-war activism. The men met over several weeks to explore the relationship between faith and action.

BERRIGAN: *I think I would like to begin by saying a few things about people whom I met recently in the Middle East. These meetings opened the question of what it is to be religious in the world.*

I was struck by two things. First, in Israel and elsewhere, the people who were thoughtful were antireligious. And the religious people we met were very closed in their suppositions about the state, in obedience to the state, and in violence. In no sense were they evil people, but they were convinced of one way of thinking, one way of acting, one attitude. They were offering very little resources in face of the suffering and the death of many innocent people. They were also convinced, to some degree at least, of the inevitability of violence.

So they found me suspect and treated me rather harshly. I regretted very often that there was so little religious sense available to deal with these terrifying human differences. I was only half-joking after one meeting in Jerusalem when I said that it was the religious people who gave us the hardest times of all, compared with the extreme rightists. I thought that that would be an important thing to try to understand— why this should be so.

NHAT HANH: Do you think that the sufferings have drawn people nearer to each other? I mean people of different religions?

BERRIGAN: *Not really; suffering has made them extremely rigid and reactionary. There is in Israel, for example, a very powerful political bloc to the right which is resisting any change, any lessening of militarization. Both sides, right and left, fear the religious people very much because they know that their influence, in the scale of political change, will be crucial. But to look on religion as some kind of a leaven, you know, of daring or of risk is almost unheard of. In the kibbutzim, for instance, they said, when we asked them, that they were antireligious. They felt that to be politically responsible they had to be so.*

NHAT HANH: And so, on the right wing there are people who are using religion as a means to achieve strength by political unity. It is suggested that that kind of alliance will protect religion as well as people.

BERRIGAN: *It's a very strange conception that religion, which is seen as a part of citizenship, is aligned to the most frightening kind of militarism, as well as to efforts to make the state more religious. The religious bloc resists the secular development of the state; it wants everybody to observe a close moral code in observance of Sabbath, dietary laws, or marriage laws. It evidently conceives of the state as a theocracy which is immersed in a sea of secularism, and it must resist this to preserve itself—and resist any possibility of living together and of welcoming Christians and Moslems and unbelieving people to an equal ground.*

NHAT HANH: I wonder what the content of sermons would be, in weekly religious meetings? Would they preach about the necessity of protecting people who are united under that religion? Or would they also speak about the spiritual dimension of life, religious principles of behavior as far as problems like killing, oppression, are concerned?

BERRIGAN: *We didn't have a chance to attend any services. But the people that we met with impressed us with their view of common problems, their view of violence, the killing even of children. I recall their vengefulness, the kind of siege mentality which religion was fostering—that the Jew and his state are caught in the midst of essentially evil people who wish their destruction.*

They are haunted by the Holocaust. This is very much part of it. They are determined that this will never happen again, and yet they feel it could happen again, any time. And the terriorists are always giving notice of that, you know, through attacks on schools and buses and settlements at the frontier. But, religion just seems to intensify the bad, bloody feelings of people and to give them a kind of blessing for feeling that way. I think such people read the Old Testament in the narrowest possible sense, as though God were a God of vengeance and wars were still religious ventures; it was a sacred thing to retaliate against the enemy—who is always accepted as the enemy. Any reconciliation work is ignored by religious people, almost unheard of. So, this is very sad.

NHAT HANH: In Israel, is there a minority who hold the Moslem belief?

BERRIGAN: *A very small, unacceptable minority. I didn't get the*

impression that they were particularly religious or that they were
offering much hope either. It seemed to me that here and there was a
Christian, Jew, or Moslem, religious or secular, especially among young
people, who was saying, "We must change, and any change in public
must begin with ourselves." It was my first experience, I think, in any
country where the religious voice was so negative. Not absent, but neg-
ative. It would almost be better if it were absent because then it wouldn't
be offering a kind of divine sanction for continuing the killing.

NHAT HANH: And when you met and discussed with leaders of the Palestinian movements, did the problem of religious people arise?

BERRIGAN: *Well, one had the impression that they were in no sense*
antireligious. They had great respect for us, for instance, as religious
people involved in resistance in our own country. They spoke of that
explicitly, and one got the impression that religious people were as
acceptable to them as anyone else was, as long as they had something to
offer. While we would not be sharing on the religious basis, they would
offer cooperation to people who came to say, "We believe also that the
state must grant you room, that your people must be accepted, and that
a settlement must be reached for you." So, they had a kind of a classical
secular view of religion, neither favorable nor hostile.

In the Arabic countries and in Israel, there's a great unspoken
longing for someone who has the courage to say, "We must change and
change rapidly; otherwise we all perish." However the feeling is one of
mixed despair and shock and depression of spirit—a sense in Israel that
they're not on the right track and haven't been for a long time, but don't
know where the right track is. And that there are very few who can help.

NHAT HANH: Has there been any effort of religious people of both sides to meet and discuss the problems?

BERRIGAN: *Well, we were the first in a long time to come into Israel and say to a rabbi, "We want to meet with some religious people. We feel it is important as outsiders to share with you our view of our struggle at home, as well as our view of the feelings of the Arabs, especially the Palestinians, about Israel. We want to share this with religious people."* So, a rabbi gathered six Jews, a Catholic, and a Protestant. They were mainly professors and chaplains. Well, it was the hardest evening of the whole trip.

NHAT HANH: They had never met Moslems of the Arab countries?

BERRIGAN: *I think that this is almost unheard of. The only person we met who was doing reconciliation work was a Maronite priest, exiled by church authorities to a small Arab village about fifty miles from Tel Aviv. We heard about him on Cyprus. He is a brilliant young theologian and lin-guist who has spoken to audiences in Europe and in the States, and he always returns to this village, to build community. He invites Jewish stu-dents and professors to come and live with the people while they're having their discussions. "Go into the village please, and live with our people. Find out what they're like—that they're not monsters or enemies, that they're very simple, beautiful, gentle, hard-working, poor people." He said that change comes from living experience and an effort to talk honestly. But it's very slow.*

A rabbi, whom we both have met—you in Ceylon and I in Jerusalem—was one of these visitors to the village. At one point, the rabbi invited the priest in return to his own home. After they had sat for a while and he had served coffee, the rabbi finally confessed that in twenty-five years, this priest was the first Arab, the first Palestinian, he had ever had in his home. The priest couldn't believe it. He exploded. "You mean that you have been teaching the Bible all these years and had never had one of us into your house?" And the rabbi was ashamed.

NHAT HANH: Did you notice anything on the part of the rabbis you talked to—any sign that they felt they were caught between religious ideals and the necessity of preserving Israel as a nation-state?

BERRIGAN: *I speak only of an impression, but it seems to me that in some cases a genuine religious understanding gets lost, you know. After a while, under these extreme crises, living so long in an atmosphere of violence, the religious person may think he retains a religious attitude. But, in reality, he has the same attitude as the state. Still, he speaks in a religious language. It's very difficult to get beyond that language and to help probe his real thinking, the real strata, the drives that lie beyond religious metaphors, religious symbols, religious ceremonies. I deeply believe that at heart, when religious people accede to violence, they become worldly, violence-oriented persons who now can invoke a religious excuse for being that way. But the fact is that, in one way or another, the state has come to embody the religious hope. The state is the expression of the religious community; the army is the natural protector of the religious community. The need for retaliation is, after a while, a religious need. The situation might change if such people can sense the distance they have moved from a religious vision, acting and living and teaching this way.*

NHAT HANH: In that case, religion plays only the role of an ideology to preserve the identity of a race, of a nation, of a group of people. But I think that any genuine religious life must express reverence toward life, nonviolence, communion between man and man, man and the absolute. You met in Tel Aviv a rabbi, a professor of scripture, whom I met in Ceylon?

BERRIGAN: *Yes.*

NHAT HANH: In Colombo, we talked for a long time. Then he asked me this question: "What would you do if you were in my position?" I told him that was a very hard question because the most I could do was to imagine that I was in his position, but imagination is not the real thing. So I said, "What I can tell you is how the Buddhists in similar conditions behaved in the past."

For instance, in India in the ninth century, Hindus and Moslems undertook a great persecution of Buddhism. They burned down Buddhist temples and killed monks and destroyed scriptures. What the Buddhist monks did in those days was to flee to Nepal, where they preserved their manuscripts. They couldn't carry the Buddha statues, which were magnificent, with them. But they did carry the scriptures. After that, Buddhism flourished in Asia—in Tibet and China and Japan. Theirs was a kind of negative resistance.

But if they had organized violent resistance and killed Moslems and Hindus, I don't think that would have been real Buddhist behavior. By organizing violent resistance, they might have preserved something that is called Buddhism, but might not be Buddhist at all in substance. By acting in the way they did, they preserved the identity of Buddhism.

I also asked him whether he thought Israel as a nation is the most important condition for the existence of the Jewish people, even when in order to protect that nation it is necessary to bomb people, to destroy life in order to protect life. A contradiction in itself. I suggested that there may be ways other than the killing of people to protect life.

BERRIGAN: *I had a sense of a kind of strange ecumenism in listening to such talk. Because I think this attitude, "kill now and pay later" or "kill now and save later," is by no means confined to any one group. I had been in Northern Ireland and seen Christians killing one another with great enthusiasm. And I had a sense of being at home, in the United States, where in the last decade the official Church has played this same game.*

I think there's a wave passing over the world—a wave of blood, of utter moral irresponsibility toward others. In such circumstances, one recognizes two things. First, that there's a diabolic ecumenism at work. The main-line religions have joined this effort to make killing acceptable and normal—at least by silence. Usually there is some kind of an obsession with their own well-being. And then more to the point, I think, for ourselves is an understanding of the importance of everyone— Buddhists and Christians and Jews and Hindus and secular people—so living that the lines are no longer drawn around churches or national- ities or religious traditions, but around the protection of the innocent, the victims. This will be a very difficult and long-term struggle.

I had it brought home to me in Israel that there is no religious group that can be relied upon, just because it's religious, to understand basic things about religion—the basic things about human life and conscience. We're in a bad time for everybody. There are very few models as to our way to be drawn upon in any community. There certainly are no states that one could look to and say, "A revolution has occurred here; they're acting better toward people." And the religions are going the way of the state; obsession with survival at any price. There is a terrible casuistry that trades off human bodies and looks on an abstract, future good as an excuse for present evil.

NHAT HANH: "Kill now and save later." That has been very true in the case of Vietnam too. Remember the time a certain village was destroyed. Someone said, "We had to destroy the village in order to save it."

BERRIGAN: *"In order to save it."*

NHAT HANH: And while bombing North Vietnam, Washington was talking about the possibility of giving aid to rebuild if North Vietnam accepted its terms.

BERRIGAN: *Then, of course, the aid never came anyway. The promise was empty.*

NHAT HANH: Returning to the Israeli professor—well, he also asked me about my loyalty to Vietnam as a nation and to Buddhism as a religion, because in our discussions I always put peace and human life above everything. So he asked, "What if Buddhism cannot survive in Vietnam? Will you accept that in order to have peace in Vietnam?" I said, "Yes. I think if Vietnam has real peace—cooperation between North and South—and if it can ban war for a long time, I would be ready to sacrifice Buddhism." He was very shocked. But I thought it was quite plain that if you have to choose between Buddhism and peace, then you must choose peace. Because if you choose Buddhism you sacrifice peace and Buddhism does not accept that. Furthermore, Buddhism is not a number of temples and organizations. Buddhism is in your heart. Even if you don't have any temple or any monks, you can still be a Buddhist in your heart and life.

The rabbi asked also, "How about your loyalty to Vietnam as a nation?" I think that question touched the very core of the problem of the Middle East. I said that if I had to choose between the survival of the Vietnamese people and the survival of Vietnam as a nation, I would choose the survival of the people. He said,

"Well, we cannot agree on that. That is why we cannot agree on other things." So that was the end of the dialogue.

BERRIGAN: *There are so many contradictions in such an attitude. I was thinking that, first of all, the only way Jews have survived is by keeping independent of institutions. They've always been able to preserve a certain spirit, a certain self-understanding, even while they were shunted into ghettoes and penalized in so many ways, even when attempts were made at exterminating them. But, also, I think that this very reproach—that of defending institutions against people—is the one they have leveled at the Catholics, and rightly so. Because during the Hitler regime, as it became clear afterward, when the Pope was confronted with the cost of defending and protecting the Jews, he hesitated. He thought of reprisals against Catholics; he thought of what Hitler could do to Catholic institutions—the schools, the seminaries, and churches. It was this threat that kept him silent.*

And now, it seems to me, this same idea—the institution is the prime meaning and symbol of the religion itself—is transferred to the state. It is said now that Israel is a sacred and secular reality which must be preserved at all costs, even at the cost of killing. They denounced the Christians for that attitude, and they have now adopted it themselves.

I know a Jewish woman in New York; she is devoted and brilliant. Her whole life has been devoted to the poor and suffering. She said one day, "I knew when Israel formed an army that is was all finished with Israel." She was speaking as a Jew who understood that there was something about being a Jew that is extinguished when you raise an army. She didn't begin from a religious point of view at all. But she realized that her people were unique because they had none of these weapons; they didn't function in the world that way. And that was a very deep truth, I thought.

The worst thing is to be in despair; there are many forms that that takes, you know. As Rabbi Heschel used to say, "The opposite of love is not violence; it is indifference." One sinks into quicksand and simply declares that there's nowhere to go, nothing to do; one washes one's hands of the human adventure.

NHAT HANH: When we were at supper, I described you as a bridge builder, a pilgrim. I told you about a Buddhist saint described in the *Lotus Sutra,* who did nothing but repair roads, build bridges so people could come together to live with each other. Well, what you have been doing—going around meeting people, listening, and building that kind of bridge—is a most important thing. And you told us about one sad experience of bridge building in the United States between the Jewish people and you. Say a few words about that so that we remember.

BERRIGAN: *The difficulty at that point, I think, Nhat Hanh, was that there already existed a bridge of illusion. This can be the most dangerous kind of all—the one that is hardest to replace. People are constantly passing over this bridge, back and forth in their dreams and ideologies and obsessions and fears; and they are being reinforced in all those things, importing and exporting to one another. The bridge of illusion grows stronger in such trade. But the bridge of illusion must be brought down before a real bridge can be constructed over which human beings can pass to and from reality—in either direction—so that the Americans going to Israel may deepen their sense of being Jews of a covenant, and the Jews coming to America may enrich and contribute to that scene, instead of trading in Phantom jets and fury and racism about Arabs and the inevitability of violence. Across this true bridge one would hope people could pass into a new way—a new land, a new direction. Well, anyway, I had sensed ever since 1967 that someday something had to be said; and when the War broke out again, I gave this speech. Someone said it would be impossible to speak in a way that would not give offense*

in these circumstances, and still tell the truth. So I managed to offend
everyone.

NHAT HANH: But the bridge of illusion has been shattered; and only after that can any real bridge be built.
The destruction of illusion is a necessity.

BERRIGAN: *I'm not at all sure whether or not that has happened. I*
hope something has happened, but I am sure I had a great deal to learn
in Israel also.

NHAT HANH: But we all see that what you said in 1973
has led people to think again, to examine again their
beliefs or their habits, their way of thinking. That is a
very positive act. We cannot say when the fruit of such
an act will come, because there are things that need
time in order to be set right. There are things that the
Buddha or Jesus said thousands of years ago; they may
begin only now to have an effect. You cannot hastily say
whether something is effective or not.

Something in you tells me that you're eager to try
and prevent pessimism from prevailing. Indeed, it is
not a good thing to be a pessimist, to say that there's
nothing beyond that. One Bodhisattra, described in
the *Lotus Sutra*, is a traveler who does nothing except
come to every person to say, "Well, I do not dare to take
you lightly; I know that you are a Buddha and you have
the capability of being a Buddha."

BERRIGAN: *I think this hope is also a kind of bridge of which the piers*
on both sides are reality rather than illusion. Hope expresses some kind
of tension between where one's feet are and the goal which is still unat-
tained. It's not that one is trying to beat somebody to the goal; it's really

that one is trying to be faithful to an impetus which is already set in motion, an invitation, the invitation from the one at the end. That invitation expresses both the urgency of living where one is as fully and really and consciously as possible; and carrying that with him so that nothing is lost as the movement goes forward. I think there's a connection between modesty—being brought down to size—and hope, as opposed to immodesty and delusion.

NHAT HANH: We must explore more about other directions. There must be other ways.

BERRIGAN: *In classrooms I doubt that things will go very far.*

NHAT HANH: I agree. I have a friend who is a Vietnamese Catholic priest. He was very open in his way of thinking concerning Christianity and society and other religions. His students liked his ideas very much. But then he came to act—he got married. That reflected his freedom, his interpretation of Christianity—that and other things he did. Some of his students accepted him for a while. But when he married, the students revolted against him.

BERRIGAN: *Why?*

NHAT HANH: Why did they accept the things that were said and not the things that were done? Do they think that discussion is life, but that when you do something you then become unacceptable?

BERRIGAN: *Bonhoeffer said that he spent a certain period of his life going around with a briefcase to religious conferences. He said that he still had to be converted to Christianity, even though he was a theologian. It was only later, when he began to suffer and be on trial and in prison, that he realized there was a deep difference between a theologian and a Christian. I think that that's a useful distinction because some people still exclude from Christianity anything but a science of Christianity. What they produce in their seminaries and classrooms is experts; but not necessarily Christians or, indeed, Jews or Buddhists. I doubt whether a Jew of the capacity of Abraham Heschel would come out of a classroom in Israel today, where the sufferings of the Palestinians would be taboo—never spoken of, you know.*

Of course, the great cry in the liberal community in the West is that international conferences illustrate the universal nature of religion, its independence of the nation-state and its ability to speak across borders. But I think this becomes very questionable, in fact, because such theologians seldom if ever face their own nation-state. It's easier to fly over the nation-state; half the fun, as they say, is getting somewhere else. But it's difficult to face the state, especially when it's making war. One could spend one's life, in the middle of the Vietnam war, flying around the world outside the United States, talking about the universal character of Christianity as some theologians and scripture scholars did. But their Christianity never quite landed, so to speak.

It's very like the liberal American secularists who are running to China as they used to run to Cuba. After Cuba, they ran to North Vietnam. They spend their lives evading the United States, seeking a kind of abstract ideal state. When it became clear that Cuba had some dark sides too—many prisoners, persecution of poets and homosexuals— there was a great flurry in the dovecote. When the revelation of torture of American pilots came out of North Vietnam, there was again a great scandal. I'm sure that if visitors ever get beyond the tourist circuit in China, they will discover some dark things too; that will be another scandal. Meantime, while the ideal state is being pursued, like an El Dorado or a mirage, the real state is never being confronted in order to make of that real state something more decent. I've seen this so often, so often. And usually this pursuit of the foreign ideal is linked to a dread, a

kind of existential dread and hatred of one's own country—an inability
to see the goodness and possibilities and hope that lie within one's own
people, so that one could work there very patiently for changes. It's a
form of alienation, I think; some theologians share it.

But I was wondering if you would speak at more length about your
recent exchanges in Ceylon. You had an exposure to religious people
very different from my own. I think that would be very helpful.

NHAT HANH: That international conference opened my
eyes a lot because in the last few years I have been living
mostly with more open-minded people in religious
circles. Because of that conference in Colombo, I was
put back into the real thing. It was difficult, the most
difficult religious meeting I have had in many, many
years. I don't know how the organizers selected the
participants. But most of the participants had degrees
in religious studies: professors, experts. And they had
a tendency to teach; but I don't think that they had
much to teach in terms of religious experiences.

During the ten days of the conference, I intervened
only three times. That means I took only about fifteen or
twenty minutes in all in order to speak. But it's so hard
to establish communication—real communication—
between people. I told a few friends I was interested
only in having a real meeting. The participants—I
wanted to know what were their problems, their difficulties, and what people could do to support one
another. But, well, that didn't succeed.

People discussed almost everything, including religious experiences. At one point, a professor of religion
said, "I don't know what you mean by religious experience. I am a professor of religion; we have things we
can think and speak of and teach on the conceptual

level. I don't think that—except on the conceptual level—we have anything to exchange."

BERRIGAN: *That's quite an admission. Did you pray together? Was there any attempt like that?*

NHAT HANH: Oh, yes. At seven o'clock in the morning, the group came together to pray under the guidance of one of the participants. That continued for some time. Then afterwards, the prayers were discontinued because of something that happened during the conference.

The change came about in this way. We were supposed to have a session on the varieties of religious experience. Father Murray Roger was asked to lead the session. He came to me and said he wouldn't like to have a discussion, because discussion of religious experiences is somehow difficult. So, I proposed to him that we make the session into a program of contemplation, meditation, and poetry. We agreed; we set up a kind of interfaith program of meditation and invited a swami to join us. The three of us made the program, divided into three parts. The first part was a meditation on a pebble. The second part was a meditation on a flower; and the third was an act of encounter.

I led the meditation on the pebble. I gave a chant, an invitation, a meditation, that lasted about three minutes. I proposed that everybody practice complete relaxation during the chant, imagining themselves as the pebble which is dropped in a river, runs down through fresh water, and finally comes to its resting place. They would do that during the chant. When the chant ended, they would be completely recovered in the holiness of their being; not trapped, not attracted to the future or the past, completely aware of the marvel of their being. And three minutes, only three minutes, would be devoted to that period.

After that, I gave a poem about the reincarnation of a flower, in order to introduce another phase of the same meditation. Father Roger came with a basket of flowers and invited each participant to come and to pick one flower to meditate on, to receive the message of the flower. He offered the name of St. Francis, who came to an almond tree in the winter and asked the tree about God. Suddenly the tree blossomed. These flowers were like the flowers of the tree. They were to try to get a message and record it in not more than seven words.

BERRIGAN: *Seven words only.*

NHAT HANH: Yes. They collected the messages and gave them to me. I made a selection of a number of messages to go with the flowers, in order to make a bouquet. And I gave it to the swami, who then led the whole group to a hospital for crippled children nearby.

Most of us had not been in that hospital before, although it was nearby. When we arrived, we saw children who were mentally and physically crippled. We listened to the doctor in charge of these children; each theologian gave his flower to a child and comforted him. Then we went nearby, near the water, near the trees, for the swami to lead us in meditation.

But, a number of participants didn't follow through. They abandoned us halfway. They had the impression that a program had been imposed on them—a program not in their traditions. But they were especially disturbed that they could not object, because of the silence and meditation.

Six of them brought the matter to the plenary session and demanded a reexamination of what had happened. As a result, the morning prayers were cancelled. We just sat in silence. That was a step backward. Before that we had had prayer together, led by a representative of each religion. It's too bad, but that's what happened. Yet it turned out that the pebble and the flowers were what they remembered most.

Then there was the fruit salad. An Indian Christian, my friend Samartha, gave a very good speech of introduction to the conference; he stressed the need to go deeper into each tradition. He tried to relieve the fears of people, to emphasize that the conference would respect religious differences—because everybody was afraid of syncretism. He said, "We are not going to make fruit salad." And everybody seemed to like that idea.

So, the first intervention of mine was on fruit salad. I said, "People here don't seem to like fruit salad, but I think fruit salad is delicious." I told them of our sharing the Eucharist here on Holy Thursday and I said, "That was possible because of the sufferings we, Vietnamese and Americans, have shared during many, many years. The sufferings brought us together; our worship didn't come out of light discussions or anything like that."

Well, a few Buddhists were very shocked at the idea that I shared the Eucharist, and I think a number of Christians were also scandalized. But I can say that there were also those who had thought hard and who understood.

I made it very plain that religious life is *life* and that I could not imagine how someone could eat only one kind of fruit. Although there are kinds of fruit that one does not like, there are many kinds that one can appreciate. Besides, only authentic fruits can make fruit salad.

BERRIGAN: *How was that received?*

NHAT HANH: Well, I cannot say. There are many things that need time to be seen. I think many shocking things were said and the negative response does not mean that people didn't receive the shock. The shock is going to work in the future. You see, one of the six who opposed the pebble said to me at the end of the conference—in a sorrowful mood—"I have learned something. On the conceptual level, we cannot know much." See, that's only the beginning.

BERRIGAN: *I think this kind of shock treatment is so important. We know so little of what we know. We have such a narrow conception of how the human soul operates. The most atrocious things can happen in public and make no difference to religious people, especially to religious experts. And yet, all religions are filled with such hope, such possibility. Ours is drenched with the idea of the corporate nature of suffering. We have Christ's words, "I am the vine, you are the branches." There must be a cutting of branches so that the vine may flourish. And then we have Paul's letters about the body—Christ's body which is one. If one member is suffering, if the hand is suffering, the whole body suffers. So many great texts and images to live by. And to think that they become the subject of textual inquiry! Like, what was the genuine text? Was there a comma here? The substance gets entirely lost, so that after a while a theologian cannot take a child in his arms.*

I like what A. J. Muste said once, "What we need in the United States is a foreign policy for children." That seems to me a deep state-ment about a future which we should not merely throw on the shoulders of young people, saying, "They must be different. They must be better."

You were saying though that you also encountered some children in Ceylon.

NHAT HANH: It has been a long time since I saw children like that. Barefoot children in that background of Ceylon—a very green island with no sign of industrial pollution. The children were not children of slums; they were of the countryside; I saw them, and to me they formed a part of nature. I had a desire to come and embrace each of them. I stood on a beach alone, and children saw me and they just ran towards me. We didn't know each other's language, so I put my arms around their shoulders—six of them. We stood like that for a long time, and night came, but that was so pleasant. So, suddenly I remembered that maybe I could emit a sound, say something. I thought, Here it is, Ceylon, country of Buddhism. I may chant a Pali prayer and they might recognize it. So, I began a chant, "I take refuge in the Buddha." They recognized that and they continued the sutra. Four of them joined hands and chanted. The two others stood by, respectfully.

BERRIGAN: *What does the sutra say?*

NHAT HANH: Just a common prayer like the "Our Father." "I take refuge in the Buddha. I take refuge in the Dhamma. I take refuge in the Samgha."

To the two children who hadn't chanted, I motioned for them to join us. They smiled and joined their hands, and chanted, "I take refuge in Mother Maria." The music of this prayer did not differ much from the Buddhist one we had just chanted. And when I embraced each child, they were a little surprised, but I felt very much with them; they gave me a feeling of serenity and sanity. We were in harmony with nature, the land, the ocean.

BERRIGAN: *One of the things that was so hard to bear in the Middle East was the fact that Israel declared, in effect, that the children of the Palestinians were worth nothing. And the Palestinians were, in effect, saying the same thing in their attacks on children. There's some deep despair about the future when one is willing to kill children too; it is as though there doesn't need to be any future. Who cares about the future? I don't know a more irreligious attitude, one more utterly bankrupt of any human content, than one which permits children to be destroyed.*

NHAT HANH: Such leaders play on whatever is left of the concern of adults—of adults vis-à-vis children. People are shocked when they see a child tortured. The leaders know that, and they want to provoke that kind of revulsion. But by such acts, they destroy everything that is left of the concern of people.

When I learned of the Israeli reprisals, bombing children and women and those who were not responsible at all for terrorism, I remembered the story of a school teacher. He was very angered by one of his students who was constantly humming in class, disturbing the class. The teacher did not know who was humming, though the class was always disturbed by that noise. He complained to another teacher, and the other proposed that whenever there was humming like that, just punish one of them, no matter who it is—just punish one. Although you do an injustice to him, you have to punish someone. Next time you punish someone else, and so on. One day the humming will stop. He followed the advice and he succeeded.

BERRIGAN: *It's called "upping the ante." You hope that through the shock waves you create, the terrorism you excite in the whole camp, you will strike at the leadership and make it less possible for them to go on. But among other considerations, even as a theory this thing does not work. Because the leadership never consulted the people anyway, before the first provocative act. You have a leadership on both sides which is acting in secret, without consultation except for a kind of terrorist ingroup, which, in Israel, would be drawn from the army and, in Lebanon, from the young commandos who are willing to go, take hostages, and die.*

But I am sure no one sits with ordinary people, either in Israel or in the camps, and says, "This is what we propose; we want to do this. This is what will happen as a result of it. You will be bombed, for instance. Do you agree?" Nobody asks the people. They are never consulted about whether they wish to die. They just die. And so, the roots of the community are cut by a leadership which is utterly indifferent to the fate of the community, and which makes its decisions entirely on its own. A kind of hardnosed fatalism is the rule; some must die, some are expendable. We were at a loss for words to describe the spiritual degradation of such actions.

And yet, of course, the acts of terrorism and reprisal are very different. This is something that is seldom considered. The technology on the Israeli side is an extension of American technology and is used no differently than the Americans used it in Vietnam. This is what is called "clean killing." It's killing which is laundered. Neither the people who commit the killing nor the people at home ever see the dead and wounded. The killing is rendered abstract; the sin is an abstract sin. There's no crime imputable. But, on the other hand, there is a great outcry when Palestinians strike in Israel because the blood is visible—the bodies of the children are visible to all. A double standard is always exercised when the technological world meets the world of immediate violence.

I said, in Israel, it was extraordinary that there was an outcry for blood after the killing of Israeli children, but that there was no word about the children the Israelis themselves had killed. One of the editors with whom we talked, who's a thoughtful, good man, said, "Don't you think all of us should address a letter to the American and European political left who have made a hero of Hawatmeh, who claimed responsibility for the attack on the children? Should we not say that this is utterly unacceptable?"

This appeared to me, in one sense, logical; I knew that, in America, elements of the left are so utterly out of contact with reality that they would elevate any violence into heroic activity. But I said, "I think we must pause. How can we address a letter to Americans and Europeans about the crimes of Hawatmeh, and say nothing about the crimes of Israeli reprisals?" A great silence followed this. It seemed that I had introduced a very complicated note into the discussion.

NHAT HANH: Just as children of today drink milk, eat vegetables, but don't know where these things come from. Various processes bring milk and vegetables and other kinds of food to the city. So, children are surprised when they see a cow or a chicken or a real cauliflower plant.

In the same way, leaders always have their machinery of propaganda behind them so that people don't see the bad side of violence. Technology helps them in that respect very much.

BERRIGAN: *Also, one notices how intellectuals become the servants of violence. This was very striking to me. On both sides, the* *justification for what was happening was formulated by an intellec-tual group that surrounded the leaders. They offered a measure of historical truth in favor of their own side. Some of their insights were extremely valuable and correct. But the devastating point is that in their study of political science and history and the analogies they draw between nations, they give a nod to the violence of the leadership. They justify the actions of the leaders before the world—in their research, in their writings—and so cause the terrorism to continue in many ways. There's very real teamwork between the tactical, militarized leadership which decides the next act of war, and those who are verbal-izing and justifying that act before the world.*

Of course the same thing goes on everywhere. Johnson needed Rostow. Kennedy needed Schlesinger. Nixon needed Kissinger. And Palestinian leaders need several scholars whom we met, who are distinguished and who well know the history of Palestine and the other states.

It occurred to me, in fact, that neither side deserved the name rev-olutionary, because from the point of view of power already pos-sessed or of power grasped at, the same tactics were going forward. The violent were in liaison with the justifiers of violence; the revolutionary appeal was no different in essence from the appeal of those in posses-sion. They were saying, "We keep our power by violence," or "We gain power by violence." And the appeal, as far as I can understand it, is an insane appeal launched in an insane world. It's as though the inmates in Marat Sade *are yelling through the bars at people who are behind other bars. There's no real difference between those in power and those who are seeking power.*

The Palestinian leaders gave it away. They said, "No one heard of us until we did these things. We were nonexistent; then we attacked a school bus or hijacked an airplane or took hostages. Now the world hears from us. Now the world knows we exist. Otherwise we would have gone on forever in the camps, you see." And I said to myself, There's a terrifying truth here. I never heard of the Palestinians until these things happened. But the appeal is insane; the world can hear only an insane call. So there is no breakthrough.

NHAT HANH: If those who seek power and those who are in power are not much different from each other, we may ask ourselves what conditions the behavior of the leadership? What part is played by free will, by strength? Why does everyone in power do very much the same thing?

When medical students and nurses are about to graduate, they think very much of helping the poor—those who have not enough money to go to fully-equipped hospitals, facilities like that. But after graduation, after a few years in ther careers, many of them begin to act like machines and pay no more attention to the poor and oppressed. The nurses become irritated at poor patients. The doctors become insensitive to the sufferings of the poor. It's very sad. To love is a difficult thing when the people try to cheat and trick you, to get the most out of you if you show compassion, goodwill; when they try to get the better of you, because you show concern. So, at one point you cannot love them any more, and you begin to treat them as you treat objects.

I think such things happen frequently. Our good-will, our intentions, play one role; social conditions play another. And there are the political and economic systems. If we try to do things faithfully, in accord with our best instincts, we have to go against all of these forces.

If you are in power, they will try to bring you down. So, you make a compromise in order to be able to continue. You compromise to the point that you become like those whom you opposed before you came to power.

BERRIGAN: *Making such a "revolution," one is almost like a person who is trying to pull himself out of quicksand. He tries to draw himself out of an awful suction of death, clean. Yet, nobody can come out clean. If you survive, you come into a new situation very much like the old—a smell, a filth of history, of human crimes. How can you stand on your feet again and say, "I am a new person, and I am now ready to begin functioning in a new way"? This is why I think there has never really been a revolution which transcended the past without submission before God, without faith.*

I think that life always is ambiguous. This we accept, the human situation being murky and conditioned by the past. But what we look for, as Camus says, is at least a world in which murder will not be legitimate. We don't look for a world in which murder will not occur; that seems unrealistic. But we don't want murder to be looked upon as virtuous and legitimate. Maybe that's a minimal definition of the kind of change we work for.

However, it seems to me that those who step out of the quicksand of bad history, by some heroic act of antigravity, still believe murder is legitimate. They call the killing of the "bad guys" a revolution. They ignore the fact that this is the most profound and bloody stereotype of history; everybody has always killed the bad guys. Nobody kills the good guys.

The Church is tainted in this way as well. The Church plays the same cards; it likes the taste of imperial power too. This is the most profound kind of betrayal I can think of. Terrible! Jews and Christians and Buddhists and all kinds of people who come from a good place, who come from revolutionary beginnings and are descended from heroes and saints. This can all be lost, you know. We can give it all up. And we do. Religion becomes another resource for the same old death-game, as we saw during the Vietnam war.

But I think maybe we're reduced to modest and small actions today, retaining some measure of sanity, some remembrance which will be viable. We must make the old stereotypes uncomfortable by asking distressing questions. I thought that that was the only thing we could do in the Middle East; perhaps it was the only thing you could do among theologians at the conference. You tried to formulate questions which were shocking and uncomfortable, which were a kind of access to the truth and to remembrance. There's not much else you can do.

Yet I don't think I have been courageous enough, lucid and visible before others, in a certain ethical position. We haven't been clear enough for our own people and for our own souls on these questions of violence. I'm humiliated to say that it has taken me so long to be willing to bear the suspicion or dislike of people whom I admire and stand with, and even to be unpopular on all sides. But now, at last, it looks as though I've gotten there!

from The Miracle of Mindfulness:

AN INTRODUCTION TO THE PRACTICE OF MEDITATION

by *Thich Nhat Hanh*

"Each act is a rite." Thich Nhat Hanh urges us to engage with each experience—to savor its beauty, ugliness, joy or pain. Whether you are brushing your teeth or taking your last breath, this moment will never come again.

Yesterday Allen came over to visit with his son Joey. Joey has grown so quickly! He's already seven years old and is fluent in French and English. He even uses a bit of slang he's picked up on the street. Raising children here is very different from the way we raise children at home. Here parents believe that "freedom is necessary for a child's development." During the two hours that Allen and I were talking, Allen had to keep a constant eye on Joey. Joey played, chattered away, and interrupted us, making it impossible to carry on a real conversation. I gave him several picture books for children but he barely glanced at them before tossing them aside and interrupting our conversation again. He demands the constant attention of grown-ups.

Later, Joey put on his jacket and went outside to play with a neighbor's child. I asked Allen, "Do you find family life easy?" Allen didn't answer directly. He said that during the past few weeks, since the birth of Ana, he had been unable to sleep any length of time. During the night, Sue wakes him up and—because she is too tired herself—asks him to check to make sure Ana is still breathing. "I get up and look at the baby and then come back and fall asleep again. Sometimes the ritual happens two or three times a night."

"Is family life easier than being a bachelor?" I asked. Allen didn't answer directly. But I understood. I asked another question: "A lot of people say that if you have a family you're less lonely and have more security. Is that true?" Allen nodded his head and mumbled something softly. But I understood.

Then Allen said, "I've discovered a way to have a lot more time. In the past, I used to look at my time as if it were divided into several parts. One part I reserved for Joey, another part was for Sue, another part to help with Ana, another part for household work. The time left over I considered my own. I could read, write, do research, go for walks.

"But now I try not to divide time into parts anymore. I consider my time with Joey and Sue as my own time. When I help Joey with his homework, I try to find ways of seeing his time as my own time. I go through his lesson with him, sharing his presence and finding ways to be interested in what we do during that time. The time for him becomes my own time. The same with

Sue. The remarkable thing is that now I have unlimited time for myself!"

Allen smiled as he spoke. I was surprised. I knew that Allen hadn't learned this from reading any books. This was something he had discovered for himself in his own daily life.

Washing the dishes to wash the dishes

Thirty years ago, when I was still a novice at Tu Hieu Pagoda, washing the dishes was hardly a pleasant task. During the Season of Retreat when all the monks returned to the monastery, two novices had to do all the cooking and wash the dishes for sometimes well over one hundred monks. There was no soap. We had only ashes, rice husks, and coconut husks, and that was all. Cleaning such a high stack of bowls was a chore, especially during the winter when the water was freezing cold. Then you had to heat up a big pot of water before you could do any scrubbing. Nowadays one stands in a kitchen equipped with liquid soap, special scrubpads, and even running hot water, which makes it all the more agreeable. It is easier to enjoy washing the dishes now. Anyone can wash them in a hurry, then sit down and enjoy a cup of tea afterwards. I can see a machine for washing clothes, although I wash my own things out by hand, but a dishwashing machine is going just a little too far!

While washing the dishes one should only be washing the dishes, which means that while washing the dishes one should be completely aware of the fact that one is washing the dishes. At first glance, that might seem a little silly: why put so much stress on a simple thing? But that's precisely the point. The fact that I am standing there and washing these bowls is a wondrous reality. I'm being completely myself, following my breath, conscious of my presence, and conscious of my thoughts and actions. There's no way I can be tossed around mindlessly like a bottle slapped here and there on the waves.

The cup in your hands

In the United States, I have a close friend named Jim Forest. When I first met him eight years ago, he was working with the Catholic Peace Fellowship. Last winter, Jim came to visit. I usually wash the dishes after we've finished the evening meal, before sitting down and drinking tea with everyone else. One night, Jim asked if he might do the dishes. I said, "Go ahead, but if you wash the dishes you must know the way to wash them." Jim replied, "Come on, you think I don't know how to wash the dishes?" I answered, "There are two ways to wash the dishes. The first is to wash the dishes in order to have clean dishes and the second is to wash the dishes in order to wash the dishes." Jim was delighted and said, "I choose the second way—to wash the dishes to wash the dishes." From then on, Jim knew how to wash the dishes. I transferred the "responsibility" to him for an entire week.

If while washing dishes, we think only of the cup of tea that awaits us, thus hurrying to get the dishes out of the way as if they were a nuisance, then we are not "washing the dishes to wash the dishes." What's more, we are not alive during the time we are washing the dishes. In fact we are completely incapable of realizing the miracle of life while standing at the sink. If we can't wash the dishes, the chances are we won't be able to drink our tea either. While drinking the cup of tea, we will only be thinking of other things, barely aware of the cup in our hands. Thus we are sucked away into the future—and we are incapable of actually living one minute of life.

Eating a tangerine

I remember a number of years ago, when Jim and I were first traveling together in the United States, we sat under a tree and shared a tangerine. He began to talk about what we would be doing in the future. Whenever we thought about a project that seemed attractive or inspiring, Jim became so immersed in it that he literally forgot about what he was doing in the present. He popped a section of tangerine in his mouth and, before he had begun chewing it, had another slice ready to pop into his mouth again. He was hardly aware he was eating a tangerine. All I had to say was, "You ought to eat the tangerine section you've already taken." Jim was startled into realizing what he was doing.

It was as if he hadn't been eating the tangerine at all. If he had been eating anything, he was "eating" his future plans.

A tangerine has sections. If you can eat just one section, you can probably eat the entire tangerine. But if you can't eat a single section, you cannot eat the tangerine. Jim understood. He slowly put his hand down and focused on the presence of the slice already in his mouth. He chewed it thoughtfully before reaching down and taking another section.

Later, when Jim went to prison for activities against

the war, I was worried about whether he could endure the four walls of prison and sent him a very short letter: "Do you remember the tangerine we shared when we were together? Your being there is like the tangerine. Eat it and be one with it. Tomorrow it will be no more."

The essential discipline

More than thirty years ago, when I first entered the monastery, the monks gave me a small book called "The Essential Discipline for Daily Use," written by the Buddhist monk Doc The from Bao Son pagoda, and they told me to memorize it. It was a thin book. It couldn't have been more than 40 pages, but it contained all the thoughts Doc The used to awaken his mind while doing any task. When he woke up in the morning, his first thought was, "Just awakened, I hope that every person will attain great awareness and see in complete clarity." When he washed his hands, he used this thought to place himself in mindfulness: "Washing my hands, I hope that every person will have pure hands to receive reality." The book is comprised entirely of such sentences. Their goal was to help the beginning practitioner take hold of his own consciousness. The Zen Master Doc The helped all of us young novices to practice, in a relatively easy way, those things which are taught in the Sutra of Mindfulness. Each time you put on your robe, washed the dishes, went to the bathroom, folded your mat, carried buckets of water, or brushed your teeth, you could use one of the thoughts from the book in order to take hold of your own consciousness.

The Sutra of Mindfulness* says, "When walking, the practitioner must be conscious that he is walking. When sitting, the practitioner must be conscious that he is sitting. When lying down, the practitioner must be conscious that he is lying down. . . . No matter what position one's body is in, the practitioner must be conscious of that position. Practicing thus, the practitioner lives in direct and constant mindfulness of the body. . . ." The mindfulness of the positions of one's body is not enough, however. We must be conscious of each breath, each movement, every thought and feeling, everything which has any relation to ourselves.

But what is the purpose of the Sutra's instruction? Where are we to find the time to practice such mindfulness? If you spend all day practicing mindfulness, how will there ever be enough time to do all the work that needs to be done to change and to build an alternative society? How does Allen manage to work, study Joey's lesson, take Ana's diapers to the laundromat, and practice mindfulness at the same time?

Allen said that since he's begun to consider Joey's and Sue's time as his own, he has "unlimited time."

---

* In the Sutras, Buddha usually teaches that one should use one's breath in order to achieve Concentration. The Sutra which speaks about the use of your breath to maintain mindfulness is the Anapanasati Sutra. This Sutra was translated and commentated on by a Vietnamese Zen Master of Central Asian origin named Khuong Tang Hoi, around the beginning of the Third Century A.D. Anapana means breath and sati means mindfulness. Tang Hoi translated it as "Guarding the Mind." The Anapanasati Sutra, that is, is the sutra on using one's breath to maintain mindfulness. The Sutra on Breath to Maintain Mindfulness is the 118th Sutra in the Majhima Nikaya collection of sutras and it teaches 16 methods of using one's breath.

But perhaps he has it only in principle. Because there are doubtless times when Allen forgets to consider Joey's time as his own time while going over homework with him, and thus Allen may lose that time. Allen might hope for the time to pass quickly, or he may grow impatient because that time seems wasted to him, because it isn't his own time. And so, if he really wants "unlimited time," he will have to keep alive the realization that "this is my time" throughout the time he's studying with Joey. But during such times, one's mind is inevitably distracted by other thoughts, and so if one really wants to keep one's consciousness alive (from now on I'll use the term "mindfulness" to refer to keeping one's consciousness alive to the present reality), then one must practice right now in one's daily life, not only during meditation sessions.

When you are walking along a path leading into a village, you can practice mindfulness. Walking along a dirt path, surrounded by patches of green grass, if you practice mindfulness you will experience that path, the path leading into the village. You practice by keeping this one thought alive: "I'm walking along the path leading into the village." Whether it's sunny or rainy, whether the path is dry or wet, you keep that one thought, but not just repeating it like a machine, over and over again. Machine thinking is the opposite of mindfulness. If we're really engaged in mindfulness while walking along the path to the village, then we will consider the act of each step we take as an infinite wonder, and a joy will open our hearts like a flower, enabling us to enter the world of reality.

I like to walk alone on country paths, rice plants and wild grasses on both sides, putting each foot down on the earth in mindfulness, knowing that I walk on the wondrous earth. In such moments, existence is a miraculous and mysterious reality. People usually consider walking on water or in thin air a miracle. But I think the real miracle is not to walk either on water or in thin air, but to walk on earth. Every day we are engaged in a miracle which we don't even recognize: a blue sky, white clouds, green leaves, the black, curious eyes of a child—our own two eyes. All is a miracle.

Sitting

Zen Master Doc The says that when sitting in meditation, one should sit upright, giving birth to this thought, "Sitting here is like sitting on the Bodhi spot." The Bodhi spot is where Lord Buddha sat when he obtained Enlightenment. If any person can become a Buddha, and the Buddhas are all those countless persons who have obtained enlightenment, then many have sat on the very spot I sit on now. Sitting on the same spot as a Buddha gives rise to happiness and sitting in mindfulness means itself to have become a Buddha. The poet Nguyen Cong Tru experienced the same thing when he sat down on a certain spot, and suddenly saw how others had sat on the same spot countless ages ago, and how in ages to come others would also come to sit there:

> On the same spot I sit today
> Others came, in ages past, to sit.
> One thousand years, still others will come.
> Who is the singer, and who the listener?

That spot and the minutes he spent there became a link in eternal reality.

But active, concerned people don't have time to spend leisurely, walking along paths of green grass and sitting beneath trees. One must prepare projects, consult with the neighbors, try to resolve a million difficulties; there is hard work to do. One must deal with every kind of hardship, every moment keeping one's attention focused on the work, alert, ready to handle the situation ably and intelligently.

You might well ask: Then how are we to practice mindfulness?

My answer is: Keep your attention focused on the work, be alert and ready to handle ably and intelligently any situation which may arise—this is mindfulness. There is no reason why mindfulness should be different from focusing all one's attention on one's work, to be alert and to be using one's best judgment. During the moment one is consulting, resolving, and dealing with whatever arises, a calm heart and self-control are necessary if one is to obtain good results. Anyone can see that. If we are not in control of ourselves but instead let our impatience or anger interfere, then our work is no longer of any value.

Mindfulness is the miracle by which we master and restore ourselves. Consider, for example: a magician who cuts his body into many parts and places each part in a different region—hands in the south, arms in the east, legs in the north, and then by some miraculous power lets forth a cry which reassembles whole every part of his body. Mindfulness is like that—it is the miracle which can call back in a flash our dispersed mind and restore it to wholeness so that we can live each minute of life.

Taking hold of one's breath

Thus mindfulness is at the same time a means and an end, the seed and the fruit. When we practice mindfulness in order to build up concentration, mindfulness is a seed. But mindfulness itself is the life of awareness: the presence of mindfulness means the presence of life, and therefore mindfulness is also the fruit. Mindfulness frees us of forgetfulness and dispersion and makes it possible to live fully each minute of life. Mindfulness enables us to live.

You should know how to breathe to maintain mindfulness, as breathing is a natural and extremely effective tool which can prevent dispersion. Breath is the bridge which connects life to consciousness, which unites your body to your thoughts. Whenever your mind becomes scattered, use your breath as the means to take hold of your mind again.

Breathe in lightly a fairly long breath, conscious of the fact that you are inhaling a deep breath. Now breathe out all the breath in your lungs, remaining conscious the whole time of the exhalation. The Sutra of Mindfulness teaches the method to take hold of one's breath in the following manner: "Be ever mindful you breathe in and mindful you breathe out. Breathing in a long breath, you know, 'I am breathing in a long breath.' Breathing out a long breath, you know, 'I am breathing out a long breath.' Breathing in a short breath, you know, 'I am breathing in a short breath.' Breathing out a short breath, you know, 'I am breathing out a short breath.'"

"Experiencing a whole breath-body, I shall breathe in," thus you train yourself. "Experiencing the whole breath-body, I shall breathe out," thus you train yourself. "Calming the activity of the breath-body, I shall breathe in," thus you train yourself. "Calming the activity of the breath-body, I shall breathe out," thus you train yourself.

In a Buddhist monastery, everyone learns to use breath as a tool to stop mental dispersion and to build up concentration power. Concentration power is the strength which comes from practicing mindfulness. It is the concentration which can help one obtain the Great Awakening. When a worker takes hold of his own breath, he has already become awakened. In order to maintain mindfulness throughout a long period, we must continue to watch our breath.

It is autumn here and the golden leaves falling one by one are truly beautiful. Taking a 10-minute walk in the woods, watching my breath and maintaining mindfulness, I feel refreshed and restored. Like that, I can really enter into a communion with each leaf.

Of course, walking alone on a country path, it is easier to maintain mindfulness. If there's a friend by your side, not talking but also watching his breath, then you can continue to maintain mindfulness without difficulty. But if the friend at your side begins to talk, it becomes a little more difficult.

If, in your mind, you think, "I wish this fellow would quit talking, so I could concentrate," you have already lost your mindfulness. But if you think, instead, "If he wishes to talk, I will answer, but I will continue in mindfulness, aware of the fact that we are walking along this path together, aware of what we say, I can continue to watch my breath as well."

If you can give rise to that thought, you will be continuing in mindfulness. It is harder to practice in such situations than when you are alone, but if you continue to practice nonetheless, you will develop the ability to maintain much greater concentration. There is a line from a Vietnamese folk song that says: "Hardest of all is to practice the Way at home, second in the crowd, and third in the pagoda." It is only in an active and demanding situation that mindfulness really becomes a challenge!

Counting one's breath and following one's breath
In the meditation sessions I recently began for non-Vietnamese, I usually suggest various methods that I myself have tried, methods that are quite simple. I suggest to beginners the method of "Following the length of the breath." The student lies, back down, on the floor. Then I invite all of the participants to gather around so I can show them a few simple points:

1) Although inhaling and exhaling are the work of the lungs, and take place in the chest area, the stomach area also plays a role. The stomach rises with the filling of the lungs. At the beginning of the breath the stomach begins to push out. But after inhaling about two-thirds of the breath, it starts to lower again.

2) Why? Between your chest and stomach there is a muscular membrane, the diaphragm. When you breathe in correctly the air fills the lower part of the lungs first, before the upper lungs fill with air, and the diaphragm pushes down

on the stomach, causing the stomach to
rise. When you have filled your upper
lungs with air, the chest pushes out and
causes the stomach to lower again.

3)   That is why, in former times, people spoke
of the breath as originating at the navel and
terminating at the nostrils.

For beginners, lying down to practice breathing is
very helpful. The important thing is to guard against
making too much of an effort: too great an effort can
be dangerous for the lungs, especially when the lungs
are weak from many years of incorrect breathing. In
the beginning, the practitioner should lie on his or her
back on a thin mat or blanket, the two arms loosely at
the sides. Don't prop your head on a pillow. Focus
your attention on your exhalation and watch how
long it is. Measure it slowly by counting in your
mind: 1, 2, 3 . . . After several times, you will know the
"length" of your breath: Perhaps it is 5. Now try to
extend the exhalation for one more count (or 2) so that
the exhalation's length becomes 6 or 7. Begin to exhale
counting from 1 to 5. When you reach 5, rather than
immediately inhaling as before, try to extend the exhalation to 6 or 7. This way you will empty your lungs
of more air. When you have finished exhaling, pause
for an instant to let your lungs take in fresh air on
their own. Let them take in just as much air as they
want without making any effort. The inhalation will
normally be "shorter" than the exhalation. Keep a
steady count in your mind to measure the length of
both. Practice several weeks like this, remaining

mindful of all your exhalations and inhalations while lying down. (If you have a clock with a loud tick you can use it to help you keep track of the length of your inhalation and exhalation.)

Continue to measure your breath while walking, sitting, standing, and especially whenever you are outdoors. While walking, you might use your steps to measure your breath. After a month or so, the difference between the length of your exhalation and inhalation will lessen, gradually evening out until they are of equal measure. If the length of your exhalation is 6, the inhalation will also be 6.

If you feel at all tired while practicing, stop at once. But even if you do not feel tired, don't prolong the practice of long, equal breaths beyond short periods of time—10 to 20 breaths are enough. The moment you feel the least fatigue, return your breathing to normal. Fatigue is an excellent mechanism of our bodies and the best advisor as to whether one should rest or continue. In order to measure your breath you can count— or use a rhythmic phrase that you like. (If the length of your breath is 6, you might use, instead of numbers, the six words, "My heart is now at peace." If the length is 7 you might use, "I walk on the new green earth." A Buddhist might say, "I take refuge in the Buddha." For a Christian it could be "Our Father who art in heaven." When you are walking, each step should correspond to one word.

Quiet breathing

Your breath should be light, even, and flowing, like a thin stream of water running through the sand. Your breath should be very quiet, so quiet that a person sitting next to you cannot hear it. Your breathing should flow gracefully, like a river, like a watersnake crossing the water, and not like a chain of rugged mountains or the gallop of a horse. To master our breath is to be in control of our bodies and minds. Each time we find ourselves dispersed and find it difficult to gain control of ourselves by different means, the method of watching the breath should always be used.

The instant you sit down to meditate, begin watching your breath. At first breathe normally, gradually letting your breathing slow down until it is quiet, even, and the lengths of the breaths are fairly long. From the moment you sit down to the moment your breathing has become deep and silent, be conscious of everything that is happening in yourself.

As the Buddhist Sutra of Mindfulness says: "Breathing in a long breath, you know, 'I am breathing in a long breath.' Breathing out a long breath, the practitioner knows, 'I am breathing out a long breath.' Breathing in a short breath, you know, 'I am breathing in a short breath.' Breathing out a short breath, you know, 'I am breathing out a short breath.' Experiencing the whole breath-body, I shall breathe in." Thus you train yourself. "Experiencing the whole breath-body, I shall breathe out." Thus you train yourself. "Calming the activity of the breath-body, I shall breathe in." Thus you train yourself. "Calming the activity of the breath-body, I shall breathe out." Thus you train yourself.

After about 10 to 20 minutes, your thoughts will have quieted down like a pond on which not even a ripple stirs.

Counting your breath

Making your breath calm and even is called the method of following one's breath. If it seems hard at first, you can substitute the method of counting your breath. As you breathe in, count 1 in your mind, and as you breathe out, count 1. Breathe in, count 2. Breathe out, count 2. Continue through 10, then return to 1 again. This counting is like a string which attaches your mindfulness to your breath. This exercise is the beginning point in the process of becoming continuously conscious of your breath. Without mindfulness, however, you will quickly lose count. When the count is lost, simply return to 1 and keep trying until you can keep the count correctly. Once you can truly focus your attention on the counts, you have reached the point at which you can begin to abandon the counting method and begin to concentrate solely on the breath itself.

In those moments when you are upset or dispersed and find it difficult to practice mindfulness, return to your breath: Taking hold of your breath is itself mindfulness. Your breath is the wondrous method of taking hold of your consciousness. As one religious community says in its rule, "One should not lose oneself in mind-dispersion or in one's surroundings. Learn to practice breathing in order to regain control of body and mind, to practice mindfulness, and to develop concentration and wisdom."

Every act is a rite

Suppose there is a towering wall from the top of which one can see vast distances—but there is no apparent means to climb it, only a thin piece of thread hanging over the top and coming down both sides. A clever person will tie a thicker string onto one end of the thread, walk over to the other side of the wall, then pull on the thread bringing the string to the other side. Then he will tie the end of the string to a strong rope and pull the rope over. When the rope has reached the bottom of one side and is secured on the other side, the wall can be easily scaled.

Our breath is such a fragile piece of thread. But once we know how to use it, it can become a wondrous tool to help us surmount situations which would otherwise seem hopeless. Our breath is the bridge from our body to our mind, the element which reconciles our body and mind and which makes possible oneness of body and mind. Breath is aligned to both body and mind and it alone is the tool which can bring them both together, illuminating both and bringing both peace and calm.

Many persons and books discuss the immense benefits that result from correct breathing. They report that a person who knows how to breathe is a person who knows how to build up endless vitality: breath builds up the lungs, strengthens the blood, and revitalizes every organ in the body. They say that proper breathing is more important than food. And all of these statements are correct.

Years ago, I was extremely ill. After several years of taking medicine and undergoing medical treatment, my condition was unimproved. So I turned to the method of breathing and, thanks to that, was able to heal myself.

Breath is a tool. Breath itself is mindfulness. The

use of breath as a tool may help one obtain immense benefits, but these cannot be considered as ends in themselves. These benefits are only the by-products of the realization of mindfulness.

In my small class in meditation for non-Vietnamese, there are many young people. I've told them that if each one can meditate an hour each day that's good, but it's nowhere near enough. You've got to practice meditation when you walk, stand, lie down, sit, and work, while washing your hands, washing the dishes, sweeping the floor, drinking tea, talking to friends, or whatever you are doing: "While washing the dishes, you might be thinking about the tea afterwards, and so try to get them out of the way as quickly as possible in order to sit and drink tea. But that means that you are incapable of living during the time you are washing the dishes. When you are washing the dishes, washing the dishes must be the most important thing in your life. Just as when you're drinking tea, drinking tea must be the most important thing in your life. When you're using the toilet, let that be the most important thing in your life." And so on. Chopping wood is meditation. Carrying water is meditation. Be mindful 24 hours a day, not just during the one hour you may allot for formal meditation or reading scripture and reciting prayers. Each act must be carried out in mindfulness. Each act is a rite, a ceremony. Raising your cup of tea to your mouth is a rite. Does the word "rite" seem too solemn? I use that word in order to jolt you into the realization of the life-and-death matter of awareness.

from Being Peace

by *Thich Nhat Hanh*

In this selection Thich Nhat Hanh discusses the "three gems" of Buddhism: Buddha (the awakened one), Dharma (the Buddha's teachings) and Sangha (the community of people who live by the teachings).

*M*any of us worry about the situation of the world. We don't know when the bombs will explode. We feel that we are on the edge of time. As individuals, we feel helpless, despairing. The situation is so dangerous, injustice is so widespread, the danger is so close. In this kind of situation, if we panic, things will only become worse. We need to remain calm, to see clearly. Meditation is to be aware, and to try to help.

I like to use the example of a small boat crossing the Gulf of Siam. In Vietnam, there are many people, called boat people, who leave the country in small boats. Often the boats are caught in rough seas or storms, the people may panic, and boats can sink. But if even one person aboard can remain calm, lucid, knowing what to do and what not to do, he or she can help the boat survive. His or her expression—face, voice—communicates clarity and calmness, and people have trust in that person. They will listen to what he or she says. One such person can save the lives of many.

Our world is something like a small boat. Compared with the cosmos, our planet is a very small boat. We are about to panic because our situation is no better than the situation of the small boat in the sea. You know that we have more than 50,000 nuclear weapons. Humankind has become a very dangerous species. We need people who can sit still and be able to smile, who can walk peacefully. We need people like that in order to save us. Mahayana Buddhism says that you are that person, that each of you is that person.

I had one student named Thich Thanh Van, who entered the monastery at the age of six, and at the age of 17, began to study with me. Later he was the first director of the School of Youth for Social Service, where he directed thousands of young people working during the war in Vietnam, rebuilding villages that were destroyed, and resettling tens of thousands of refugees fleeing the war-zones. He was killed in an accident. I was in Copenhagen when I heard of the death of my student. He was a very gentle monk, very brave.

When he was a novice, six or seven years old, he saw people come to the temple and bring cakes and bananas to offer to the Buddha. He wanted to know how the Buddha eats bananas, so he waited until everyone went home and the shrine was closed, and then he peered through the door, waiting for the Buddha to reach out his hand, take a banana, peel it, and eat it. He waited and waited, but nothing happened. The Buddha did not seem to eat bananas, unless he realized that someone was spying on him.

Thich Thanh Van told me several other stories about when he was a young boy. When he discovered that the statue of the Buddha is not the Buddha, he began to ask where the Buddhas are, because it did not seem to him that Buddhas were living among humans. He concluded that Buddhas must not be very nice, because when people became Buddhas, they would leave us to go to a far-away country. I told him that Buddhas are us. They are made of flesh and bones, not copper or silver or gold. The Buddha statue is just a symbol of the Buddha, in the same way the American flag is a symbol of America. The American flag is not the American people.

The root-word *buddh* means to wake up, to know, to understand; and he or she who wakes up and understands is called a Buddha. It is as simple as that. The capacity to wake up, to understand, and to love is called Buddha nature. When Buddhists say, "I take refuge in the Buddha," they are expressing trust in their own capacity of understanding, of becoming awake. The Chinese and the Vietnamese say, "I go back and rely on the Buddha in me." Adding "in me" makes it very clear that you yourself are the Buddha.

In Buddhism, there are three gems: Buddha, the awakened one; Dharma, the way of understanding and loving; and Sangha, the community that lives in harmony and awareness. The three are interrelated, and at times it is hard to distinguish one from another. In everyone there is the capacity to wake up, to understand, and to love. So in ourselves we find Buddha, and we also find Dharma and Sangha. I will explain more about Dharma and Sangha, but first I want to say something about Buddha, the one who develops his or her understanding and loving to the highest degree. (In Sanskrit, understanding is *prajña* and love is *karuna* and *maitri*.)

Understanding and love are not two things, but just one. Suppose your son wakes up one morning and sees that it is already quite late. He decides to wake up his younger sister, to give her enough time to eat breakfast before going to school. It happens that she is grouchy and instead of saying, "Thank you for waking me up," she says, "Shut up! Leave me alone!" and kicks him. He will probably get angry, thinking, "I woke her up nicely. Why did she kick me?" He may want to go to the kitchen and tell you about it, or even kick her back. But then he remembers that during the night his sister coughed a lot, and he realizes that she must be sick. Maybe she has a cold, maybe that is why she behaved so meanly. He is not angry any more. At that moment there is *buddh* in him. He understands, he is awake. When you understand, you cannot help but love. You cannot get angry. To develop understanding, you have to practice looking at all living beings with the eyes of compassion. When you understand, you love. And when you love, you naturally act in a way that can relieve the suffering of people.

Someone who is awake, who knows, who understands, is called a Buddha. Buddha is in every one of us. We can become awake, understanding, and also loving. I often tell children that if their mother or father is very understanding and loving, working, taking care of the family, smiling, being lovely, like a flower, they can say, "Mommy (or Daddy), you are all Buddha today."

Two thousand five hundred years ago there was a person who practiced in a way that his understanding and love became perfected, and everyone in the world recognized this. His name was Siddhartha. When Siddhartha was very young, he began to think that life had a lot of suffering in it, that people do not love each other enough, do not understand each other enough. So he left his home to go to the forest to practice meditating, breathing and smiling. He became a monk, and he tried to practice in order to develop his awakening, his understanding, and his love to the highest levels. He practiced sitting meditation and walking meditation for several years with five friends who were also monks. Although they were intelligent people, they made mistakes. For instance, each day they ate only one piece of fruit—one mango, or one guava, or one star fruit. Sometimes people exaggerate, and say that Siddhartha ate only one sesame seed a day, but I went to the forest in India where he practiced, and I know that is silly because there are no sesame seeds there. I saw also the Anoma River, in which he bathed several times, and the Bodhi tree where he sat and became a Buddha. The Bodhi tree I saw is not the same tree, it is the great-great-great-grandchild of the first Bodhi tree.

One day Siddhartha became so weak that he could not practice, and as he was an intelligent young man, he decided to go to the village and get something to eat—bananas or cake or anything. But as soon as he took four or five steps, he stumbled and fainted; he lost consciousness because he was too hungry. He would have died, but a milkmaid carrying milk to the village saw him and came over. She found that he was still alive, still breathing, but very weak, and so she took a bowl and poured some milk into his mouth. At first Siddhartha did not react, but then his lips moved and he began to drink the milk. He drank a whole bowl of milk, and he felt much better and slowly sat up. He looked beautiful, because Siddhartha was a very, very handsome person. Nowadays people make statues of him which are not very handsome. Sometimes they are even grouchy, without any smile on his face. But he was a very beautiful person, and the milkmaid thought that he must be the god of the mountain. She kneeled down and was about to worship, but he stretched out his arm to tell her not to, and he told her something. What do you think he must have said to her?

He said, "Please give me another bowl of milk." Because he saw that the milk was doing wonderful things, and he knew that once our body is strong enough, we can succeed in meditation. The young lady was so happy, she poured him another bowl of milk. After that, she inquired about him, and he said that he was a monk, trying to meditate to develop his compassion and his understanding to the highest level so that he could help other people. She asked if there was anything she could do to help, and Siddhartha said, "Each day at noon-time, can you give me a small bowl of rice? That would help me very much." So from that day on, she brought him some rice wrapped in banana leaves, and sometimes she also brought milk.

The five other monks Siddhartha had been practicing

with despised him and thought him worthless. "Let us go somewhere else to practice. He drinks milk, and he eats rice. He has no perseverance." But Siddhartha did very well. Day in and day out he meditated, and he developed his insight, his understanding, and his compassion very, very quickly as he recovered his health.

One day, after taking a swim in the Anoma River, he had the impression that he only needed one more sitting to come to a total breakthrough, to become a fully enlightened person. When he was about to sit down, still practicing walking meditation, a buffalo boy came by. In India 2,500 years ago, buffaloes were used to pull the plows, and a buffalo boy's job was to watch them, bathe and take care of them, and cut grass for them to eat.

As the buffalo boy came by, he saw Siddhartha walking very peacefully, and he liked him immediately. Sometimes we see someone we like very much, even if we don't know why. The boy wanted to say something, but he was shy, so he came near Siddhartha three or four times before saying, "Gentleman, I like you very much." Siddhartha looked at him and said, "I like you also." Encouraged by this response, the boy told him, "I really want to give you something, but I have nothing I can give you." And Siddhartha said, "You do have something that I need. You have very beautiful green grass that you just cut. If you want to, please give me an armful of that grass." The boy was so happy to be able to give him something, and Siddhartha thanked him very much. After the buffalo boy left, Siddhartha spread the grass into a kind of cushion that he could sit on. As he sat down, he made a firm vow, "Until I get true enlightenment, I shall not stand up." With this strong determination, he meditated all night, and when the morning star appeared in the sky, he became a fully enlightened person, a Buddha, with the highest capacity to understand and to love.

The Buddha stayed at that spot for two weeks, smiling and enjoying his breathing. Every day the milkmaid brought him rice and the buffalo boy also came by to see him. He taught them about understanding, loving, and being awake. There is a scripture in the Pali Canon called *Sutta of Tending Buffaloes*, which lists eleven skills a buffalo boy must have, such as recognizing his own buffaloes, making smoke to keep mosquitoes away, taking care of wounds on the body of buffaloes, helping buffaloes cross rivers, and finding places with enough grass and water to eat. After listing eleven skills, the Buddha tells the monks that meditation is also like this, and he lists eleven parallel skills for monks—recognizing the five components of a human being, and so on. Most stories of the life of the Buddha overlook the two weeks he stayed near the Bodhi tree, meeting with the milkmaid and the buffalo boy, walking slowly, enjoying themselves. But I am sure it happened this way. Otherwise how could the Buddha have delivered the *Sutta of Tending Buffaloes*? In fact, when the buffalo boy grew up, he must have become a disciple of the Buddha, and one day, as he sat in the front of the assembly, the Buddha delivered that sutta.

After two weeks, the Buddha realized he had to get up from his seat under the Bodhi tree and share his understanding and compassion with other people. He told the milkmaid and the buffalo boy, "I am sorry, but I have to leave now. We are so happy together, but I must go and work with the adults."

He thought about who he could share his understanding and compassion with, and he thought of the five friends who had practiced with him. He walked an entire day in order to find them, and when he happened upon their camp, they had just finished their afternoon sitting meditation. They sat a lot. They were very thin by now, as you can imagine. One of them saw the Buddha coming and said to the others, "Don't stand up if he comes. Don't go to the gate to welcome him. Don't go and fetch water for him to wash his feet and his hands. He didn't persevere. He ate rice, and he drank milk." But when he arrived he was so attractive and so peaceful that they could not help themselves from offering him water to wash his feet and his hands and giving him a special seat. The Buddha told them, "Friends, I have found a way to develop understanding and loving. Please sit down, I'll teach you." They did not believe, at first. They said, "Siddhartha, while we practiced together, you gave up. You drank milk, you ate rice. How is it possible you have become a fully enlightened person? Please tell us. We cannot believe it." The Buddha said, "Friends, have I ever told you a lie?" In fact, he had never lied to anyone, and these five friends remembered that. "I have never told you a lie. Now I am not telling you a lie. I have become a fully enlightened person, and I'll be your teacher. Sit down, and listen to me." And the five of them sat down and listened to the Buddha. He gave his first Dharma talk for adults. If you want to read his words, they are available in a wonderful sutta explaining the basic doctrines of Buddhism: suffering, the causes of suffering, the removal of suffering, and the way to do it.

I have read many accounts of the life of the Buddha, and I see him as a person like us. Sometimes artists draw a Buddha in a way that we cannot recognize him as a human being. In fact, he is a human being. I have seen so many Buddha statues, but not many really beautiful and simple ones. If anytime you want to draw a picture of a Buddha, please sit down and breathe for five or ten minutes, smiling, before you pick up the pen to draw a Buddha. Then draw a simple Buddha, beautiful but simple, with a smile. And if you can, draw some children sitting with him. Buddha is young, not too grim, not too solemn, with a very light smile on his face. We have to go in this direction, because, when we look at the Buddha, we have to like him just as the buffalo boy and the milkmaid did.

When we say, "I take refuge in the Buddha," we should also understand that "The Buddha takes refuge in me," because without the second part the first part is not complete. The Buddha needs us for awakening, understanding, and love to be real things and not just concepts. They must be real things that have real effects on life. Whenever I say, "I take refuge in the Buddha," I hear "Buddha takes refuge in me." There is a verse for planting trees and other plants:

I entrust myself to earth,
Earth entrusts herself to me.
I entrust myself to Buddha,
Buddha entrusts herself to me.

"I entrust myself to earth" is like "I take refuge in the Buddha." (I identify myself with the plant.) The plant will die or be alive because of the earth. The plant takes refuge in the earth, the soil. But earth entrusts herself to me because each leaf that falls down and decomposes makes the soil richer. We know that the layer of soil that is rich and beautiful has been made by the vegetation. If our earth is green and beautiful, it is because of this vegetation. Therefore, while the vegetation needs the earth, the earth also needs the vegetation to express herself as a beautiful planet. So when we say, "I entrust myself to earth," I, the plant, have to hear the other version also: "Earth entrusts herself to me." "I entrust myself to Buddha, Buddha entrusts herself to me." Then it is very clear that the wisdom, the understanding and love of Shakyamuni Buddha needs us to be real again in life. Therefore, we have a very important task: to realize awakening, to realize compassion, to realize understanding.

We are all Buddhas, because only through us can understanding and love become tangible and effective. Thich Thanh Van was killed during his effort to help other people. He was a good Buddhist, he was a good Buddha, because he was able to help tens of thousands of people, victims of the war. Because of him, awakening, understanding, and love were real things. So we can call him a Buddha body, in Sanskrit *Buddhakaya*. For Buddhism to be real, there must be a Buddhakaya, an embodiment of awakened activity. Otherwise Buddhism is just a word. Thich Thanh Van was a Buddhakaya. Shakyamuni was a Buddhakaya. When we realize awakening, when we are understanding and loving, each of us is a Buddhakaya.

. . .

The second gem is the Dharma. Dharma is what the Buddha taught. It is the way of understanding and love—how to understand, how to love, how to make understanding and love into real things. Before the Buddha passed away, he said to his students, "Dear people, my physical body will not be here tomorrow, but my teaching body will always be here to help. You can consider it as your own teacher, a teacher who never leaves you." That is the birth of *Dharmakaya*. The Dharma has a body also, the body of the teaching, or the body of the way. As you can see, the meaning of Dharmakaya is quite simple, although people in Mahayana have made it very complicated. Dharmakaya just means the teaching of the Buddha, the way to realize understanding and love. Later it became something like the ontological ground of being.

Anything that can help you wake up has Buddha nature. When I am alone and a bird calls me, I return to myself, I breathe, and I smile, and sometimes it calls me once more. I smile and I say to the bird, "I hear already." Not only sounds, but sights can remind you to return to your true self. In the morning when you open your window and see the light streaming in, you can recognize it as the voice of the Dharma, and it becomes part of the Dharmakaya. That is why people who are awake see the manifestation of the Dharma in everything. A pebble, a bamboo tree, the cry of a baby, anything can be the voice of the Dharma calling. We should be able to practice like that.

One day a monk came to Tue Trung, the most illustrious teacher of Buddhism in Vietnam in the 13th century, a time when Buddhism was flourishing in

Vietnam. The monk asked him, "What is the pure, immaculate Dharmakaya?" and Tue Trung pointed to the excrement of a horse. This was an irreverent approach to Dharmakaya, because people were using the word immaculate to describe it. You cannot use words to describe the Dharmakaya. Even though we say that it is immaculate, pure, that does not mean it is separate from things that are impure. Reality, ultimate reality, is free from all adjectives, either pure or impure. So his response was to shake up the mind of the monk, for him to cleanse himself of all these adjectives in order to see into the nature of the Dharmakaya. A teacher is also part of the Dharmakaya because she or he helps us be awake. The way she looks, the way she lives her daily life, the way she deals with people, animals, and plants helps us realize understanding and love in our life.

There are many ways of teaching: teaching by words, teaching by books, teaching by tape recorders. I have a friend who is a Zen teacher in Vietnam, quite well-known, but not many people can come and study with him. Therefore, they make tape recordings of his talks, and he has become known as Cassette Monk! He is still in Vietnam. The government just chased him away from his monastery, so he had to go to another place to teach. He is not allowed to preach in Ho Chi Minh City, because if he teaches there, too many people come to hear him, and the government doesn't like that.

Even if he does not teach, his being is very helpful to us in being awake, for he is part of the Dharmakaya. Dharmakaya is not just expressed in words, in sounds. It can express itself in just being. Sometimes if we don't do anything, we help more than if we do a lot. We call that non-action. It is like the calm person on a small boat in a storm. That person does not have to do much, just to be himself and the situation can change. That is also an aspect of Dharmakaya: not talking, not teaching, just being.

This is true not only of humans, but other species as well. Look at the trees in our yard. An oak tree is an oak tree. That is all it has to do. If an oak tree is less than an oak tree, then we are all in trouble. Therefore, the oak tree is preaching the Dharma. Without doing anything, not serving in the School of Youth for Social Service, not preaching, not even sitting in meditation, the oak tree is very helpful to all of us just by being there. Everytime we look at the oak tree we have confidence. During the summer we sit under it and we feel cool, relaxed. We know that if the oak tree is not there, and all the other trees are not there, we will not have good air to breathe.

We also know that in our former lives we were trees. Maybe we have been an oak tree ourselves. This is not just Buddhist; this is scientific. The human species is a very young species—we appeared on the earth only recently. Before that, we were rock, we were gas, we were minerals, and then we were single-celled beings. We were plants, we were trees, and now we have become humans. We have to recall our past existences. This is not difficult. You just sit down and breathe and look, and you can see your past existences. When we shout at the oak tree, the oak tree is not offended. When we praise the oak tree, it doesn't raise its nose. We can learn the Dharma from the oak tree; therefore, the oak tree is part of our Dharmakaya. We can learn from everything that is around, that is in us. Even if we are not at a meditation center, we can still practice at home, because around us the Dharma is present. Everything is preaching the Dharma. Each pebble, each leaf, each flower is preaching the *Saddharma Pundarika Sutra.*

The Sangha is the community that lives in harmony and awareness. Sanghakaya is a new Sanskrit term. The Sangha needs a body also. When you are with your family and you practice smiling, breathing, recognizing the Buddha body in yourself and your children, then your family becomes a Sangha. If you have a bell in your home, the bell becomes part of your Sanghakaya, because the bell helps you to practice. If you have a cushion, then the cushion also becomes part of the Sanghakaya. Many things help us practice. The air, for breathing. If you have a park or a river bank near your home, you are very fortunate because you can enjoy practicing walking meditation. You have to discover your Sanghakaya, inviting a friend to come and practice with you, have tea meditation, sit with you, join you for walking meditation. All those efforts are to establish your Sanghakaya at home. Practice is easier if you have a Sanghakaya.

Siddhartha, the Buddha-to-be, while practicing with other people, began to drink milk, and the five monks who were with him went away. So he made the Bodhi tree into his Sanghakaya. He made the buffalo boy, the milkmaid, the river, the trees, and the birds around him into his Sanghakaya. There are those in Vietnam who live in re-education camps. They don't have a Sangha. They don't have a Zen Center. But they practice. They have to look upon other things as part of their Sanghakaya. I know of people who practiced

walking meditation in their prison cells. They told me
this after they got out of the camp. So while we are
lucky, while we are still capable of finding so many elements to set up our Sanghakaya, we should do so. A
friend, our own children, our own brother or sister,
our house, the trees in our back yard, all of them can
be part of our Sanghakaya.

Practicing Buddhism, practicing meditation is for us
to be serene and happy, understanding and loving. In
that way we work for the peace and happiness of our
family and our society. If we look closely, the Three
Gems are actually one. In each of them, the other two
are already there. In Buddha, there is Buddhahood,
there is the Buddha body. In Buddha there is the
Dharma body because without the Dharma body, he
could not have become a Buddha. In the Buddha there is
the Sangha body because he had breakfast with the bodhi
tree, with the other trees, and birds and environment.
In a meditation center, we have a Sangha body, Sanghakaya, because the way of understanding and compassion is practiced there. Therefore the Dharma body is
present, the way, the teaching is present. But the
teaching cannot become real without the life and body of
each of us. So the Buddhakaya is also present. If Buddha
and Dharma are not present, it is not a Sangha. Without
you, the Buddha is not real, it is just an idea.

Without you, the Dharma cannot be practiced. It has
to be practiced by someone. Without each of you, the
Sangha cannot be. That is why when we say, "I take
refuge in the Buddha," we also hear, "the Buddha takes
refuge in me." "I take refuge in the Dharma. The
Dharma takes refuge in me. I take refuge in the
Sangha. The Sangha takes refuge in me."

A Rose for Your Pocket

by *Thich Nhat Hanh*

Thich Nhat Hanh reflects on motherhood and love in this 1987 prose poem.

*T*he thought "mother" cannot be separated from that of "love." Love is sweet, tender, and delicious. Without love, a child cannot flower, an adult cannot mature. Without love, we weaken, wither.

The day my mother died, I made this entry in my journal: "The greatest misfortune of my life has come!" Even an old person, when he loses his mother, doesn't feel ready. He too has the impression that he is not yet ripe, that he is suddenly alone. He feels as abandoned and unhappy as a young orphan.

All songs and poems praising motherhood are beautiful, effortlessly beautiful. Even songwriters and poets without much talent seem to pour their hearts into these works, and when they are recited or sung, the performers also seem deeply moved, unless they have lost their mothers too early even to know what love for mother is. Writings extolling the virtues of motherhood have existed since the beginning of time throughout the world.

When I was a child I heard a simple poem about losing your mother, and it is still very important for me. If your mother is still alive, you may feel tenderness for her each time you read this, fearing this distant yet inevitable event.

> That year, although I was still very young
> My mother left me.
> And I realized
> That I was an orphan.
> Everyone around me was crying.
> I suffered in silence . . .
>
> Allowing the tears to flow,
> I felt my pain soften.
> Evening enveloped Mother's tomb,
> The pagoda bell rang sweetly.
>
> I realized that to lose your mother
> Is to lose the whole universe.

We swim in a world of tender love for many years, and, without even knowing it, we are quite happy there. Only after it is too late do we become aware of it.

People in the countryside do not understand the complicated language of city people. When people from the city say that mother is "a treasure of love," that is already too complex for them. Country people in Vietnam compare their mothers to the finest varieties of bananas or to honey, sweet rice, or sugar cane. They express their love in these simple and direct ways. For me, a mother is like a *ba huong* banana of the highest quality, like the best *nep mot* sweet rice, the most delicious *mia lau* sugar cane!

There are moments after a fever when you have a bitter, flat taste in your mouth, and nothing tastes good. Only when your mother comes and tucks you in, gently pulls the covers over your chin, puts her hand on your burning forehead (Is it really a hand, or is it the silk of heaven?), and gently whispers, "My poor darling!" do you feel restored, surrounded with the sweetness of maternal love. Her love is so fragrant, like a banana, like sweet rice, like sugar cane.

Father's work is enormous, as huge as a mountain. Mother's devotion is overflowing, like water from a mountain spring. Maternal love is our first taste of love, the origin of all feelings of love. Our mother is the teacher who first teaches us love, the most important subject in life. Without my mother I could never have known how to love. Thanks to her I can love my neighbors. Thanks to her I can love all living beings. Through her I acquired my first notions of understanding and compassion. Mother is the foundation of all love, and many religious traditions recognize this and pay deep honor to a maternal figure, the Virgin Mary, the goddess Kwan Yin. Hardly an infant has opened her mouth to cry without her mother already running to the cradle. Mother is a gentle and sweet spirit who makes unhappiness and worries disappear. When the word "mother" is uttered, already we feel our hearts overflowing with love. From love, the distance to belief and action is very short.

In the West, we celebrate Mother's Day in May. I am from the countryside of Vietnam, and I had never heard of this tradition. One day, I was visiting the Ginza district of Tokyo with the monk Thien An, and we were met outside a bookstore by several Japanese students who were friends of his. One discretely asked him a question, and then took a white carnation from her bag and pinned it on my robe. I was surprised and a little embarrassed. I had no idea what this gesture meant, and I didn't dare ask. I tried to act natural, thinking this must be some local custom.

When they were finished talking (I don't speak Japanese), Thien An and I went into the bookstore, and he told me that today was what is called Mother's Day. In Japan, if your mother is still alive, you wear a red flower on your pocket or your lapel, proud that you still have your mother. If she is no longer alive, you wear a white flower. I looked at the white flower on my robe and suddenly I felt so unhappy. I was as much an orphan as any other unhappy orphan; we orphans could no longer proudly wear red flowers in our buttonholes. Those who wear white flowers suffer, and their thoughts cannot avoid returning to their mothers. They cannot forget that she is no longer there. Those who wear red flowers are so happy, knowing their mothers are still alive. They can try to please her before she is gone and it is too late. I find this a beautiful custom. I propose that we do the same thing in Vietnam, and in the West as well.

Mother is a boundless source of love, an inexhaustible treasure. But unfortunately, we sometimes forget. A mother is the most beautiful gift life offers us. Those of you who still have your mother near, please don't wait for her death to say, "My God, I have lived beside my mother all these years without ever looking closely at her. Just brief glances, a few words exchanged—asking for a little pocket money or one thing or another." You cuddle up to her to get warm, you sulk, you get angry with her. You only complicate her life, causing her to worry, undermining her health, making her go to sleep late and get up early. Many mothers die young because of their children. Throughout her life we expect her to cook, wash, and clean up after us, while we think only about our grades and our careers. Our mothers no longer have time to look deeply at us, and we are too busy to look closely at her. Only when she is no longer there do we realize that we have never been conscious of having a mother.

This evening, when you return from school or work or, if you live far away, the next time you visit your mother, you may wish to go into her room and, with a calm and silent smile, sit down beside her. Without saying anything, make her stop working. Then, look at her for a long time, look at her deeply. Do this in order to see her, to realize that she is there, she is alive, beside you. Take her hand and ask her one short question to capture her attention, "Mother, do you know something?" She will be a little surprised and will probably smile when she asks you, "What, dear?" Keep looking into her eyes, smiling serenely, and say, "Do you know that I love you?" Ask this question without waiting for an answer. Even if you are thirty or forty years old, or older, ask her as the child of your mother. Your mother and you will be happy, conscious of living in eternal love. Then tomorrow, when she leaves you, you will have no regrets.

In Vietnam, on the holiday of Ullambana, we listen to stories and legends about the bodhisattva Maudgalyayana, and about filial love, the work of the father, the devotion of the mother, and the duty of the child. Everyone prays for the longevity of his or her parents, or if they are dead, for their rebirth in the heavenly Pure Land. We believe that a child without filial love is without worth. But filial devotion also arises from love itself. Without love, filial devotion is just artificial. When love is present, that is enough, and there is no need to talk of obligation. To love your mother is enough. It is not a duty, it is completely natural, like drinking when you are thirsty. Every child must have a mother, and it is totally natural to love her. The mother loves her child, and the child loves his mother. The child needs his mother, and the mother needs her child. If the mother doesn't need her child, nor the child his mother, then this is not a mother, and this is not a child. It is a misuse of the words "mother" and "child."

When I was young, one of my teachers asked me, "What do you have to do when you love your mother?" I told him, "I must obey her, help her, take care of her when she is old, and pray for her, keeping the ancestral altar when she has disappeared forever behind the mountain." Now I know that the word "What" in his question was superfluous. If you love your mother, you don't have to *do* anything. You love her; that is enough. To love your mother is not a question of morality or virtue.

Please do not think I have written this to give a lesson in morality. Loving your mother is a question of profit: A mother is like a spring of pure water, like the very finest sugar cane or honey, the best quality sweet rice. If you do not know how to profit from this, it is unfortunate for you. I simply want to bring this to your attention, to help you avoid one day complaining that there is nothing left in life for you. If a gift such as the presence of your own mother doesn't satisfy you, even if you are president of a large corporation or king of the universe, you probably will not be satisfied. I know that the Creator is not happy, for the Creator arises spontaneously and does not have the good fortune to have a mother.

I would like to tell a story. Please don't think that I am thoughtless. It could have been that my sister didn't marry, and I didn't become a monk. In any case, we both left our mother—one to lead a new life beside the man she loved, and the other to follow an ideal of life that he adored. The night my sister married, my mother worried about a thousand and one things, and didn't even seem sad. But when we sat down at the table for some light refreshments, while waiting for our in-laws to come for my sister, I saw that my mother hadn't eaten a bite. She said, "For eighteen years she has eaten with us and today is her last meal here before going to another family's home to take her meals." My sister cried, her head bowing barely above her plate, and she said, "Mama, I won't get married." But she married nonetheless. As for me, I left my mother to become a monk. To congratulate those who are firmly resolved to leave their families to become monks, one says that they are following the way of understanding, but I am not proud of it. I love my mother, but I also have an ideal, and to serve it I had to leave her—so much the worse for me.

In life, it is often necessary to make difficult choices. We cannot catch two fish at the same time, one in each hand. It is difficult, because if we accept growing up, we must accept suffering. I don't regret leaving my mother to become a monk, but I am sorry I had to make such a choice. I didn't have the chance to profit fully from this precious treasure. Each night I pray for my mother, but it is no longer possible for me to savor the excellent *ba huong* banana, the best quality *nep mot* sweet rice, and the delicious *mia lau* sugar cane. Please don't think that I am suggesting that you not follow your career and remain home at your mother's side. I have already said I do not want to give advice or lessons in morality. I only want to remind you that a mother is like a banana, like good rice, like honey, like sugar. She is tenderness, she is love; so you, my brothers and sisters, please do not forget her. Forgetting creates an immense loss, and I hope you do not, either through ignorance or through lack of attention, have to endure such a loss, I gladly put a red flower, a rose, on your lapel so that you will be happy. That is all.

If I were to have any advice, it would be this:

Tonight, when you return from school or work, or the next time you visit your mother, go into her room calmly, silently, with a smile, and sit down beside her. Without saying anything, make her stop working, and look at her for a long time. Look at her well, in order to see her well, in order to realize she is there, alive, sitting beside you. Then take her hand and ask her this short question, "Mother, do you know something?" She will be a little surprised, and will ask you, smiling, "What, dear?" Continuing to look into her eyes with a serene smile, tell her, "Do you know that I love you?" Ask her this question without waiting for an answer. Even if you are thirty, forty years old, or older, ask her simply, because you are the child of your mother. Your mother and you will both be happy, conscious of living in eternal love. And tomorrow when she leaves you, you will not have any regrets.

This is the refrain I give you to sing today. Brothers and sisters, please chant it, please sing it, so that you won't live in indifference or forgetfulness. This red rose, I have already placed it on your lapel. Please be happy.

Self-Immolation

from The Raft Is Not the Shore:

CONVERSATIONS TOWARD A BUDDHIST
CHRISTIAN AWARENESS

by *Daniel Berrigan and Thich Nhat Hanh*

More than one hundred Vietnamese Buddhist monks and nuns during the 1960's and early 1970's doused themselves with gasoline and lit themselves on fire to protest the war in Vietnam. Father Daniel Berrigan asked Thich Nhat Hanh to discuss the meaning of this action and its relationship to faith. This exchange occurred during a series of conversations in Paris during the mid 1970's.

BERRIGAN: *I was wondering, could we discuss, even briefly, a question which is so vexing and mysterious for people—the question of self-immolation? As you know, we've had a number of these tragic events in the United States. And while it's been a source, I think, of inspiration and life to some, it's also been a great scandal. I can remember, one of the first of these events occurred in 1965. A young Catholic worker named Roger Laporte burned himself in front of the UN as a protest against the war. I was asked to speak at a service for him at the Catholic Worker. And I raised the question of whether or not this death could be called a suicide, because I felt that it shouldn't be. Suicide proceeds from despair and from the loss of hope, and I felt that this young person did not die in that spirit. So my sermon became a source of scandal, because the official line of the Church was that this was suicide and was not to be called anything else.*

Consequently, I was in severe trouble as a result of that friendship and his death and that sermon. We had to deal with the same agony on successive occasions. Some of the people who died became known, and some did not. But I think such tragedies widened the conception of death as a gift of life in a way we had not known before in the West. We had never known an occasion where a person freely offered his life, except on the field of battle or to save another person. But the deliberate self-giving, a choice which didn't depend upon some immediate crisis but upon thoughtful revaluation of life—this was very new to us and was, indeed, an unprecedented gift.

NHAT HANH: I think, first, we should consider a few things. We should examine each particular case. I see in the act of self-immolation the willingness to take suffering on yourself, to make yourself suffer for the sake of purification, for the sake of communication. And in that respect, I think self-immolation by fire is not very different from fasting. Fasting is also to purify, to establish communication, to take suffering on yourself. And if you fast too long, you also die.

The Coconut Monk—you have heard of him—has many hundreds of disciples who have become conscientious objectors. When I asked him to write an article about Nhat Chi Mai, a woman who immolated herself, he said something like this, as if he were speaking to Mai: "Your uncle is also burning himself, in a slower way. I am burning myself with austerity, with active resistance against the war. I am doing exactly what you have done, but in a different way."

I think of Nhat Chi Mai and Thich Quang Duc—Vietnamese who immolated themselves. I knew both personally, and I think I understand the nature of their acts. I was a visitor in Thich Quang Duc's temple for many months. There were nights when I was busy writing. He would come to my room and just sit there and watch me, not saying anything for fear that he would interrupt me. I would continue, then stop and talk to him. Nhat Chi Mai loved life as much as Thich Quang Duc. She wanted to live. She was young, she had good friends, she loved life. Thich Quang Duc also. He was head of a community that looked upon him as a brother or father, someone you leaned on, relied on. Both have left very lucid poetry and letters. When you read them, you sense their desire to live. But they could not bear the suffering of others. They wanted to do something or to be something for others.

As Phuong once put it, "If you want to buy something, you should pay something. And now you want to buy something very, very precious like the understanding of people. So you don't have anything more precious than your life. You pay by your own life. You try to exchange your life for understanding of peace, brotherhood, and cooperation." So, they gave their lives in payment. But they still wanted to be alive. It was because of life that they acted, not because of death.

I would say that Jesus knew the things that were to happen to Him. Why didn't He try to avoid them? Why did He allow Himself to be caught in that situation—to be judged, to be crucified, to die? I think he did so because of others.

Nhat Chi Mai and Thich Quang Duc immolated themselves for others. Because of life. Because they saw their lives in the lives of others. And in a moment of perception of that deep, deep truth, they suddenly lost all fear and gave themselves. I wouldn't want to describe these acts as suicide or even as sacrifice. Maybe they didn't think of it as a sacrifice. Maybe they did. They may have thought of their act as a very natural thing to do, like breathing. The problem is to understand the situation and the context in which they acted.

BERRIGAN: *I think when one gets beyond names and cultural differences, there's a great clue here to the life and death of Jesus. Especially since we're discussing this on Good Friday. (In fact, it's now 12:20 on Good Friday.) And one thinks of the proud and self-conscious statements of Jesus about His own death. He is anxious to free His action from any misunderstanding about His being a victim of circumstances or of evil. He is always asserting His self-possession—the deliberate nature of the death He is about to enter. So He says, "No one takes My life from Me, but I give My life freely." There are many occasions when they try to seize Him and He evades them. He says, "My hour has not yet come." In other words, He dies when He chooses to die. He doesn't die when they choose to take Him. And I think this is similar to the deaths we are trying to understand. The Son of man goes to His death freely, and His death is a gift to many, given in view of the lives of others and their possibilities. It is never a defeat or a base bargain or something exacted of Him against His will. I think the person who is capable of dying well is the one who is capable of living. The one who dies well is the one who gives his life with this free and full consciousness.*

NHAT HANH: Nobody can persuade another to give his or her life in that way. Still I think we must try to understand those who have sacrificed themselves. We do not intend to say that self-immolation is good, or that it is bad. It is neither good nor bad. When you say something is good, you say that you should do that. But nobody can urge another to do such a thing. So such a discussion is not pursued in order to decide whether self-immolation is a good tactic in the nonviolent struggle or not. It is apart from all that. It is done to wake us up.

BERRIGAN: *You know, once when I was underground, there was a very disturbing occurrence in the nieghborhood. A young boy about fourteen years old had been so brokenhearted by the war that he immolated himself one night in his own yard, in the front garden. He left a note to his family, went out, and immolated himself about three o'clock in the morning. His father came out to go to work, walked into the garden, and found the boy's body. This was another example of so many who went through that death alone—young people, especially, who couldn't bear the horror of the war and, as you say, not do something. They found themselves at their wit's end about what could be done and finally decided on this course. And this was a Catholic boy, as so many of these people were.*

Another boy I knew immolated himself, lived for forty days, and finally died. He was very brilliant and religious. He decided on this all alone, as you said of the Vietnamese woman. All alone, not letting even his own family know.

I think in Christianity that something very great has been lost. Jesus' death, I think, in a very deep sense can be called a self-immolation. I mean that He went consciously to death, choosing that death for the sake of others, reasonably and thoughtfully. But the only way such a death continues in history as an example to others is in the military. Except for a few saints here and there who die for others; but that's very exceptional. In war, soldiers always go and die. And in many cases they die in religious wars. They die with the blessing: you will attain eternal life because you gave your life. But they die with weapons in their hands; they die at the hands of others with weapons. This seems to be so contrary to the example of Jesus, who refused to take up the sword.

So the Church loses any capacity to deal with the kind of death the Vietnam war brought home to us, in the case of a number of people in our country and, of course, in Vietnam, who chose this way. However, I think that these deaths were a nonviolent counterpart to those who killed and who died in armed violence. But would you say something about the circumstances under which your friends died?

NHAT HANH: Nhat Chi Mai, for instance, prepared everything for her immolation by herself—absolutely by herself. Her most intimate friends didn't know a thing about it. She spent a whole month with her parents in order to be a source of joy and pleasure. She was, as we say, honey and sweet rice for her parents. And after that, she came to visit our community. She wore a beautiful dress. We had never seen her in that dress before, and many thought that she was going to marry and that was why she had deserted the community for one month. She brought a banana cake that she had made at home. She divided it up and gave it to every one of us. And how she laughed! Many suspected that she was going to get married. She was so joyful. And then two days later they heard the news.

One remarkable thing is that when she knelt to die, she put in front of her a statue of the Virgin Mary and a statue of woman Bodhisattva Quan Am, the Buddhist saint of compassion. And she put a poem there: "Joining my hands, I kneel before Mother Mary and Bodhisattva Quan Am. Please help me to realize fully my vow." In the situation of Vietnam, that meant very much, because unless the people of the two major

religions in Vietnam—Buddhists and Catholics—
cooperate, it will be very hard to alter the course of the
war. She saw that.

BERRIGAN: *It seems to me those gestures are a counterpart to the gestures of Jesus Himself. The joyful service of others at the point of death
makes it apparent that this death is a fully human gesture—a human
death, one that is taking everything into account. There are very few
people who are given to die that way, that well, that consciously, that
knowingly. Most people die fearfully or unhappily or grudgingly or in
terror. But to die in such deep, deep joy and sense of oneself—that's a
marvelous thing.*

NHAT HANH: She also wrote poems, but nobody knew
that until she died. Because she was shy, she didn't want
to show off her poems. And so, they were surprised to
see that most of the things she left behind were poems,
and a few letters. She wrote letters to her family, to her
father and mother, one letter to her coworkers, and a
very brief letter to me. I was not there at the time. She
wrote, "Tomorrow I will sacrifice myself for peace."
And then she said, "I wish to contribute my part, and I
ask you not to worry because very soon peace will
come." Dying and yet trying to encourage others.

BERRIGAN: *Yes. Yes. That's so. But this is typical, I think, of the
resources of people like that. They have enough to give themselves in
every direction.*

NHAT HANH: When Thich Quang Duc and Nhat Chi
Mai immolated themselves, they were in perfect control of themselves. They sat in the lotus position in full
control of their bodies and, I believe, of their spirits.

According to the people who were there, Thich Quang Duc sat very straight, very stable like a mountain, until he passed away. And Mai passed away very beautifully; she leaned forward in a position of worship in front of her two statues.

BERRIGAN: *No cry, no sound?*

NHAT HANH: No.

BERRIGAN: *Silence? A great silence.*

NHAT HANH: I know that during that period they had a very high degree of concentration. Once I went to a dentist and because I do not like anesthesia I asked him not to inject it when he pulled my tooth. All that time I looked at my hand with total concentration in order not to feel the pain. I believe that in the lotus position while they burned, they also had that kind of concentration, only in a greater, more intense degree. Because in my case it was only a tooth which gave pain; in theirs, it was the whole body.

BERRIGAN: *What was the effect of such a death, offered by such an extraordinary woman?*

NHAT HANH: One Catholic friend of mine, Father Lan, was so moved by her death that he undertook to publish her writings. And he was attacked by many Catholics.

BERRIGAN: *Why were the Catholics angry?*

NHAT HANH: Oh, a number of them thought of her death as a Communist trick—as propaganda. When you want to buy understanding, at the price of your life, you can buy it only to a certain degree.

BERRIGAN: *Were the Catholics calling these deaths suicide too? As in the States?*

NHAT HANH: Yes.

BERRIGAN: *Therefore, beneath consideration?*

NHAT HANH: Do you remember Madame Nhu? She spoke of the immolation as a barbecue.

BERRIGAN: *You know, tonight, I see a clue that I didn't see before. It's very strange. I think it's because of our worship together and Holy Week and the very deep things in this community which I have gained some sense of. I see how these deaths would be so much better understood in the Buddhist community than in the Christian community. And this says something very deep about how our communities understand the offering of Jesus.*

Why is it, for instance, that the Buddha's death was not at the hands of the violent, and the death of Jesus was? This is a very great difference, isn't it? Is it a matter merely of society and the culture of their time?

NHAT HANH: You might say that, but I also think that there is a basic similarity in their deaths. They both knew the time of their death had come and they were both completely prepared.

The Buddha was old and He knew that His time was coming. So He asked His beloved disciples to find a place between the two blooming trees and He made a last recommendation. Then He asked whether they had any questions before He went: "Have I forgotten to tell you anything?"

BERRIGAN: *And then He died quietly?*

NHAT HANH: One of the things He said was, "Light your own torch, carry your own light, and go." The Buddhist tradition speaks of the continuation of the lamp because of that: the torch of wisdom, the torch of light. When a Master transmits this, we call it the seal of spirit. If the disciple receives it, it is called the transmission of the lamp.

To Veterans

from Love in Action:

WRITINGS ON NONVIOLENT SOCIAL CHANGE

by *Thich Nhat Hanh*

Thich Nhat Hanh extends his compassion to everyone affected by war. Here is a selection taken from talks he gave during retreats for American Vietnam veterans during 1989 and 1991.

On the final day of a mindfulness retreat for 200 Americans in Massachusetts, Jon Kabat-Zinn read an insight poem that said, "The Vietnam War ends today." That was in 1987, and since then, I have begun to lead retreats for war veterans. I want veterans to realize how important they are.

I, too, am a veteran. I lost many friends—many brothers and sisters—during the Vietnam War, and I experienced much suffering. Grenades were thrown into my room, but were deflected by a curtain. Social service workers under my direction were killed and maimed. We did our best to confront the violence with love, but we had to cry a lot.

I have been practicing to transform my suffering and share my insight with others. I do not feel any more blame. I feel peace and compassion, and that allows me to help other people.

Veterans are the light at the tip of the candle, illuminating the way for the whole nation. If veterans can achieve awareness, transformation, understanding, and peace, they can share with the rest of society the realities of war. And they can teach us how to make peace with ourselves and each other, so we never have to use violence to resolve conflicts again. To make the world a peaceful place, to ensure for our children and grandchildren a life worth living, we need a transformation.

When you touch fire and your hand gets burned, it is not the responsibility of the hand alone. It is the responsibility of the whole person. The hand did not touch the fire by itself. It was commanded to do so by the brain, and the whole body got hurt at the same time. If the body blames the hand, that is not just. The hand acted because the body ordered it to do so. When there is good communication between the hand and the rest of the body, both the hand and the body will feel better. If the body says, "You must bear the burden of your actions by yourself; I cannot forgive what you have done," that is the lack of understanding.

When you went to war, you went for the whole nation. The whole nation was responsible for what happened there, not you alone. Your hand was the hand of the whole nation. If you made mistakes, the whole nation made mistakes. If you went to war believing you were doing something important—trying to save a people, fighting evil—it was not your thinking alone; it was the thinking of the whole nation. You were sent there to fight, destroy, kill, and die. You were not the only one responsible. We cannot just shout at you and say, "You did that!" We all did it collectively.

Our individual consciousness is a product of our society, ancestors, education, and many other factors. Your sense of duty, service, and freedom were handed to you by society, and you went to war as representatives of your people, not just as individuals. You have to look deeply to understand what really happened. Your personal healing will be the healing of the whole nation, your children, and their children.

When the hand gets burned, if there is good communication with the rest of the body, blood and other fluids will rush to the wound and begin the process of healing. If the nation comes to understand the true nature of the war, loving kindness will begin to surface, and healing will begin. As long as there is no communication, there is no insight or compassion, and you will continue to suffer. Non-veterans do not understand veterans, and they refuse to listen to you. You know the truth about war, but you have not been able to share your insight with them. You have suffered so much, but you have not been able to find ways to tell people about it, and they have not been ready to listen.

You continue to suffer, because you feel guilty about your actions in Vietnam. Shame, guilt, and regret can be helpful or harmful; it depends how you use them. When you realize that you have caused a lot of damage, if you vow not to do it again, that regret is wholesome and beneficial. But if your guilt persists for too long and becomes a complex, it blocks the way to joy and peace. The way to liberate yourself is to look deeply into the nature of the guilt and self-hatred and see the seeds of the suffering—your ancestors, your parents, and the violence and lack of understanding in our society and its institutions. If you went to Vietnam with such a heritage of suffering, your actions were dictated by those forces. That is also true of those who opposed the war.

The seeds of suffering come from many directions. When your parents conceived you, you already had many seeds of happiness and suffering handed down by your ancestors. In your mother's womb, you received more seeds. If your parents were not happy together, you received seeds of suffering.

As you grew up, if your parents argued and made each other unhappy, you received those seeds of suffering, too. If your parents were alcoholic, they made you suffer. If your father abused you, you suffered. Violent films and TV programs also watered the seeds of fear and hatred in you. By the time you became a soldier, you were already filled with suffering. Then, in the army you were told that the Vietnamese were beasts and you had to kill them. You cannot kill another human being without visualizing him as a beast. The mass media reinforced this image, watering the seeds of hatred and fear in order to help you kill. So many seeds of violence were watered before you were a soldier and during the time you were a soldier.

With such a heritage of suffering, it is no surprise that you committed atrocities during the war. You knew you could be killed at any time. You saw your friends killed in ambushes. You became more and more angry and more and more afraid. You may have killed children and women. You may have raped women or destroyed villages out of the fear, hatred, and rage that were pouring into you from so many directions. If you committed atrocities in Vietnam, it was the act of everyone—your father who abused you, the press, your commander, everyone who watered the seeds of anger in you so that you could kill.

We do not need to go overseas to a war zone to see such violence. The Los Angeles policemen beating Rodney King, that was also Vietnam. War manifests itself in so many ways here and now. It is a reflection of our collective consciousness, which is filled with suffering. With this heritage, the violence will repeat itself over and over. There will be other Vietnams, other Gulf Wars. It is our task to look deeply into the violence, hatred, and fear to see their roots.

Many soldiers who went to Vietnam had almost no contact with the Vietnamese people, culture, or life. They were told that the Vietnamese needed to be killed because they were evil and they were killers. Because it was a high-tech war, you just pushed buttons to complete many of your missions. You did not know or see the damage you were inflicting on the people and the country of Vietnam. If you flew one hundred missions, you might have been successful as a soldier, but you did not know what was happening on the ground, because you were so far away. Once you realized what was happening on the ground, you began to have guilt.

Who did that bombing? Your President, your Congress, your Senate, your people, everyone. You were only the hand ordered to do it. Why keep the regret for yourself? Why keep the shame for yourself? When you begin to see that, you will be free, and we need you to share your insight with everyone so we will not be tempted to do it again.

When you came home after the war, the American people were cool, neglectful, and unappreciative, and of course you became angry. But your people did not know anything about the war. Both hawks and doves had a very wrong view. You experienced the reality firsthand, and when you see that they were speaking out of ignorance, you will stop being angry at them. You were ignorant too, but now you have learned, and you are liberated from your anger. Now you can offer your compassion.

We who have experienced war directly have a responsibility to share our insight and experience concerning the truth of war. We are the light at the tip of the candle. It is very hot, but it has the power of shining and illuminating. We can gather into groups to support each other. Practicing mindfulness, we will know how to look deeply into the nature of the war and, with our insight, awaken our own people. We know what war is. We also know that the war is not only in us; it is in everyone—veterans and non-veterans. We must share our insight, not out of anger, but out of love. Our people need us to do it. I am trying my best, and I hope my friends will do the same.

During the war, one portion of the American population had to confront one portion of the Vietnamese population. These were the soldiers, the combatants. But the combatants and the non-combatants were not so different. In both, there were conflicts, and we have to look deeply to recognize these conflicts so that we can transform them into understanding and compassion, the fruit of insight. Insight can be brought about by mindfulness and looking deeply. If we do not have enough mindfulness, if we do not make enough effort to look deeply, we will not have enough insight to transform the conflicts that are within us, not to mention those between people and those with other nations.

The basic condition for happiness is to be understood. Our pain, hope, and despair have to be understood by someone for us to be happy. Vietnam veterans do not feel understood by their society, not even by members of their own families. Consciously or unconsciously, veterans blame the non-veterans for not understanding them. There is so much misunderstanding to be dissolved. Veterans have suffered so much, and they have to take the time to understand their own suffering. It may look as if the people of America understand Gulf War veterans better, but I don't think so. Our ignorance about the nature of war is exactly the same. The war in Vietnam and the war in the Gulf were the same. It does not change just by the way people welcome you back. Whether they shout at you or wave flags and welcome you, the true nature of the war is the same. We have to see that.

Many years have now passed since the Vietnam War. We are calm enough to realize that the Vietnam War was not necessary. We spent so much energy, so many human lives—millions of people died in Vietnam. There are still a lot of mines and bombs in Vietnam that have not been defused, and there are also many bombs in our souls that have not been defused. We need to defuse the bombs in our souls first. Then we can go to Vietnam to help defuse the bombs there.

When we look deeply, we can see that all wars have

their roots in the lack of understanding. We may be a little wiser now that twenty years have passed since the Vietnam War, but are we wise enough to prevent another war? In fact, we have already had another unnecessary war. In order to prevent yet another, we have to be prepared. We need time, of course, but we also need a way. If we know what to do, how to prepare, time is of secondary importance. We have to practice in a way that helps the whole nation see deeply into the nature of war.

When you look into your consciousness and see your own pain, you also see the suffering and confusion of your society and your government. You have been embracing your suffering for many years, but when you see it directly, it will transform itself into a positive source of energy that will empower you to share your insight. To help others, we have to go to them with arms extended, filled with loving kindness and compassion. Blaming others or blaming ourselves can never help. The moment we have this insight, we will stop blaming, we will stop suffering, and we will have the energy to serve our people, even if they are still ignorant about the nature of the war.

No one ever wins a war. The Vietnamese did not win the war. Millions of people in Vietnam are still suffering, and the country has been destroyed. Vietnam did not win anything. We cannot call it a victory. You cannot call the Gulf War a victory either. But many Americans did call it a victory, so they could have the feeling once again that America is the greatest power on Earth. They organized parades welcoming the soldiers back, trying to overcome what they called a defeat many years ago.

I don't see any difference between a Vietnam

veteran and a Gulf War veteran. I don't see any difference between the nature of the war in Vietnam
and the nature of the Gulf War. I don't see any difference between the consciousness of the people
during the Vietnam War and the consciousness of the
people during the Gulf War. Please look deeply and
remove all of these false distinctions. Look deeply to
see the true nature of our society and our collective
consciousness. If the people are educated, if the
truth can break into their souls, we will all be able to
go in the direction of peace.

As long as the American people believe that the Gulf
War was moral, just, and liberating, they will be tempted
to do the same thing the next time there is a conflict.
How can we prevent that? By telling the truth, by sharing
our insight. We need to look deeply and to share our
insights. We do not have time to embrace our pain in
private anymore. We have to reveal ourselves. We have
to allow ourselves to be the light at the tip of the candle,
and to join with other veterans. We who have had firsthand experience can share the reality with everyone.

Transformation is the key. Looking just into the
ocean of suffering, you see that it is immense. But if
you turn around, you see the land. It is possible to
transform our hearts right in the present moment. If
we do it, if we vow to go in the direction of peace and
service, a rose will be born in us at that very moment.
My brothers and sisters who died during the war have
been reborn as flowers. We have to harvest those
flowers and form a beautiful bouquet. Please don't
dwell on your memory of guilt. If we can learn from
our suffering, all of those flowers will smile deeply at
us, and we will be free.

from Present Moment
Wonderful Moment:
MINDFULNESS VERSES FOR DAILY LIVING

by *Thich Nhat Hanh*

Smiling, breathing, pausing. One becomes aware of the beauty of each moment by mindfully practicing these simple actions. In this passage from his 1990 book Thich Nhat Hanh offers practical advice about how to achieve such mindfulness.

1. Waking Up

Waking up this morning, I smile.
Twenty-four brand new hours are before me.
I vow to live fully in each moment
and to look at all beings with eyes of compassion.

If you really know how to live, what better way to start the day than with a smile? Your smile affirms your awareness and determination to live in peace and joy. How many days slip by in forgetfulness? What are you doing with your life? Look deeply, and smile. The source of a true smile is an awakened mind.

How can you remember to smile when you wake up? You might hang a reminder—such as a branch, a leaf, a painting, or some inspiring words—in your window or from the ceiling above your bed, so that you notice it when you wake up. Once you develop the practice of smiling, you may not need a sign. You will smile as soon as you hear a bird sing or see the sunlight stream through the window. Smiling helps you approach the day with gentleness and understanding.

The last line of this gatha comes from the "Universal Door" chapter of the *Lotus Sutra*. The one who "looks at all beings with eyes of compassion" is Avalokitesvara, the *bodhisattva* of compassion. In the sutra, this line reads: "Eyes of loving kindness look on all living beings." Love is impossible without understanding. In order to understand others, we must know them, "be inside their skin." Then we can treat them with loving kindness. The source of love is our fully awakened mind.

2. Taking the First Step of the Day

Walking on the Earth
is a miracle!
Each mindful step
reveals the wondrous Dharmakaya.

This poem can be recited as we get out of bed and our feet touch the floor. It can also be used during walking meditation or any time we stand up and walk.

Walking on the Earth is a miracle! We do not have to walk in space or on water to experience a miracle. The real miracle is to be awake in the present moment. Walking on the green Earth, we can realize the wonder of being alive. If we make steps like this, the sun of the *Dharmakaya* will shine.

3. Opening the Window

Opening the window,
I look out onto the Dharmakaya.
How wondrous is life!
Attentive to each moment,
my mind is clear like a calm river.

After you wake up, you probably open the curtains and look outside. You may even like to open the window and feel the cool morning air with the dew still on the grass. But is what you see really "outside"? In fact, it is your own mind. As the sun sends its rays through the window, you are not just yourself. You are also the beautiful view from your window. You are the *Dharmakaya*.

Dharmakaya literally means the "body" *(kaya)* of the Buddha's teachings *(Dharma)*, the way of understanding and love. Before passing away, the Buddha told his disciples, "Only my physical body will pass away. My Dharma body will remain with you forever." In Mahayana Buddhism, the word has come to mean "the essence of all that exists." All phenomena—the song of a bird, the warm rays of the sun, a cup of hot tea—are manifestations of the Dharmakaya. We, too, are of the same nature as these wonders of the universe.

When we open the window and look out onto the Dharmakaya, we see that life is infinitely marvelous. At that very moment, we can vow to be awake all day long, realizing joy, peace, freedom, and harmony throughout our lives. When we do this, our mind becomes clear like a calm river.

4. Looking in the Mirror

Awareness is a mirror
reflecting the four elements.
Beauty is a heart that generates love
and a mind that is open.

The moments during the day of looking in a mirror can be moments of deep awareness. The mirror can serve as a tool for cultivating mindfulness so that we develop a broad capacity to understand and love others. Anyone who maintains awareness in the present moment becomes beautiful and naturally emanates peace, joy, and happiness. A calm half smile and a loving heart are refreshing, and they allow miracles to unfold. The Buddha's smile is beautiful because it expresses tolerance, compassion, and loving kindness.

In traditional cultures, the four great elements were earth, water, fire, and air. The Vietnamese poet Tru Vu wrote:

The flower, whose fragrance is ephemeral,
is made of the four elements.
Your eyes, shining with love,
are also made of the four elements.

The poet is saying that the four elements are neither mind nor matter. They are the universe itself revealed to us. When your mind is the clear mirror of meditative awareness, you will know that you are the outward expression of the essence of reality. So please smile. Smile with your eyes, not just with your lips. Smile with your whole being, reflecting the four elements in the mirror of mindful awareness.

5. Using the Toilet

Defiled or immaculate,
increasing or decreasing—
these concepts exist only in our minds.
The reality of interbeing is unsurpassed.

Life is always changing. Each thing relies on every other thing for its very existence. If our mind is calm and clear, using the toilet can be as sacred as lighting incense. To accept life is to accept both birth and death, gain and loss, joy and sorrow, defilement and purity. The *Heart Sutra* teaches us that when we see things as they are, we do not discriminate between seeming opposites such as these.

Everything "inter-is." Understanding the truth of nonduality allows us to overcome all pain. Reciting this gatha can help us apply the teachings of the *Heart Sutra*, even during what is usually regarded as a mundane act.

6. Turning on the Water

Water flows from high in the mountains.
Water runs deep in the Earth.
Miraculously, water comes to us,
and sustains all life.

Even if we know the source of our water, we still take its appearance for granted. But it is thanks to water that life is possible. Our bodies are more than seventy percent water. Our food can be grown and raised because of water. Water is a good friend, a bodhisattva, which nourishes the many thousands of species on Earth. Its benefits are numberless.

Reciting this gatha before turning on the faucet or drinking a glass of water enables us to see the stream of fresh water in our own hearts so that we feel completely refreshed. To celebrate the gift of water is to cultivate awareness and help sustain our life and the lives of others.

7. Washing Your Hands

Water flows over these hands.
May I use them skillfully
to preserve our precious planet.

Our beautiful Earth is endangered. We are about to exhaust her resources by polluting her rivers, lakes, and oceans, thus destroying the habitats of many species, including our own. We are destroying the forests, the ozone layer, and the air. Because of our ignorance, fears, and hatred of one another, our planet may be destroyed as an environment hospitable to human life.

The Earth stores water, and water gives life. Observe your hands as the water runs over them. Do you have enough clear insight to preserve and protect this beautiful planet, our Mother Earth?

8. Brushing Your Teeth

Brushing my teeth and rinsing my mouth,
I vow to speak purely and lovingly.
When my mouth is fragrant with right speech,
a flower blooms in the garden of my heart.

Each toothpaste manufacturer tells us that his brand will make our mouth clean and our breath fragrant. But if we do not practice "Right Speech," our breath can never be completely fragrant. In Vietnamese we say, "Your words smell bad!" to mean "Your words are not kind or constructive, but rather they are sharp, slanderous, and misleading." Our speech can build a world of peace and joy in which trust and love can flourish, or it can create discord and hatred. "Right Speech" means that our words are both truthful and beautiful.

In 1964, several of us founded a new Buddhist order, the Order of Interbeing. The ninth precept of the Order reads:

Do not say untruthful things for the sake of personal interest or to impress people. Do not utter words that can cause division and hatred. Do not spread news that you do not know to be certain. Do not criticize or condemn things that you are not sure of. Always speak truthfully and constructively. Have the courage to speak out about situations of injustice, even when doing so may threaten your own safety.

When we remember to speak words which are true, kind, and constructive, we nourish a beautiful flower in our hearts, and we can offer its sweet fragrance to everyone.

9. Bathing

Unborn and indestructible,
beyond time and space—
both transmission and inheritance
lie in the wonderful nature of the Dharmadhatu.

Whenever we take a bath or a shower, we can look at our body and see that it is a gift from our parents and their parents. Many of us in the West do not want to have much to do with our parents. They may have hurt us so much. But when we look deeply, we discover that it is impossible to drop all identity with them. As we wash each part of our body, we can meditate on the nature of the body and the nature of consciousness, asking ourselves, "To whom does this body belong? Who has transmitted this body to me? What has been transmitted?"

If we meditate in this way, we will discover that there are three components: the transmitter, that which is transmitted, and the one who receives the transmission. The transmitter is our parents. We are the continuation of our parents and their ancestors. The object of transmission is our body itself, and the one who receives the transmission is us. As we continue to meditate on this, we see clearly that the transmitter, the object transmitted, and the receiver are one. All three are present in our body. When we are deeply in touch with the present moment, we can see that all our ancestors and all future generations are present in us. Seeing this, we will know what to do and what not to do—for ourselves, our ancestors, our children, and their children.

The Dharmadhatu is all that is manifested from the Dharmakaya, having Dharmakaya as its essence, just as all waves are manifestations of water. The Dharmadhatu is neither born nor destroyed. It has no previous existence and no future existence. Its existence is beyond time and space. When we understand this truth of existence with our whole being, we will begin to transcend the fear of death, and we will not be disturbed by unnecessary discriminations.

10. Looking at Your Hand

Whose hand is this
that has never died?
Who is it who was born in the past?
Who is it who will die in the future?

If you look deeply into the palm of your hand, you will see your parents and all generations of your ancestors. All of them are alive in this moment. Each is present in your body. You are the continuation of each of these people.

To be born means that something which did not exist comes into existence. But the day we are "born" is not our beginning. It is a day of continuation. But that should not make us less happy when we celebrate our "Happy Continuation Day."

Since we are never born, how can we cease to be? This is what the *Heart Sutra* reveals to us. When we have a tangible experience of non-birth and non-death, we know ourselves beyond duality. The meditation on "no separate self" is one way to pass through the gate of birth and death.

Your hand proves that you have never been born and you will never die. The thread of life has never been interrupted from time without beginning until now. Previous generations, all the way back to single-celled beings, are present in your hand at this moment. You can observe and experience this. Your hand is always available as a subject for meditation.

11. Washing Your Feet

Peace and joy in each toe—
my own peace and joy.

We take our toes for granted. We worry about so many things, but we seldom think about our toes. If one small toe steps on a thorn, however, our whole body will feel the pain. Holding one toe in our hand, we can feel its peace and joy. It has been a good friend. It is not broken. It does not have cancer. We can thank our toe for its health and well-being.

Our toe and each cell of our body exist interdependently, not separately. If our body becomes ill or injured, the cause may be external, such as bacteria from contaminated food, alcohol in another driver's bloodstream, or a bomb dropped from a plane. If the sun were to stop shining, life on earth would cease. We must understand that our body also includes all of these things. The sun is our heart outside of our body. Our life and the life of all existence are one continuous life. The peace and joy of our small toe are the peace and joy of our whole body and mind, and the peace and joy of the entire universe. Once we identify with our toe, we can proceed further to identify ourselves with all life. Life comes from the whole universe. When we identify with the life of all that exists, we realize that birth and death are minor fluctuations in an ever-changing cosmos.

12. Getting Dressed

Putting on these clothes,
I am grateful to those who made them
and to the materials from which they were made.
I wish everyone could have enough to wear.

This gatha is an adaptation of a Vietnamese folk song: "My father works the land for the rice we eat. My mother sews the clothes I wear at every season." Today, not many of our fathers work the land; we buy our food in a store. Nor do many of our mothers sew our clothes; we buy manufactured clothes. By introducing the word "grateful," which is not in the folk song, the meaning becomes wider. In Zen monasteries, before eating, the monks reflect on the sources of their food. As we get dressed in the morning, we can contemplate the sources of our clothing and the fact that not everyone has enough to wear.

from Touching Peace:

PRACTICING THE ART OF MINDFUL LIVING

by *Thich Nhat Hanh*

Thich Nhat Hanh describes anger, fear, depression and hatred as "compost." Meditation and mindfulness help us put that compost to work cultivating the flowers of love and understanding, which lead to peace.

When we look deeply at a flower, we can see that it is made entirely of non-flower elements, like sunshine, rain, soil, compost, air, and time. If we continue to look deeply, we will also notice that the flower is on her way to becoming compost. If we don't notice this, we will be shocked when the flower begins to decompose. When we look deeply at the compost, we see that it is also on its way to becoming flowers, and we realize that flowers and compost "inter-are." They need each other. A good organic gardener does not discriminate against compost, because he knows how to transform it into marigolds, roses, and many other kinds of flowers.

When we look deeply into ourselves, we see both flowers and garbage. Each of us has anger, hatred, depression, racial discrimination, and many other kinds of garbage in us, but there is no need for us to be afraid. In the way that a gardener knows how to transform compost into flowers, we can learn the art of transforming anger, depression, and racial discrimination into love and understanding. This is the work of meditation.

According to Buddhist psychology, our consciousness is divided into two parts, like a house with two floors. On the ground floor there is a living room, and we call this "mind consciousness." Below the ground level, there is a basement, and we call this "store consciousness." In the store consciousness, everything we have ever done, experienced, or perceived is stored in the form of a seed, or a film. Our basement is an archive of every imaginable kind of film stored on a videocassette. Upstairs in the living room, we sit in a chair and watch these films as they are brought up from the basement.

Certain movies, such as *Anger, Fear,* or *Despair,* seem to have the ability to come up from the basement all by themselves. They open the door to the living room and pop themselves into our videocassette recorder whether we choose them or not. When that happens, we feel stuck, and we have no choice but to watch them. Fortunately, each film has a limited length, and when it is over, it returns to the basement. But each time it is viewed by us, it establishes a better position on the archive shelf, and we know it will return soon.

Sometimes a stimulus from outside, like someone saying something that hurts our feelings, triggers the showing of a film on our TV screen. We spend so much of our time watching these films, and many of them are destroying us. Learning how to stop them is important for our well-being.

Traditional texts describe consciousness as a field, a plot of land where every kind of seed can be planted—seeds of suffering, happiness, joy, sorrow, fear, anger, and hope. Store consciousness is also described as a storehouse filled with all our seeds. When a seed manifests in our mind consciousness, it always returns to the storehouse stronger. The quality of our life depends on the quality of the seeds in our store consciousness.

We may be in the habit of manifesting seeds of anger, sorrow, and fear in our mind consciousness; seeds of joy, happiness, and peace may not sprout up much. To practice mindfulness means to recognize each seed as it comes up from the storehouse and to practice watering the most wholesome seeds whenever possible, to help them grow stronger. During each moment that we are aware of something peaceful and beautiful, we water seeds of peace and beauty in us, and beautiful flowers bloom in our consciousness. The length of time we water a seed determines the strength of that seed. For example, if we stand in front of a tree, breathe consciously, and enjoy it for five minutes, seeds of happiness will be watered in us for five minutes, and those seeds will grow stronger. During the same five minutes, other seeds, like fear and pain, will not be watered. We have to practice this way every day. Any seed that manifests in our mind consciousness always returns to our store consciousness stronger. If we water our wholesome seeds carefully, we can trust that our store consciousness will do the work of healing.

Our bodies have a healing power. Every time we cut our finger, we wash the wound carefully and leave the work of healing to our body. In a few hours or a day, the cut is healed. Our consciousness also has a healing power. Suppose you see someone on the street you knew twenty years ago, and you cannot remember his name. The seed of him in your memory has become quite weak, since it has not had the chance to manifest in the upper level of your consciousness in such a long time. On your way home, you look throughout your basement to find the seed of his name, but you cannot find it. Finally you get a headache from looking so hard, so you stop looking and listen to a tape or a compact disc of beautiful music. Then you enjoy a delicious dinner and get a good night's sleep. In the morning, while you are brushing your teeth, his name just pops up. "Oh yes, that's his name." This means that during the night while your mind consciousness ceased the search, the store consciousness continued to work, and in the morning it brought you the results.

Healing has many avenues. When we feel anger, distress, or despair, we only need to breathe in and out consciously and recognize the feeling of anger, distress, or despair, and then we can leave the work of healing to our consciousness. But it is not only by touching our pain that we can heal. In fact, if we are not ready to do that, touching it may only make it worse. We have to strengthen ourselves first, and the easiest way to do this is by touching joy and peace. There are many wonderful things, but because we have focused our attention on what is wrong, we have not been able to touch what is *not* wrong. If we make some effort to breathe in and out and touch what is not wrong, the healing will be easier. Many of us have so much pain that it is difficult for us to touch a flower or hold the hand of a child. But we must make some effort so that we can develop the habit of touching what is beautiful and wholesome. This is the way we can assist our store consciousness to do the work of healing. If we touch what is peaceful and healing in us and around us, we help our store consciousness do the work of transformation. We let ourselves be healed by the trees, the birds, and the beautiful children. Otherwise, we will only repeat our suffering.

One wonderful seed in our store consciousness—the seed of mindfulness—when manifested, has the capacity of being aware of what is happening in the present moment. If we take one peaceful, happy step and we know that we are taking a peaceful, happy step, mindfulness is present. Mindfulness is an important agent for our transformation and healing, but our seed of mindfulness has been buried under many layers of forgetfulness and pain for a long time. We are rarely aware that we have eyes that see clearly, a heart and a liver that function well, and a non-toothache. We live in forgetfulness, looking for happiness somewhere else, ignoring and crushing the precious elements of happiness that are already in us and around us. If we breathe in and out and see that the tree is there, alive and beautiful, the seed of our mindfulness will be watered, and it will grow stronger. When we first start to practice, our mindfulness will be weak, like a fifteen-watt light-bulb. But as soon as we pay attention to our breathing, it begins to grow stronger, and after practicing like that for a few weeks, it becomes as bright as a one-hundred-watt bulb. With the light of mindfulness shining, we touch many wonderful elements within and around us, and while doing so, we water the seeds of peace, joy, and happiness in us, and at the same time, we refrain from watering the seeds of unhappiness.

When we start out, the seeds of unhappiness in us are quite strong, because we have been watering them every day. Our seeds of anger have been watered by our spouse and our children. Because they themselves suffer, they only know how to water our seeds of suffering. When those seeds of unhappiness are strong, even if we do not invite them up from the basement, they will push the door open and barge into the living room. When they enter, it is not at all pleasant. We may try to suppress them and keep them in the basement, but because we have watered them so much, they are strong enough to just show up in the upper level of our consciousness even without an invitation.

Many of us feel the need to do something all the time—listen to a Walkman, watch TV, read a book or a magazine, pick up the telephone. We want to keep ourselves busy in our living room so we can avoid dealing with the worries and anxieties that are in our basement. But if we look deeply into the nature of the guests we are inviting into the living room, we will see that many carry the same toxins as are present in the negative seeds we are trying so hard to avoid. Even as we prevent these negative seeds from coming up, we are watering them and making them stronger. Some of us even do social and environmental work to avoid looking at our real problems.

For us to be happy, we need to water the seed of mindfulness that is in us. Mindfulness is the seed of enlightenment, awareness, understanding, care, compassion, liberation, transformation, and healing. If we practice mindfulness, we get in touch with the refreshing and joyful aspects of life in us and around us, the things we are not able to touch when we live in forgetfulness. Mindfulness makes things like our eyes, our heart, our non-toothache, the beautiful moon, and the trees deeper and more beautiful. If we touch these wonderful things with mindfulness, they will reveal their full splendor. When we touch our pain with mindfulness, we will begin to transform it. When a baby is crying in the living room, his mother goes in right away to hold him tenderly in her arms. Because mother is made of love and tenderness, when she does that, love and tenderness penetrate the baby and, in only a few minutes, the baby will probably stop crying. Mindfulness is the mother who cares for your pain every time it begins to cry.

While the pain is in the basement, you can enjoy many refreshing and healing elements of life by producing mindfulness. Then, when the pain wants to come upstairs, you can turn off your Walkman, close your book, open the living room door, and invite your pain to come up. You can smile to it and embrace it with your mindfulness, which has become strong. If fear, for example, wishes to come up, don't ignore it. Greet it warmly with your mindfulness. "Fear, my old friend, I recognize you." If you are afraid of your fear, it may overwhelm you. But if you invite it up calmly and smile at it in mindfulness, it will lose some of its strength. After you have practiced watering the seeds of mindfulness for a few weeks, you will be strong enough to invite your fear to come up any time, and you will be able to embrace it with your mindfulness. It may not be entirely pleasant, but with mindfulness you are safe.

If you embrace a minor pain with mindfulness, it will be transformed in a few minutes. Just breathe in and out, and smile at it. But when you have a block of pain that is stronger, more time is needed. Practice sitting and walking meditation while you embrace your pain in mindfulness, and, sooner or later, it will be transformed. If you have increased the quality of your mindfulness through the practice, the transformation will be quicker. When mindfulness embraces pain, it begins to penetrate and transform it, like sunshine penetrating a flower bud and helping it blossom. When mindfulness touches something beautiful, it reveals its beauty. When it touches something painful, it transforms and heals it.

Another way to accelerate the transformation is called looking deeply. When we look deeply at a flower, we see the non-flower elements that help it to be—the clouds, the Earth, the gardener, the soil. When we look deeply at our pain, we see that our suffering is not ours alone. Many seeds of suffering have been handed down to us by our ancestors, our parents, and our society. We have to recognize these seeds. One boy who practices at Plum Village told me this story. When he was eleven, he was very angry at his father. Every time he fell down and hurt himself, his father would get angry and shout at him. The boy vowed that when he grew up, he would be different. But a few years ago, his little sister was playing with other children and she fell off a swing and scraped her knee. It was bleeding, and the boy became very angry. He wanted to shout at her, "How stupid! Why did you do that?" But he caught himself. Because he had been practicing mindfulness, he knew how to recognize his anger as anger, and he did not act on it.

A number of adults who were present were taking good care of his sister, washing her wound and putting a bandage on it, so he walked away slowly and practiced looking deeply. Suddenly he saw that he was exactly like his father, and he realized that if he did not do something about his anger, he would transmit it to his children. It was a remarkable insight for an eleven-year-old boy. At the same time, he saw that his father may have been a victim just like him. The seeds of his father's anger might have been transmitted by his grandparents. Because of the practice of looking deeply in mindfulness, he was able to transform his anger into insight. Then he went to his father, and told him that because he now understood him, he was able to really love him.

When we are irritated and we say something unkind to our child, we water the seeds of suffering in him. When he reacts, he waters the seeds of suffering in us. Living this way escalates and strengthens the suffering. In mindfulness, calmly breathing in and out, we can practice looking deeply at the types of suffering we have in ourselves. When we do so, we also begin to understand our ancestors, our culture, and our society. The moment we see this, we can go back and serve our people with loving kindness and compassion, and without blame. Because of our insight, we are capable of practicing real peace and reconciliation. When you remove the conflict between yourself and others, you also remove the conflict within yourself. One arrow can save two birds at the same time—if you strike the branch, both birds will fly away. First, take care of yourself. Reconcile the conflicting elements within yourself by being mindful and practicing loving kindness. Then reconcile with your own people by understanding and loving them, even if they themselves lack understanding.

The seeds of suffering are always trying to emerge. If we try to suppress them, we create a lack of circulation in our psyche and we feel sick. Practicing mindfulness helps us get strong enough to open the door to our living room and let the pain come up. Every time our pain is immersed in mindfulness, it will lose some of its strength, and later, when it returns to the store consciousness, it will be weaker. When it comes up again, if our mindfulness is there to welcome it like a mother greeting her baby, the pain will be lessened and will go back down to the basement even weaker. In this way, we create good circulation in our psyche, and we begin to feel much better. If the blood is circulating well in our body, we experience well-being. If the energy of our mental formations is circulating well between our store consciousness and mind consciousness, we also have the feeling of well-being. We do not need to be afraid of our pain if our mindfulness is there to embrace it and transform it.

Our consciousness is the totality of our seeds, the totality of our films. If the good seeds are strong, we will have more happiness. Meditation helps the seed of mindfulness grow and develop as the light within us. If we practice mindful living, we will know how to water the seeds of joy and transform the seeds of sorrow and suffering so that understanding, compassion, and loving kindness will flower in us.

Interbeing:

AN INTERVIEW WITH THICH NHAT HANH

by the editors of *Tricycle: The Buddhist Review*

Thich Nhat Hanh discusses the challenges, especially for those in the West, of practicing engaged Buddhism, and offers suggestions on how to integrate the basic precepts of Interbeing into daily life.

TRICYCLE: *Hundreds of thousands of people are in touch with Buddhism only through you. What is important for them to know?*

THICH NHAT HANH: [Laughing] To know about Buddhism—or to know about themselves? It is important that we understand that Buddhism is a way of life. People may be interested in learning about Buddhism because they have had some difficulties with their own religion. But for me, Buddhism is a very old, broad tradition. It is part of the heritage of humankind, and if you don't know what it is, you don't profit from its wisdom.

TRICYCLE: *Can everyone benefit?*

THICH NHAT HANH: Buddhism is more of a way of life than a religion. It is like a fruit. You may like a number of fruits, like bananas, oranges, mandarins, and so on. You are committed to eating these fruits. But then someone tells you that there is a fruit called mango and it would be wonderful for you to try that fruit. It will be a pity if you don't know what a mango is. But eating a mango does not require you to abandon your habit of eating oranges. Why not try it? You may like it a lot. Buddhism is a kind of mango, you see—a way of life, an experience that is worth trying. It is open for everyone. You can continue to be a Jew or a Catholic while enjoying Buddhism. I think that's a wonderful thing.

TRICYCLE: *Originally, in your book* Interbeing, *you published the Fourteen Precepts for the first time. I'm curious about the transition from those fourteen to the five that you have been emphasizing more recently. It seems that the five are perhaps more disciplined. Is that because of your perception of your students, that we need more discipline?*

THICH NHAT HANH: The five precepts are very old and date back to the time of the Buddha. But we feel that they should be rephrased; represented again in a way that can be understood more easily for the people, especially the young in the West. If you say, "Don't do this, don't do that," people don't like that. They feel they are being forced to do something. In Asia we also profit from that rewording of the five precepts, because Asia is now in touch with the West and westernized in their daily life.

TRICYCLE: *What is the practice of the precepts?*

THICH NHAT HANH: To practice the precepts is to protect yourself and to protect people you love; to protect society. That is why "Compassion" is the first precept, instead of "Do not kill." It is worded like this because it is a practice of protecting life. I vow to refrain from killing, from encouraging people to kill. I vow to do whatever I can in order to protect life and to prevent the killing, not only with my body, with my speech, but also with my way of life, with my thinking. By practicing awareness, mindfulness, you know that suffering is born from the destruction of life. People are ready to accept this as a guideline of their life. And the same is true with the other four precepts.

TRICYCLE: *You said, "to protect yourself and to protect your family."* *What did you mean, exactly?*

THICH NHAT HANH: I'm using everyday language. When you practice not drinking alcohol, you not only protect yourself, you protect your family, your husband, your wife, your children—you protect your society. If you don't get drunk while driving, you protect people—not only yourself, but your family, too. If you die in an accident, your family will have to suffer. And you protect the person who you might injure just by your practice of not drinking. It's very simple.

TRICYCLE: *Can you explain what you mean when you talk about "ancestors" or "heritage" with regard to karma? There's a sense that what we call "karma" is somehow genetic, biological, is within genetic transmission.*

THICH NHAT HANH: Karma is action, and action of the father can affect the children. When you practice, you transform the karma. You practice like that not only for *your* transformation but for the transformation of your parents, your ancestors. In Vietnam there is a saying that when the father eats too much salt, the son has to drink a lot of water. Karma, or action, is like that. Not only do you have to suffer, your children have to suffer also. That is why to practice the precepts is to protect yourself and to protect future generations.

TRICYCLE: *Is this idea of genetic lineage compatible with reincarnation?*

THICH NHAT HANH: I can only smile. Reincarnation means that there is something to enter into the body. That something might be called the "soul," or "consciousness," whatever name you might like to use. *Re* means again—*reincarnation* means "into the body again." The understanding is that the "soul" can go out and "you" can be gone into. Maybe it's not the best word, not a very Buddhist word. In Buddhism there is the word *rebirth* or *reborn,* and then the basic teaching of the Buddha is "no-self." Everything manifests itself because of conditions. If there is no body, our perceptions, our feelings, and our consciousness cannot be manifested.

TRICYCLE: *Not born, but manifested?*

THICH NHAT HANH: Yes. So, body is one condition. There are many other conditions. There are at least two kinds of Buddhism; popular Buddhism and deep

Buddhism. Which kind of Buddhism you're talking about is very important. It requires learning and practice, because anything you say in the second may be misunderstood and can create damage. The true teaching is the kind of teaching that conforms to two things: First, it is consistent with the Buddhist insight. And secondly, it is appropriate for the person who is receiving it. It's like medicine. It has to be true medicine, and it must fit the person who is receiving it. Sometimes you can give someone a very expensive treatment, but they still die. That is why when the Buddha meets someone and offers the teaching, he has to know that person in order to be able to offer the appropriate teaching. Even if the teaching is very valuable, if you don't make it appropriate to the person, it is not Buddhist teaching. To some other people, it is excellent teaching. But, to this person, it's not Buddhist teaching because it does damage, does more damage than good. If you offer the things that are not appropriate, you destroy people.

TRICYCLE: *At what level are you addressing the thousands of people reading your books?*

THICH NHAT HANH: Most of these books have a specific kind of audience, or reader. *Being Peace*, for example, was first spoken to children and to people who come for a retreat. When you read the book, you can see what kind of audience the book is intended for. That should be true of everything, every sutra, or the Bible. When Jesus Christ talked to someone, he had to know and to talk to that particular person. The same is true with the sutras. You have to know who the Buddha is speaking to. Maybe the Buddha is not speaking to you. He's speaking to another person. But if you know what the Buddha is speaking to in that person, the Buddha can speak to you, also. This is very important.

TRICYCLE: *Is there a problem with making teachings appropriate for so many, many people in the West who have no Buddhist background at all?*

THICH NHAT HANH: We all have to examine the problem of appropriateness of the teaching, because it is a big problem. As I said, the five precepts had been presented in China and Vietnam and Tibet for a long time, just as they were—there was no problem with the wording [Laughing]. But when we present them to the young people here, they say, "I don't like to be ordered around."

TRICYCLE: *How has living your life affected the way you present the teachings? Has the importance of things shifted over time in terms of how you say it, or what you say, or what you feel the world needs to know?*

THICH NHAT HANH: In Plum Village, Vietnamese refugees come to study and practice alongside Europeans and Americans. During the summer opening, I used to give dharma talks in three languages: Vietnamese, French, and English. Our Western friends were very curious about the dharma talks I gave in Vietnamese. They came and listened to the translation with earphones and realized that when I give a teaching in Vietnamese, it's quite different. I am aware that I'm addressing people with a background of a particular kind of suffering. Their suffering is not exactly the same kind of suffering which Westerners have had to undergo.

TRICYCLE: *Can you speak about the difference?*

THICH NHAT HANH: Suppose we were talking about a family of refugees that had undergone suffering as boat people. They might have people dying during the dangerous trip. Sometimes a child is alive, and his or her parents are dead. They have suffered the loss of a loved one, but the circumstances are different.

So I had the impression that dharma talks given to the Vietnamese would feel a little strange to Westerners. But in fact, from time to time, Western friends say, "Why don't you talk to us about the same problems?" And the same is true of the Vietnamese—each is curious what I tell the other. It turns out that there are things that are common to both cultures, and each profits from the other's teaching.

TRICYCLE: *Can awakening be realized through mindful breathing—which seems to be at the heart of all your teaching?*

THICH NHAT HANH: Of course. Mindful breathing helps you see your anger, your frustration, your suffering. When you breathe mindfully, you practice looking deeply into yourself. You are made of feelings, perceptions, mental formations, and consciousness. Your true nature is what—if not these things? Because it is wrong perceptions that make you suffer, and if you don't know the nature of your own perceptions, you are not likely to get free of your suffering. So your true nature is the nature of your feelings, your perceptions, your mental formations, and your consciousness.

True nature does not point to something abstract, but to your nature as the nature of the One. If, while practicing meditation, you ignore the presence of social injustice and the fact that people are dying every day, you are not looking at your true nature because all of this is the manifestation of our collective consciousness, our true nature.

TRICYCLE: *So much of your teachings seems to be about behavior.*

THICH NHAT HANH: Why don't you say "daily life," or "being in the moment and responding to what is there"?

TRICYCLE: *Well, for example, you talk a lot about being happy, as if creating happiness in a very deliberate way is itself beneficial, whereas so much of "daily life" seems to be about anger, frustration, despair.*

THICH NHAT HANH: I have noticed that people are dealing too much with the negative, with what is wrong. They do not touch enough on what is not wrong—it's the same as some psychotherapists. Why not try the other way, to look into the patient and see positive things, to just touch those things and make them bloom?

Waking up in the morning, you can recognize "I'm alive" and that there are twenty-four hours for me to live, to learn how to look at living beings with the eyes of compassion. If you are aware that you are alive, that you have twenty-four hours to create new joy, this would be enough to make yourself happy and the people around you happy. This is a practice of happiness.

TRICYCLE: *It's very hard to imagine that somebody could come out of Vietnam the way you did and be completely free of anger. Do you think of yourself as being free from anger?*

THICH NHAT HANH: You have to practice in order to diminish your anger, to help non-anger prevail. Non-anger is a wholesome mental formation that you can touch. When you have seen your whole country destroyed, millions of people dying, it's natural that you get angry. But through the practice of looking deeply, you can see things that other people cannot see. You can see that the American soldiers were very scared too, and because of this they dropped lots of bombs. They didn't know what happened down there when a bomb exploded.

If you practice looking deeply, you ask, Why have they come here? Have they come with the intention to kill? To destroy our country? If you had had any contact with the soldiers, you would see that they had been sent in order to kill or to be killed, and that the Vietnamese soldiers also don't want to be killed, don't want to kill, but are forced to do so. When you practice looking like that, you see that the deep cause of the war is a policy that is based on a wrong perception of the situation—in Vietnam and in the world—and wrong perception is the real criminal.

TRICYCLE: *Do you still get angry about things, whether it's about the war from thirty years ago or about contemporary things? Do you still have to practice dissolving anger?*

THICH NHAT HANH: The seeds of anger are *always* there. But when you notice, when you keep alive your understanding, they have no chance to manifest. Understanding is something that stays with you, and practicing the precepts, practicing meditation, helps you deepen your understanding all the time.

You know, in Vietnam, when you sat during the war, when you sat in the meditation hall and heard the bombs falling, you had to be aware that the bombs were falling and people were dying. That is part of the practice. Meditation means to be aware of what is happening in the present moment—to your body, to your feelings, to your environment. But if you see and you don't do anything, where is your awareness? Then where would your enlightenment be?—Your compassion? In order not to get lost, you have to be able to continue the practice there, in the midst of all that. But no one can be completely there twenty-four hours a day. I find that after having talked to two or three people who have deep suffering, I, myself, feel the need to withdraw in order to recuperate.

TRICYCLE: *You have become so popular that I have heard people say "Thich Nhat Hanh is a movement, not a teacher."*

THICH NHAT HANH: That's not my impression. I see myself as a very lazy teacher, as a very lazy monk.

TRICYCLE: *I don't think very many people see you that way.*

THICH NHAT HANH: I have a lot of time for myself. And that's not easy. My nature is that I don't like to disappoint people, and it is very difficult for me to say no to invitations. But I have learned to know my limit, learned to say no and to withdraw to my hermitage to have time for my walking meditation, my sitting, my time with the garden, with the flowers and things like that. I have not used the telephone for the last twenty-five years.

My schedule is free. It is a privilege. Sometimes I remember a Catholic father in Holland who keeps a beeper. I asked him, "Why do you have to keep that?" and he said "I have no right to be disconnected from my people." Well, in that case, you need an assistant. Because you cannot continue to be of help to other people if you do not take care of yourself. Your solidity, your freedom, your happiness, are crucial for other people. Taking good care of yourself is very important. I have learned to protect myself. That does not mean that I have to be unkind to people, but sharing the teaching with helping professionals, well, I always say, "You work so hard. Doctors and nurses and social workers, you work too hard. And if you face so much stress, you cannot go on, you have burned out. So please find ways—by all means—in order to protect yourself. Come together and discuss strategies of self-protection. Otherwise you cannot help people for a long time." Because I urge other people to do so, I do so myself.

TRICYCLE: *You are often called the "father of engaged Buddhism." But there is concern that the engaged Buddhist movement in the United States is very different from what you're talking about for your own life, that people don't come back to protecting themselves through their practice enough. There seems to be some confusion around your work with regard to this; the ideal that is sometimes projected in the West is that social action is practice, but this has been used as a way of replacing contemplative forms of practice with social action.*

THICH NHAT HANH: Well, in a difficult situation like the situation of war, you cannot dissociate yourself from a society that suffers. You have to be engaged and do whatever you can in order to help. Everyone is capable of having time to sit, to walk, to eat mindfully, to eat silently or alone or with the sangha. If you abandon basic things like that, how can you call yourself a practicing Buddhist? If you are smart, you find a lot of time to practice during your day, even cooking your dinner or preparing a pot of tea. There's no boundary between practice and non-practice.

For those who only talk about it, I have nothing much to offer. But for those who really want to practice, I would say that it is possible to practice meditation the whole day. Even if I am only taking three steps or five steps, I always practice walking meditation. I do it, I don't just say it. Even during a one-hundred-day trip in North America, the most difficult environment for practice, I have done that.

TRICYCLE: *North America is the most difficult environment for practice?*

THICH NHAT HANH: Yes, because it's so busy, people are so quick. During that one hundred days of teaching retreats and dharma talks, I always followed my breathing. I always practice walking meditation, even at the airport.

TRICYCLE: *What is the difference between three steps of mindful walking and three steps of not mindful walking?*

THICH NHAT HANH: Mindful walking is walking in such

a way that you know you are walking. You are aware of every step. There is solidity, mindfulness, the awareness that you are alive—it is you who are walking, not a ghost walking. You are completely alive. You walk not only to arrive somewhere, but to be entirely present in every step you make.

TRICYCLE: *Is it possible that engaged Buddhism in North America is being used in the United States to create a more diluted Buddhism, or what some people call "Buddhism Lite"?*

THICH NHAT HANH: I think everything is possible. Anything can turn out to be like that. If you practice, that's all right. The question is whether people practice enough. Engaged Buddhism is engaged because you are urged and encouraged to do sitting meditation to produce joy and stability, for yourself and for the people around you.

I sometimes say, "Sit for your father. Sit for your mother. Sit for your sister. Sit for me." Because when you sit like that you get the joy, the stability, and all your ancestors in you get the joy and the stability. If I, your teacher, am sick that day, you sit for me also, because from the outcome of your sitting, we all profit. So sitting silently in the meditation hall, alone or with the sangha, is already engaged Buddhism. When you smile, that is engaged Buddhism, because smiling like that is to relax and to bring joy. When you smile, all your ancestors smile with you; your children and grandchildren also. And, if you can be smiling, you are building your sangha with your smile.

A smiling person is very crucial for the sangha. When a smiling person comes to visit your sangha, very fresh, very pleasant, you should beg her to stay, beg him to stay, because that is a plus to the sangha. The happiness of a person is very important to the world. That is why engaged Buddhism means that you practice sitting meditation or walking meditation in the monastery not only for your so-called "self" but you do it wherever you are and for the whole society.

TRICYCLE: *In the United States, many people now talk about "engaged Buddhism" as if it replicates a Christian sense of charity, a sense that you are "engaged" if you're working with homeless people, if you're working with AIDS projects.*

THICH NHAT HANH: I think that we need dharma teachers to help explain more about engaged Buddhism. One of the things I have been trying to do is to urge people to set up sanghas. There is a kind of practice we call "sangha building." Sangha building is so crucial. If you are without a sangha, you lose your practice very soon. In our tradition we say that without the sangha you are like a tiger that has left his mountain and gone to the lowland—he will be caught and killed by humans. If you practice without sangha you are abandoning your practice.

Whether you are a psychotherapist, a doctor, a nurse, a social worker, whoever you are, you can only survive as a practitioner if you have a sangha. So, building a sangha is the first thing you have to do. That is what we always urge in retreats. On the last day of every retreat we organize sangha-building sessions. We say that the first thing you should do when you go home after retreat is to build a sangha for the practice to be able to continue. If you are surrounded by a sangha, you have the chance to sit together, to walk together, to learn together, and you won't lose your practice. Otherwise, in just a few weeks or few months, you will be carried away and you can no longer talk about practice— engaged or not engaged. No practice at all. Although I speak about engaged Buddhism, I still live like a monastic, and I feel very engaged. I don't feel disconnected with anyone.

The Fourteen Precepts of the Order of Interbeing

1. Do not be idolatrous about or bound to any doctrine, theory, or ideology, even Buddhist ones. Buddhist systems of thought are guiding means; they are not absolute truth.

2. Do not think the knowledge you presently possess is changeless, absolute truth. Avoid being narrowminded and bound to present views. Learn and practice non-attachment from views in order to be open to receive others' viewpoints. Truth is found in life and not merely in conceptual knowledge. Be ready to learn throughout your entire life and to observe reality in yourself and in the world at all times.

3. Do not force others, including children, by any means whatsoever, to adopt your views, whether by authority, threat, money, propaganda, or even education. However, through compassionate dialogue, help others renounce fanaticism and narrowness.

4. Do not avoid contact with suffering or close your eyes before suffering. Do not lose awareness of the existence of suffering in the life of the world. Find

ways to be with those who are suffering, including personal contact, visits, images, and sounds. By such means, awaken yourself and others to the reality of suffering in the world.

5. Do not accumulate wealth while millions are hungry. Do not take as the aim of your life fame, profit, wealth, or sensual pleasure. Live simply and share time, energy, and material resources with those who are in need.

6. Do not maintain anger or hatred. Learn to penetrate and transform them when they are still seeds in your consciousness. As soon as they arise, turn your attention to your breath in order to see and understand the nature of your anger and hatred and the nature of the persons who have caused your anger and hatred.

7. Do not lose yourself in dispersion and in your surroundings. Practice mindful breathing to come back to what is happening in the present moment. Be in touch with what is wondrous, refreshing, and healing both inside and around you. Plant seeds of joy, peace, and understanding in yourself in order to facilitate the work of transformation in the depths of your consciousness.

8. Do not utter words that can create discord and cause the community to break. Make every effort to reconcile and resolve all conflicts, however small.

9. Do not say untruthful things for the sake of personal interest or to impress people. Do not utter words that cause division and hatred. Do not spread news that you do not know to be certain. Do not criticize or condemn things of which you are not sure. Always speak truthfully and constructively. Have the

courage to speak out about situations of injustice, even when doing so may threaten your own safety.

10. Do not use the Buddhist community for personal gain or profit, or transform your community into a political party. A religious community, however, should take a clear stand against oppression and injustice and should strive to change the situation without engaging in partisan conflicts.

11. Do not live with a vocation that is harmful to humans and nature. Do not invest in companies that deprive others of their chance to live. Select a vocation that helps realize your ideal of compassion.

12. Do not kill. Do not let others kill. Find whatever means possible to protect life and prevent war.

13. Possess nothing that should belong to others. Respect the property of others, but prevent others from profiting from human suffering or the suffering of other species on Earth.

14. Do not mistreat your body. Learn to handle it with respect. Do not look on your body only as an instrument. Preserve vital energies (sexual, breath, spirit) for the realization of the Way. (For brothers and sisters who are not monks and nuns:) Sexual expression should not take place without love and a long-term commitment.

from For a Future to Be Possible:
COMMENTARIES ON THE FIVE WONDERFUL PRECEPTS

by *Thich Nhat Hanh*

The Third Precept of Buddhism calls upon us to refrain from sexual misconduct. The definition of "sexual misconduct" is complex and potentially confusing in our contemporary, secular society. Thich Nhat Hanh in this selection explores the relationship between love, trust, responsibility and sexual intimacy.

ware of the suffering caused by sexual misconduct, I vow to cultivate responsibility and learn ways to protect the safety and integrity of individuals, couples, families, and society. I am determined not to engage in sexual relations without love and a long-term commitment. To preserve the happiness of myself and others, I am determined to respect my commitments and the commitments of others. I will do everything in my power to protect children from sexual abuse and to prevent couples and families from being broken by sexual misconduct.

So many individuals, children, couples, and families have been destroyed by sexual misconduct. To practice the Third Precept is to heal ourselves and heal our society. This is mindful living.

The Fifth Precept—not to consume alcohol, toxins, or drugs—and the Third Precept are linked. Both concern destructive and destabilizing behavior. These precepts are the right medicine to heal us. We need only to observe ourselves and those around us to see the truth. Our stability and the stability of our families and society cannot be obtained without the practice of these two precepts. If you look at individuals and families who are unstable and unhappy, you will see that many of them do not practice these precepts. You can make the diagnosis by yourself and then know that the medicine is there. Practicing these precepts is the best way to restore stability in the family and in society. For many people, this precept is easy to practice, but for others, it is quite difficult. It is important for these people to come together and share their experiences.

In the Buddhist tradition, we speak of the oneness of body and mind. Whatever happens to the body also happens to the mind. The sanity of the body is the sanity of the mind; the violation of the body is the violation of the mind. When we are angry, we may think that we are angry in our feelings, not in our body, but that is not true. When we love someone, we want to be close to him or her physically, but when we are angry at someone, we don't want to touch or be touched by that person. We cannot say that body and mind are separate.

A sexual relationship is an act of communion between body and spirit. This is a very important encounter, not to be done in a casual manner. You know that in your soul there are certain areas—memories, pain, secrets— that are private, that you would only share with the person you love and trust the most. You do not open your heart and show it to just anyone. In the imperial city, there is a zone you cannot approach called the forbidden city; only the king and his family are permitted to circulate there. There is a place like that in your soul that you do not allow anyone to approach except the one you trust and love the most.

The same is true of our body. Our bodies have areas that we do not want anyone to touch or approach unless he or she is the one we respect, trust, and love the most. When we are approached casually or carelessly, with an attitude that is less than tender, we feel insulted in our body and soul. Someone who approaches us with respect, tenderness, and utmost care is offering us deep communication, deep communion. It is only in that case that we will not feel hurt, misused, or abused, even a little. This cannot be attained unless there is true love and commitment. Casual sex cannot be described as love. Love is deep, beautiful, and whole.

True love contains respect. In my tradition, husband and wife are expected to respect each other like guests, and when you practice this kind of respect, your love and happiness will continue for a long time. In sexual relationships, respect is one of the most important elements. Sexual communion should be like a rite, a ritual performed in mindfulness with great respect, care, and love. If you are motivated by some desire, that is not love. Desire is not love. Love is something much more responsible. It has care in it.

We have to restore the meaning of the word "love." We have been using it in a careless way. When we say, "I love hamburgers," we are not talking about love. We are

talking about our appetite, our desire for hamburgers.
We should not dramatize our speech and misuse words
like that. We make words like "love" sick that way. We
have to make an effort to heal our language by using
words carefully. The word "love" is a beautiful word.
We have to restore its meaning.

*"I am determined not to engage in sexual relations without love and
a long-term commitment."* If the word "love" is understood
in the deepest way, why do we need to say "long-term
commitment"? If love is real, we do not need long or
short-term commitments, or even a wedding ceremony. True love includes the sense of responsibility,
accepting the other person as he is, with all his
strengths and weaknesses. If we like only the best
things in the person, that is not love. We have to
accept his weaknesses and bring our patience, understanding, and energy to help him transform. Love is
maitri, the capacity to bring joy and happiness, and
karuna, the capacity to transform pain and suffering.
This kind of love can only be good for people. It
cannot be described as negative or destructive. It is
safe. It guarantees everything.

Should we cross out the phrase "long-term commitment" or change it to "short-term commitment"?
"Short-term commitment" means that we can be
together for a few days and after that the relationship
will end. That cannot be described as love. If we have
that kind of relationship with another person, we
cannot say that the relationship comes out of love and
care. The expression "long-term commitment" helps
people understand the word love. In the context of real
love, commitment can only be long-term. "I want to
love you. I want to help you. I want to care for you. I

want you to be happy. I want to work for happiness. But just for a few days." Does this make sense?

You are afraid to make a commitment—to the precepts, to your partner, to anything. You want freedom. But remember, you have to make a long-term commitment to love your son deeply and help him through the journey of life as long as you are alive. You cannot just say, "I don't love you anymore." When you have a good friend, you also make a long-term commitment. You need her. How much more so with someone who wants to share your life, your soul, and your body. The phrase "long-term commitment" cannot express the depth of love, but we have to say something so that people understand.

A long-term commitment between two people is only a beginning. We also need the support of friends and other people. That is why, in our society, we have a wedding ceremony. The two families join together with other friends to witness the fact that you have come together to live as a couple. The priest and the marriage license are just symbols. What is important is that your commitment is witnessed by many friends and both of your families. Now you will be supported by them. A long-term commitment is stronger and more long-lasting if made in the context of a Sangha.

Your strong feelings for each other are very important, but they are not enough to sustain your happiness. Without other elements, what you describe as love may turn into something sour rather soon. The support of friends and family coming together weaves a kind of web. The strength of your feelings is only one of the strands of that web. Supported by many elements, the couple will be solid, like a tree. If a tree wants to be strong, it needs a number of roots sent deep into the soil. If a tree has only one root, it may be blown over by the wind. The life of a couple also needs to be supported by many elements—families, friends, ideals, practice, and Sangha.

In Plum Village, the practice community where I live in France, every time we have a wedding ceremony, we invite the whole community to celebrate and bring support to the couple. After the ceremony, on every full moon day, the couple recites the Five Awarenesses together, remembering that friends everywhere are supporting their relationship to be stable, long-lasting, and happy.* Whether or not your relationship is bound by law, it will be stronger and more long-lasting if made in the presence of a Sangha—friends who love you and want to support you in the spirit of understanding and loving kindness.

Love can be a kind of sickness. In the West and in Asia, we have the word "lovesick." What makes us sick is attachment. Although it is a sweet internal formation, this kind of love with attachment is like a drug. It makes us feel wonderful, but once we are addicted, we cannot have peace. We cannot study, do our daily work, or sleep. We only think of the object of our love. We are sick with love. This kind of love is linked to our

---

* The Five Awarenesses are: 1. We are aware that all generations of our ancestors and all future generations are present in us. 2. We are aware of the expectations our ancestors, our children, and their children have of us. 3. We are aware that our joy, peace, freedom, and harmony are the joy, peace, freedom, and harmony of our ancestors, our children, and their children. 4. We are aware that understanding is the very foundation of love. 5. We are aware that blaming and arguing never help us and only create a wider gap between us, that only understanding, trust, and love can help us change and grow.

willingness to possess and monopolize. We want the object of our love to be entirely ours and only for us. It is totalitarian. We do not want anyone to prevent us from being with him or her. This kind of love can be described as a prison, where we lock up our beloved and create only suffering for him or her. The one who is loved is deprived of freedom—of the right to be him or herself and enjoy life. This kind of love cannot be described as maitri or karuna. It is only the willingness to make use of the other person in order to satisfy our own needs.

When you have sexual energy that makes you feel unhappy, as though you are losing your inner peace, you should know how to practice so that you do not do things that will bring suffering to other people or yourself. We have to learn about this. In Asia, we say there are three sources of energy—sexual, breath, and spirit. *Tinh*, sexual energy, is the first. When you have more sexual energy than you need, there will be an imbalance in your body and in your being. You need to know how to reestablish the balance, or you may act irresponsibly. According to Taoism and Buddhism, there are practices to help reestablish that balance, such as meditation or martial arts. You can learn the ways to channel your sexual energy into deep realizations in the domains of art and meditation.

The second source of energy is *khi*, breath energy. Life can be described as a process of burning. In order to burn, every cell in our body needs nutrition and oxygen. In his *Fire Sermon*, the Buddha said, "The eyes are burning, the nose is burning, the body is burning." In our daily lives, we have to cultivate our energy by practicing proper breathing. We benefit from the air and its oxygen, so we have to be sure that non-polluted air is available to us. Some people cultivate their khi by refraining from smoking and talking, or by practicing conscious breathing after talking a lot. When you speak, take the time to breathe. At Plum Village, every time we hear the bell of mindfulness, everyone stops what they are doing and breathes consciously three times. We practice this way to cultivate and preserve our khi energy.

The third source of energy is *thân*, spirit energy. When you don't sleep at night, you lose some of this kind of energy. Your nervous system becomes exhausted and you cannot study or practice meditation well, or make good decisions. You don't have a clear mind because of lack of sleep or from worrying too much. Worry and anxiety drain this source of energy.

So don't worry. Don't stay up too late. Keep your nervous system healthy. Prevent anxiety. These kinds of practices cultivate the third source of energy. You need this source of energy to practice meditation well. A spiritual breakthrough requires the power of your spirit energy, which comes about through concentration and knowing how to preserve this source of energy. When you have strong spirit energy, you only have to focus it on an object, and you will have a breakthrough. If you don't have thân, the light of your concentration will not shine brightly, because the light emitted is very weak.

According to Asian medicine, the power of thân is linked to the power of tinh. When we expend our sexual energy, it takes time to restore it. In Chinese medicine, when you want to have a strong spirit and concentration, you are advised to refrain from having sexual relationships or overeating. You will be given herbs, roots, and medicine to enrich your source of thân, and, during the time you are taking this medicine, you are asked to refrain from sexual relationships. If your source of spirit is weak and you continue to have sexual relations, it is said that you cannot recover your spirit energy. Those who practice meditation should try to preserve their sexual energy, because they need it during meditation. If you are an artist, you may wish to practice channeling your sexual energy together with your spirit energy into your art.

During his struggle against the British, Gandhi undertook many hunger strikes, and he recommended to his friends who joined him on these fasts not to have sexual intercourse. When you fast for many days, if you have sexual relations, you may die; you have to preserve your energies. Thich Tri Quang, my friend who fasted for one hundred days in the hospital in Saigon in 1966, knew very well that not having sexual intercourse was very basic. Of course, as a monk, he did not have any problem with that. He also knew that speaking is an energy drain, so he refrained from speaking. If he needed something, he said it in one or two words or wrote it down. Writing, speaking, or making too many movements draws from these three sources of energy. So, the best thing is to lie down on your back and practice deep breathing. This brings into you the vitality that you need to survive a hundred-day hunger strike. If you don't eat, you cannot replenish this energy. If you refrain from studying, doing research, or worrying, you can preserve these resources. These three sources of energy are linked to each other. By practicing one, you help the other. That is why *anapanasati*, the practice of conscious breathing, is so important for our spiritual life. It helps with all of our sources of energy.

Monks and nuns do not engage in sexual relationships because they want to devote their energy to having a breakthrough in meditation. They learn to channel their sexual energy to strengthen their spirit energy for the breakthrough. They also practice deep breathing to increase the spirit energy. Since they live alone, without a family, they can devote most of their time to meditation and teaching, helping the people who provide them with food, shelter, and so on. They have contact with the population in the village in order to share the Dharma. Since they do not have a house or a family to care for, they have the time and space to do the things they like the most—walking, sitting, breathing, and helping fellow monks, nuns, and laypeople—and to realize what they want. Monks and nuns don't marry in order to preserve their time and energy for the practice.

"Responsibility" is the key word in the Third Precept. In a community of practice, if there is no sexual misconduct, if the community practices this precept well, there will be stability and peace. This precept should be practiced by everyone. You respect, support, and protect each other as Dharma brothers and sisters. If you don't practice this precept, you may become irresponsible and create trouble in the community and in the community at large. We have all seen this. If a teacher cannot refrain from sleeping with one of his or her students, he or she will destroy everything, possibly for several generations. We need mindfulness in order to have that sense of responsibility. We refrain from sexual misconduct because we are responsible for the well-being of so many people. If we are irresponsible, we can destroy everything. By practicing this precept, we keep the Sangha beautiful.

In sexual relationships, people can get wounded. Practicing this precept is to prevent ourselves and others from being wounded. Often we think it is the woman who receives the wound, but men also get deeply wounded. We have to be very careful, especially in short-term commitments. The practice of the Third Precept is a very strong way of restoring stability and peace in ourselves, our family, and our society. We should take the time to discuss problems relating to the practice of this precept, like loneliness, advertising, and even the sex industry.

The feeling of loneliness is universal in our society. There is no communication between ourselves and other people, even in the family, and our feeling of loneliness pushes us into having sexual relationships. We believe in a naive way that having a sexual relationship will make us feel less lonely, but it isn't true. When there is not enough communication with another person on the level of the heart and spirit, a sexual relationship will only widen the gap and destroy us both. Our relationship will be stormy, and we will make each other suffer. The belief that having a sexual relationship will help us feel less lonely is a kind of superstition. We should not be fooled by it. In fact, we will feel more lonely afterwards.

The union of the two bodies can only be positive when there is understanding and communion on the level of the heart and the spirit. Even between husband and wife, if the communion on the level of heart and spirit does not exist, the coming together of the two bodies will only separate you further. When that is the case, I recommend that you refrain from having sexual relationships and first try to make a breakthrough in communication.

There are two Vietnamese words, *tinh* and *nghiã*, that are difficult to translate into English. They both mean something like love. In tinh, you find elements of passion. It can be very deep, absorbing the whole of your being. Nghiã is a kind of continuation of tinh. With nghiã you feel much calmer, more understanding, more willing to sacrifice to make the other person happy, and more faithful. You are not as passionate as in tinh, but your love is deeper and more solid. Nghiã will keep you and the other person together for a long time. It is the result of living together and sharing difficulties and joy over time.

You begin with passion, but, living with each other, you encounter difficulties, and as you learn to deal with them, your love deepens. Although the passion diminishes, nghiã increases all the time. Nghiã is a deeper love, with more wisdom, more interbeing, more unity. You understand the other person better. You and that person become one reality. Nghiã is like a fruit that is already ripe. It does not taste sour anymore; it is only sweet.

In nghiã, you feel gratitude for the other person. "Thank you for having chosen me. Thank you for being my husband or my wife. There are so many people in society, why have you chosen me? I am very thankful." That is the beginning of nghiã, the sense of thankfulness for your having chosen me as your companion to share the best things in yourself, as well as your suffering and your happiness.

When we live together, we support each other. We begin to understand each other's feelings and difficulties. When the other person has shown his or her understanding of our problems, difficulties, and deep aspirations, we feel thankful for that understanding. When you feel understood by someone, you stop being unhappy. Happiness is, first of all, feeling understood. "I am grateful because you have proved that you understand me. While I was having difficulty and remained awake deep into the night, you took care of me. You showed me that my well-being is your own well being. You did the impossible in order to bring about my well-being. You took care of me in a way that no one else in this world could have. For that I am grateful to you."

If the couple lives with each other for a long time, "until our hair becomes white and our teeth fall out," it is because of nghiã, and not because of tinh. Tinh is passionate love. Nghiã is the kind of love that has a lot of understanding and gratitude in it.

All love may begin by being passionate, especially for younger people. But in the process of living together, they have to learn and practice love, so that selfishness— the tendency to possess—will diminish, and the elements of understanding and gratitude will settle in, little by little, until their love becomes nourishing, protecting, and reassuring. With nghiã, you are very sure that the other person will take care of you and will love you until your teeth fall out and your hair becomes white. Nothing will assure you that the person will be with you for a long time except nghiã. Nghiã is built by both of you in your daily life.

To meditate is to look into the nature of our love to see the kind of elements that are in it. We cannot call our love just tinh or nghiã, possessive love or altruistic love, because there may be elements of both in it. It may be ninety percent possessive love, three percent altruistic love, two percent gratitude, and so on. Look deeply into the nature of your love and find out. The happiness of the other person and your own happiness depend on the nature of your love. Of course you have love in you, but what is important is the nature of that love. If you realize that there is a lot of maitri and karuna in your love, that will be very reassuring. Nghiã will be strong in it.

Children, if they observe deeply, will see that what keeps their parents together is nghiã and not passionate love. If their parents take good care of each other, look after each other with calmness, tenderness, and care, nghiã is the foundation of that care. That is the kind of love we really need for our family and for our society.

In practicing the Third Precept, we should always look into the nature of our love in order to see and not be fooled by our feelings. Sometimes we feel that we have love for the other person, but maybe that love is only an attempt to satisfy our own egoistic needs. Maybe we have not looked deeply enough to see the needs of the other person, including the need to be safe, protected. If we have that kind of breakthrough, we will realize that the other person needs our protection, and therefore we cannot look upon him or her just as an object of our desire. The other person should not be looked upon as a kind of commercial item.

Sex is used in our society as a means for selling products. We also have the sex industry. If we don't look at the other person as a human being, with the capacity of becoming a Buddha, we risk transgressing this precept. Therefore the practice of looking deeply into the nature of our love has a lot to do with the practice of the Third Precept.

"I will do everything in my power to protect children from sexual abuse and to prevent couples and families from being broken by sexual misconduct." Adults who were molested as children continue to suffer very much. Everything they think, do, and say bears the mark of that wound. They want to transform themselves and heal their wound, and the best way to do this is to observe the Third Precept. Because of their own experience, they can say, "As a victim of sexual abuse, I vow to protect all children and adults from sexual abuse." Our suffering becomes a kind of positive energy that will help us become a bodhisattva. We vow to protect all children and other people. And we *also* vow to help those who abuse children sexually, because they are sick and need our help. The ones who made us suffer become the object of our love and protection. The ones who will molest children in the future become the objects of our love and protection.

We see that until the sick people are protected and helped, children are going to continue to be abused sexually. We vow to help these people so that they will not molest children any longer. At the same time, we vow to help children. We take not only the side of children who are being molested, but the other side also. These molesters are sick, the products of an unstable society. They may be an uncle, an aunt, a grandparent, or a parent. They need to be observed, helped, and, if possible, healed. When we are determined to observe this precept, the energy that is born helps us transform into a bodhisattva, and that transformation may heal us even before we begin to practice. The best way for anyone who was molested as a child to heal is to take this precept and vow to protect children and adults who may be sick, who may be repeating the kind of destructive actions that will cause a child to be wounded for the rest of his or her life.

from Living Buddha, Living Christ

by *Thich Nhat Hanh*

Thich Nhat Hanh is deeply interested in the relationship between Buddhism and Christianity. Here he con-
siders what happens after we die, drawing upon both
traditions to explore the ideas of resurrection, reincarnation and rebirth.

Continuation

Recent polls show that nearly one-fourth of all Europeans and North Americans believe in some form of
reincarnation. We seem to feel there must be a next life
so that those who have acted improperly in this life will
pay for their misdeeds. Or we feel that this earthly life
is just too brief to be decisive for all of eternity. Or we
are afraid that when we die we might be reduced to nothingness. So, revolting against the fact that we have to
die, we prefer the idea of continuing with a new body,

like changing our clothes. Will we continue or not after death? How? Where? When?

Reincarnation implies a re-entrance of the soul into the body. The third-century Christian theologian Origen taught about the pre-existence of the soul from all eternity before its incorporation into a body, a kind of "pre-incarnation." This idea is actually close to reincarnation, because if you are incarnated once, you might be incarnated twice, or more. The sixth-century Council of Constantinople condemned Origen for this teaching. Even today, most Christian leaders say the idea of reincarnation does not fit with Christianity. But resurrection does have to do with reincarnation. An immortal soul does not need to be resurrected. It is the body that does. According to the teaching of the Last Judgment, everyone will have his or her *body* resurrected. Elements of reincarnation are certainly present in the teachings of Christianity.

Manifestation and Remanifestation

At first, we might think of reincarnation as a soul entering a body. The body is seen as impermanent and the soul as permanent, and when we get rid of one body, we re-enter another. You may be surprised to know that people in Buddhist Asia are not fond of reincarnation. They want the circle of birth and death to end because they know it represents suffering without end. In popular Buddhism, reincarnation is accepted literally, without much examination, but as we continue to study and practice, the idea of an immortal soul gives way to another idea that is closer to reality. If we study the teachings of the Buddha and if we observe our own mind, we will find there is nothing permanent within the constituents of what we call our "self." The Buddha taught that a so-called "person" is really just five elements (*skandhas*) that come together for a limited period of time: our body, feelings, perceptions, mental states, and consciousness. These five elements are, in fact, changing all the time. Not a single element remains the same for two consecutive moments.

Not only is our body impermanent, but our so-called soul is also impermanent. It, too, is comprised only of elements like feelings, perceptions, mental states, and consciousness. When the idea of an *immortal* soul is replaced, our understanding of reincarnation gets closer to the truth. The idea of reincarnation is somehow still there, but our understanding is different. We see that there are only rapidly changing constituents.

In Buddhism, we do not actually use the word "reincarnation." We say "rebirth." But even rebirth is problematic. According to the teachings of the Buddha, "birth" does not exist either. Birth generally means from nothing you become something, and death generally means from something you become nothing. But if we observe the things around us, we find that nothing comes from nothing. Before its so-called birth, this flower already existed in other forms— clouds, sunshine, seeds, soil, and many other elements. Rather than birth and rebirth, it is more accurate to say "manifestation" (*vijñapti*) and "remanifestation." The so-called birthday of the flower is really a day of its remanifestation. It has already been here in other forms, and now it has made an effort to remanifest. Manifestation means its constituents have always been here in some form, and now, since conditions are sufficient, it is capable of manifesting itself as a flower. When things have manifested, we commonly say that they are born, but in fact, they are not. When conditions are no longer sufficient and the flower ceases to manifest, we say the flower has died, but that is not correct either. Its constituents have merely transformed themselves into other elements, like compost and soil. We have to transcend notions like birth, death, being, and non-being. Reality is free from all notions.

True Faith Is Alive

In the beginning, we might have embarked upon the path of Buddhism thanks to a belief in reincarnation, but as we continue to practice and touch reality, our beliefs change. We needn't be afraid of this. In the course of our study and practice, as we touch reality more and more deeply, our beliefs naturally evolve and become more solid. When our beliefs are based on our own direct experience of reality and not on notions offered by others, no one can remove these beliefs from us. Making a long-term commitment to a concept is much more dangerous. If ten years pass without the growth of our belief, one day we will wake up and discover that we can no longer believe in what we did. The notion of ten years ago is no longer sound or adequate, and we are plunged into the darkness of disbelief.

Our faith must be alive. It cannot be just a set of rigid beliefs and notions. Our faith must evolve every day and bring us joy, peace, freedom, and love. Faith implies practice, living our daily life in mindfulness. Some people think that prayer or meditation involves only our minds or our hearts. But we also have to pray with our bodies, with our actions in the world. And our actions must be modeled after those of the living Buddha or the living Christ. If we live as they did, we will have deep understanding and pure actions, and we will do our share to help create a more peaceful world for our children and all of the children of God.

Each Moment Is a Moment of Renewal

All of us possess the energy of mindfulness, the energy of the Holy Spirit, only its intensity and strength vary in each person. Our daily practice is to increase, to strengthen that power. There is no need to wait until Easter to celebrate. When the Holy Spirit is present, Jesus is already here: He does not have to be resurrected. We can feel Him right now. It is not a matter of reincarnation, rebirth, or even resurrection. Dwelling mindfully, we know that each moment is a moment of renewal. I wish I could be like Asita and Simeon, the holy men who came to see the Buddha and Jesus, and tell you how important your birth is.

Enlightenment Grows

Several years ago, after practicing walking meditation with three children in Switzerland, I asked them, "Do you think the enlightenment of the Buddha can grow?" They answered, "Yes," and I was very happy. The children affirmed something I also believe, that enlightenment is alive, like a tree. If it does not continue to grow, it will die. The enlightenment of the Buddha, the compassion and loving-kindness of Jesus, grow every day. We ourselves are responsible for their growth. Our bodies are the continuation of the Buddha's body. Our compassion and understanding are the compassion and understanding of Jesus. Awareness is the Buddha in person. If we live mindfully, we encounter the Buddha and Jesus Christ all the time.

Nirvana Is Available Now

Some waves on the ocean are high and some are low. Waves appear to be born and to die. But if we look more deeply, we see that the waves, although coming and going, are also water, which is always there. Notions like high and low, birth and death can be applied to waves, but water is free of such distinctions. Enlightenment for a wave is the moment the wave realizes that it is water. At that moment, all fear of death disappears. If you practice deeply, one day you will realize that you are free from birth and death, free from many of the dangers that have been assaulting you. When you see that, you will have no trouble building a boat that can carry you across the waves of birth and death. Smiling, you will understand that you do not have to abandon this world in order to be free. You will know that nirvana, the Kingdom of Heaven, is available here and now.

The Buddha seldom talked about this because he knew that if he talked about nirvana, we would spend too much time talking about it and not practicing. But he did make a few rare statements, such as this one from *Udana* viii, 3: "Verily, there is an unborn, unoriginated, uncreated, unformed. If there were not this unborn, unoriginated, uncreated, unformed, then an escape from the world of the born, the originated, the created, and the formed would not be possible." Early Buddhism did not have the ontological flavor we find in later Buddhism. The Buddha dealt more with the phenomenal world. His teaching was very practical.

Theologians spend a lot of time, ink, and breath talking about God. This is exactly what the Buddha did not want his disciples to do, because he wanted them to have time to practice samatha (stopping, calming), vipasyana (looking deeply), taking refuge in the Three Jewels, the Five Precepts, and so on.

The Extinction of Notions

The philosopher Ludwig Wittgenstein said, "Concerning that which cannot be talked about, we should not say anything." We cannot talk about it, but we can experience it. We can experience the non-born, non-dying, non-beginning, non-ending because it is reality itself. The way to experience it is to abandon our habit of perceiving everything through concepts and representations. Theologians have spent thousands of years talking about God as one representation. This is called onto-theology, and it is talking about what we should not talk about.

Protestant theologian Paul Tillich said that God is not a person, but also not less than a person. Whether we speak of God as not a person, as a non-person, as not less than a person, or as more than a person, these attributes do not mean very much. One flower is made of the whole cosmos. We cannot say that the flower is less than this or more than that. When we extinguish our ideas of more and less, is and is not, we attain the extinction of ideas and notions, which in Buddhism is called nirvana. The ultimate dimension of reality has nothing to do with concepts. It is not just absolute reality that cannot be talked about. Nothing can be conceived or talked about. Take, for instance, a glass of apple juice. You cannot talk about apple juice to someone who has never tasted it. No matter what you say, the other person will not have the true experience of apple juice. The only way is to drink it. It is like a turtle telling a fish about life on dry land. You cannot describe dry land to a fish. He could never understand how one might be able to breathe without water. Things cannot be described by concepts and words. They can only be encountered by direct experience.

More Time for Your Tea

Wittgenstein's statement, "Concerning that which cannot be talked about, we should not say anything," might lead you to think there are things we can talk about and things we cannot. But, in fact, nothing can be talked about, perceived, or described by representation. If you talk about things you have not experienced, you are wasting your and other people's time. As you continue the practice of looking deeply, you will see this more and more clearly, and you will save a lot of paper and publishing enterprises and have more time to enjoy your tea and live your daily life in mindfulness.

Rohitassa asked the Buddha whether it is possible to get out of this world of birth and death by traveling, and the Buddha said no, not even if you were to travel at the speed of light. But he did not say it is impossible to transcend the world of birth and death. He said that we only need to look deeply into our body to touch the world of no-birth and no-death. But we cannot just talk about it. We have to practice, to experience it in our own being. The world of no-birth and no-death is not something apart from the world of birth and death. In fact, they are identical.

The Other Shore Is This Other Shore

When the Buddha spoke of salvation or emancipation, he used the word *parayana,* "the other shore." The other shore represents the realm of no-birth, no-death, and no suffering. Sometimes the concept "other shore" is not clear enough, so the Buddha also used the word *tathata,* which means "reality as it is." We cannot talk about it, we cannot conceive it. Sometimes we call it nirvana, the extinction of all words, ideas, and concepts. When the concept "other shore" is misunderstood, nirvana comes to the rescue. When we think of another shore, we may think that it is completely different from this shore, that to reach it we have to abandon this shore completely. The true teaching is that the other shore is this very shore. In all schools of Buddhism, the teaching of no-coming, no-going, no-being, no-nonbeing, no-birth, and no-death exists. Mahayana Buddhists remind us that this teaching is only a finger pointing to the moon. It is not the moon itself.

Everything Can Be Spiritual

Jesus pointed to that same reality of no-birth, no-death. He called it the Kingdom of God. The Kingdom of God is not something distinct from God, whom he called *Abba,* "Father." Just as the concept "other shore" can create the misunderstanding that the other shore is not this shore, the concept "Father" can also be misleading. For instance, feminists in our time ask why "Father" and not "Mother"? Eternal life is the kind of life that includes death. In fact, eternal life without death is not possible. It is like two sides of a coin. Eternal life is the whole coin. Noneternal life is just one side of the coin. Once you choose eternal life, you choose death as well, and both are life. But if you want to take only one side of the coin, you have no coin.

Theology has gone a long way trying to describe "God" or the "Kingdom of God," that wonderful reality that, in fact, cannot be talked about. Over many centuries, theology has thus become metaphysical theology or onto-theology to such an extent that we neglect the true teaching of Jesus concerning the way to live that reality. Since German philosopher Martin Heidegger, theologians have been trying to go back to the beginning and have been more careful in making statements about God.

Many people in our time want to go back to Jesus and His teaching. Sometimes terms like "secular Christianity" or "atheistic Christianity" are used to describe this movement. There are those who worry that secular or atheistic Christianity is no longer real Christianity. To me, if you live deeply the teaching of Jesus, everything you say and do in your daily life will be deeply spiritual. I would not call it secular or atheistic at all. Suppose we do not celebrate a Eucharist in a church, but sit together in the open air to share our bread, eating it mindfully and gratefully, aware of the marvelous nature of the bread. Such an act cannot be described as secular or atheistic.

Touching the Living Buddha

God as the ground of being cannot be conceived of. Nirvana also cannot be conceived of. If we are aware when we use the word "nirvana" or the word "God" that we are talking about the ground of being, there is no danger in using these words. But if we say,

"According to Buddhism, this exists," or, "This does not exist," it is not Buddhism, because the ideas of being and non-being are extremes that the Buddha transcended. When we share the Dharma, we must speak carefully so that we and our listeners do not get stuck in words or concepts. It is our duty to transcend words and concepts to be able to encounter reality. To be in touch with the source of our own wisdom is the most eloquent way to show that Buddhism is alive. We can touch the living Buddha. We can also touch the living Christ. When we see someone overflowing with love and understanding, someone who is keenly aware of what is going on, we know that they are very close to the Buddha and to Jesus Christ.

Trees and Birds Preaching the Dharma

The Buddha is often described as having "three bodies": Dharmakaya, Sambhogakaya, and Nirmanakaya. Dharmakaya is the embodiment of the Dharma, always shining, always enlightening trees, grass, birds, human beings, and so on, always emitting light. It is this Buddha who is preaching now and not just 2,500 years ago. Sometimes we call this Buddha Vairochana, the ontological Buddha, the Buddha at the center of the universe.

The Sambhogakaya is the body of bliss. Because the Buddha practices mindfulness, he has immeasurable peace, joy, and happiness, and that is why we can touch his body of bliss, sometimes called the body of enjoyment or body of rewards. The Sambhogakaya represents the peace and happiness of the Buddha, the fruit of his practice. When you practice mindfulness, you enjoy within you the fruit of the practice. You are happy and peaceful, and your happiness and peace radiate around you for others to enjoy. When you do this, you are sending many Sambhogakayas into the world to help relieve the suffering of living beings. Each of us has the capacity of transforming many living beings if we know how to cultivate the seed of enlightenment within ourselves.

Shakyamuni, the historical Buddha, is the Nirmanakaya, the transformation body, a light ray sent by the sun of the Dharmakaya. Those in touch with Vairochana are also in touch with Shakyamuni. But if that ray is not apparent to us, we do not need to worry. The sun is still there. If we cannot listen directly to Shakyamuni, if we are open enough we can listen to Vairochana. In addition, many other transformation Buddhas are also expounding the same Dharma—the trees, the birds, the violet bamboo, and the yellow chrysanthemums are all preaching the Dharma that Shakyamuni taught 2,500 years ago. We can be in touch with him through any of these. He is a living Buddha, always available.

In Christianity, mystery is often described as darkness. When Victor Hugo lost his daughter, he complained, "Man sees only one side of things, the other side is plunged into the night of frightening mystery." In many Buddhist sutras, everyone in the assembly experiences bliss when they are touched by the beams of light emanating from the Buddha. In Buddhism, the word "*avidya*," ignorance, means literally "the lack of light." *Vidya*, understanding, is made of light.

Rinsing the Mouth, Washing the Ears
In the Greek Orthodox church, theologians talk about

"apophatic theology," or "negative theology." "Apophatic" is from the Greek *apophasis,* which means "denying." You say that God is not this, God is not that, until you get rid of all your concepts of God. The second-century Buddhist philosopher Nagarjuna developed a similar dialectic to remove our ideas concerning reality. He did not describe reality, because reality is what it is and cannot be described. Buddhism teaches us that reality is quite different from our concepts. The reality of a table is quite different from the concept "table." Every word we use has a concept behind it. The word "God" is based on a concept of "God." According to Buddhism, meditation on a rabbit's horns or a tortoise's hair, things we do not believe exist, can also lead to enlightenment. These concepts are comprised of real elements that we can merge in our imagination. We have an image of horns and an image of rabbit, so why not have a rabbit with horns? The concept "rabbit's horn" is a true concept, as real as any other concept.

One Buddhist teacher said that every time he pronounced the word "Buddhism," he had to rinse his mouth out three times. Even the word "Buddhism" can cause misunderstanding. People may think of Buddhism as something that can exist by itself, independent of Christianity, Judaism, or anything else. Rinsing his mouth was a kind of preventive medicine to remind himself (and his students) not to cling to the concept "Buddhism" as something that can exist all by itself. One day someone in the congregation stood up and said, "Teacher, every time I hear you pronounce the word 'Buddhism,' I have to go to the river and wash my ears three times!" The teacher approved that statement.

In Buddhist circles, we are careful to avoid getting stuck in concepts, even the concepts "Buddhism" and "Buddha." If you think of the Buddha as someone separate from the rest of the world, you will never recognize a Buddha even if you see him on the street. That is why one Zen Master said to his student, "When you meet the Buddha, kill him!" He meant that the student should kill the *Buddha-concept* in order for him to experience the *real Buddha* directly.

Another Zen teacher said, "To end suffering, you must touch the world of no-birth and no-death." His student asked, "Where is the world of no-birth and no-death?" The master replied, "It is right here in the world of birth and death." The world of impermanence and non-self *is* the world of birth and death. The world of nirvana is also the world of birth and death. Salvation is possible. It is possible to enter the world of no-birth and no-death through the practice of living each moment of your life in awareness. Jewish theologian Abraham Heschel said that to live by the Torah, the Jewish law, is to live the life of eternity within time. We live in the historical dimension and yet touch the ultimate dimension. But if we talk too much about it, we move far from the ultimate dimension. That is why in Zen Buddhist circles people are urged to experience and not to talk a lot.

The Holy Spirit Can Be Identified
In every school of Christianity, we see people who follow the same spirit, who do not want to speculate on what cannot be speculated about. "Negative theology" is an effort and practice to prevent Christians from being caught by notions and concepts that prevent them from

touching the living spirit of Christianity. When we speak of negative theology, the theology of the Death of God, we are talking about the death of every concept we may have of God in order to experience God as a living reality directly.

A good theologian is one who says almost nothing about God, even though the word "theology" means "discourse about God." It is risky to talk about God. The notion of God might be an obstacle for us to touch God as love, wisdom, and mindfulness. The Buddha was very clear about this. He said, "You tell me that you are in love with a beautiful woman, but when I ask you, 'What is the color of her eyes? What is her name? What is the name of her town?' you cannot tell me. I don't believe you are really in love with something real." Your notion of God may be vague like that, not having to do with reality. The Buddha was not against God. He was only against notions of God that are mere mental constructions that do not correspond to reality, notions that prevent us from developing ourselves and touching ultimate reality. That is why I believe it is safer to approach God through the Holy Spirit than through the door of theology. We can identify the Holy Spirit whenever it makes its presence felt. Whenever we see someone who is loving, compassionate, mindful, caring, and understanding, we know that the Holy Spirit is there.

Touching the Ultimate Dimension

One day as I was about to step on a dry leaf, I saw the leaf in the ultimate dimension. I saw that it was not really dead, but that it was merging with the moist soil in order to appear on the tree the following spring in another form. I smiled at the leaf and said, "You are pretending." Everything is pretending to be born and pretending to die, including that leaf. The Buddha said, "When conditions are sufficient, the body reveals itself, and we say the body exists. When conditions are not sufficient, the body cannot be perceived by us, and we say the body does not exist." The day of our "death" is a day of our continuation in many other forms. If you know how to touch your ancestors in the ultimate dimension, they will always be there with you. If you touch your own hand, face, or hair and look very deeply, you can see that they are there in you, smiling. This is a deep practice. The ultimate dimension is a state of coolness, peace, and joy. It is not a state to be attained after you "die." You can touch the ultimate dimension right now by breathing, walking, and drinking your tea in mindfulness. Everything and everyone is dwelling in nirvana, in the Kingdom of God. A farmer looking at his land in winter can already see his crop, because he knows that all of the conditions are there—land, seeds, water, fertilizer, farm equipment, and so on—except one, warm weather, and that will come in a matter of months. So it would be inaccurate to say his crop does not exist. It *is* already there. It needs only one more condition to manifest. When St. Francis asked the almond tree to tell him about God, in just a few seconds the tree was covered with beautiful flowers. St. Francis was standing on the side of the ultimate dimension. It was winter. There were no leaves, flowers, or fruits, but he saw the flowers.

We are entirely capable of touching the ultimate dimension. When we touch one thing with deep awareness, we touch everything. Touching the present moment, we realize that the present is made of the past and is creating the future. When we drink a cup of tea very deeply, we touch the whole of time. To meditate, to live a life of prayer, is to live each moment of life deeply. Through meditation and prayer, we see that waves are made only of water, that the historical and the ultimate dimensions are one. Even while living in the world of waves, we touch the water, knowing that a wave is nothing but water. We suffer if we touch only the waves, but if we learn how to stay in touch with the water, we feel the greatest relief. Touching nirvana, touching the Kingdom of God, liberates us from many worries. We enter a spiritual practice seeking relief in the historical dimension. We calm our body and mind and establish our stillness, our freshness, and our solidity. We practice loving-kindness, concentration, and transforming our anger, and we feel some relief. But when we touch the ultimate dimension of reality, we get the deepest kind of relief. Each of us has the capacity to touch nirvana and be free from birth and death, one and many, coming and going.

Christian contemplation includes the practice of resting in God, which, I believe, is the equivalent of touching nirvana. Although God cannot be described by using concepts and notions, that does not mean you cannot experience God the Father. If the wave does not have to die to become water, then we do not have to die to enter the Kingdom of God. The Kingdom of God is available here and now. The energy of the Holy Spirit is the energy that helps us touch the Kingdom of God. Tillich has said that speaking of God as a person is just a figure of speech. He said that God is the ground of being. This makes me think of the water that is the ground of being for the wave. He also said that God is the ultimate reality, and that makes me remember nirvana. I do not think there is that much difference between Christians and Buddhists. Most of the boundaries we have created between our two traditions are artificial. Truth has no boundaries. Our differences may be mostly differences in emphasis.

You are born in your tradition, and naturally you become a Buddhist or a Christian. Buddhism or Christianity is part of your culture and civilization. You are familiar with your culture and appreciate the good things in it. You may not be aware that in other cultures and civilizations there are values that people are attached to. If you are open enough, you will understand that your tradition does not contain all truths and values. It is easy to get caught in the idea that salvation is not possible outside of your tradition. A deep and correct practice of your tradition may release you from that dangerous belief.

In the Gospel according to Matthew, the Kingdom of God is described as a mustard seed. "The Kingdom of Heaven is like a mustard seed that someone took and sowed in the field. It is the smallest of all the seeds, but when it has grown it is the greatest of shrubs and becomes a tree so that the birds of the air come and make nests in its branches." What is that seed? Where is the soil? What is it if not our own consciousness? We hear repeatedly that God is within us. To me, it means that God is within our consciousness. Buddha nature, the seed of mindfulness, is in the soil of our consciousness. It may be small, but if we know how to care for it, how to touch it, how to water it moment after moment, it becomes an important refuge for all the

birds of the air. It has the power of transforming everything. In Buddhist practice, we learn how to touch that
seed in every moment, how to help it grow, how to
make it into the light that can guide us.

In the Gospel according to Matthew, the Kingdom
of Heaven is also described as yeast: "The Kingdom of
Heaven is like yeast that a woman took and mixed in
with three measures of flour until all of it was leav-
ened." A little yeast has the power to leaven a lot of
flour. The flour is our consciousness. Inside that consciousness are negative seeds: seeds of fear, hatred, and
confusion. But if you have the seed of the Kingdom of
God inside and know how to touch it, it will have the
power to leaven, to transform everything.

Touching the Water within the Waves
The Kingdom of God is also said to be like a treasure
that someone finds and hides in a field. Then, in his
joy, he sells all he has and buys that field. If you are
capable of touching that treasure, you know that nothing
can be compared to it. It is the source of true joy, true
peace, and true happiness. Once you have touched it,
you realize that all the things you have considered to be
conditions for your happiness are nothing. They may
even be obstacles for your own happiness, and you can
get rid of them without regret. We are all looking for
the conditions for our own happiness, and we know
what things have made us suffer. But we have not yet
seen or touched the treasure of happiness. When we
touch it, even once, we know that we have the capacity of
letting go of everything else.

That treasure of happiness, the Kingdom of
Heaven, may be called the ultimate dimension of

reality. When you see only waves, you might miss the water. But if you are mindful, you will be able to touch the water within the waves as well. Once you are capable of touching the water, you will not mind the coming and going of the waves. You are no longer concerned about the birth and the death of the wave. You are no longer afraid. You are no longer upset about the beginning or the end of the wave, or that the wave is higher or lower, more or less beautiful. You are capable of letting these ideas go because you have already touched the water.

Mindfulness Bell:

A PROFILE OF THICH NHAT HANH

by *Trevor Carolan*

Trevor Carolan is an author, journalist, translator, poet and teacher specializing in East-West arts and letters. He has been a student of Buddhism for more than twenty years, and has worked as a media advocate for international human rights and refugees. This profile of Thich Nhat Hanh describes Carolan's personal response to the presence and teachings of this quiet, compassionate man.

*T*hich Nhat Hanh's ringing call to practice mindfulness and interconnection has inspired a worldwide movement of politically engaged Buddhists. "Where there is suffering," says the Vietnamese zen master, "mindfulness responds with the energy of compassion." Somewhere during most experiences there occurs a climactic moment in which all that has gone before, and will come after, becomes fixed in the mind. For whatever reason, this defining moment thrives in the psyche as a kind of touchstone, and again and again we return to it in search of magic.

I was reminded of this during a recent gathering in

San Francisco, where a global brain trust had been convened by the Mikhail Gorbachev Foundation USA for a "State of the World Forum."

The colloquium's luminaries were many and mixed: Nobel Peace Prize Laureate Rigoberta Menchu, South African Vice-President Thabo Mbeki, Jane Goodall, Dutch Prime Minister Ruud Lubbers, Fritjof Capra, Ted Turner, Sam Keen, Shirley MacLaine, Joan Halifax, Zbigniew Brzezinski, President Oscar Arias of Costa Rica and the remarkable Mr. Gorbachev himself.

It was an obvious case of beatnik genius at the controls, the breakthrough pow-wow linking up the Esalen Institute, the Pentagon, the Fortune 500 and a grab-bag of stray cosmic tracers. Their purpose was to search for and articulate answers to certain fundamental challenges as humanity prepares to enter its next historic phase of development on this precious planet.

On the third day of this Forum heaviosity, though, a little man appeared as magically as Rumpelstiltskin. He arrived late at a mid-morning dialogue addressing the topic "Expanding the Boundaries of Humanness." The guest panel was Rupert Sheldrake, Deepak Chopra, Esalen Institute founder Michael Murphy and Episcopalian Dean Alan Jones. The late arrival was a Vietnamese Buddhist monk named Thich Nhat Hanh.

Discussion was free-ranging and abstract: how Descartes' three hundred year old notions of mechanistic science still impact on the Western world view of self, place and spiritual relevance; how pilgrimage became tourism; how telepathic communication with other star worlds is worth a shot. Michael Murphy discoursed on golf and Sri Aurobindo; Deepak Chopra thought the rational mind was inadequate to comprehend non-linear intelligence. Whew. Some-where between Dr. Chopra's scientific mysticism (or was it mystical science?) and someone else's view of Celtic pre-Christian pagan consciousness, I became aware of an increasing buzzy muddification of my frontal lobes. Then Dean Alan Jones introduced the final presenter.

A small man garbed in the drab brown robes of his Order, Thich Nhat Hanh spoke quietly, plaintively, in good English with occasional French inflections. His words and speech were restful, like a balm to the ears and conscience. Most everything about Thich Nhat Hanh was marked by calmness, a soft yin-ness that goes beyond simple stillness. When he spoke, it was with great mindfulness—a word, an action to which he is especially devoted.

Thich Nhat Hanh began with a story. "One day I was practicing mindful movement in a wood with the people of our community," he said softly. "Every day we practice this, walking slowly, mindfully, to enjoy every step; then we sit down.

"One day, I suddenly realized that the tree standing in front of me allowed my movement to be possible. I saw very clearly that I was able to breathe in because of its presence in front of me. It was standing there for me, and I was breathing in and out for the tree. I saw this connection very profoundly.

"In my tradition we speak of 'interbeing.' We cannot 'be' by ourself alone; we must be with everything else," he continued. "So, for example, we 'inter-are' with a tree: if it is not there, we are not there either.

"In the Diamond Sutra the Buddha advises us to consider four notions: the notions of self, of humanity, of living beings, and of life span. He also advises that the practice of removing these notions from mind is not difficult; anyone can do it."

After the previous discussion, what Thich Nhat Hanh had to say, and how he said it—without pyrotechnics or bombast; without jewelled elephants or eight-nectared realms; without pseudoscience or systems—was like a glass of hot tea on a raw day.

"If we observe things mindfully and profoundly," he explained, "we find out that self is made up only of non-self elements. If we look deeply into a flower, what do we see? We also see sunshine, a cloud, the earth, minerals, the gardener, the complete cosmos. Why? Because the flower is composed of these non-flower elements: that's what we find out. And, like this flower, our body too is made up of everything else— except for one element: a separate self or existence. This is the teaching of 'non-self' in Buddhism.

"In order to just be ourself, we must also take care of the non-self elements. We all know this, that we cannot be without other people, other species, but very often we forget that being is really inter-being; that living beings are made only of non-living elements.

"This is why we have to practice meditation—to keep alive this vision. The shamatha practice in my tradition is to nourish and keep alive this kind of insight twenty-four hours a day with the whole of our being."

About then, a radio correspondent leaned over to whisper inquiringly. "What exactly is his tradition anyway? Is it zen he's talking about, or is all of Buddhism like this?" The hard-boiled Capitol Hill reporter had been told that to understand what the environmental lobby was fuelled by these days, she ought to check out what the Buddhist monk from Vietnam had to say. I had queries of my own, however, since to rework a line from Andrei Codrescu, as a teacher Thich Nhat Hanh appears to cultivate anonymity with the kind of passion with which others cultivate publicity.

His students call him "Thay," Vietnamese for "Teacher." Born in 1926, Thich Nhat Hanh (pronounced Tick-Not-Hawn) has been a monk for fifty-three years, dedicating himself to the practice and transmission of "Engaged Buddhism," a root insight tradition melding meditation, awareness of the moment and compassionate action as a means of taking care of our lives and society. In 1967, he was nominated for the Nobel Peace Prize by Dr. Martin Luther King for his peace work in Vietnam.

Arnie Kotler seemed like a good source of answers to my questions about Thich Nhat Hanh. Kotler is the publisher of many of Thich Nhat Hanh's seventy-five books and a board member of the Community of Mindful Living, a loose-knit umbrella organization of more than one hundred groups of students around the world practicing in Thich Nhat Hanh's tradition of living mindfully, daily, in the moment.

"Thay is a zen teacher," Kotler related. "He's lived in Plum Village, a contemplative community near Bordeaux, France, since 1966. Originally he's from Vietnam—Indochina—so there may be an assumption that he's from a Theravada tradition. Thay likes to remind people that Indochina was influenced by both India and China, and that Indian Buddhism especially means a lot to him. Vietnam's Unified Buddhist Church, which is suppressed there by the government,

is a combination of mahayana and Theravada traditions." Placing Thich Nhat Hanh's background in
context is useful, Kotler says, "because we tend to think
of zen mostly as Japanese; yet that's only one manifestation, the one best known in the West. Thay practices
in the forty-second generation of Lin-Chi's (in
Japanese, Rinzai) chan/zen Buddhism. The particular
Vietnamese offshoot of this original Tang Chinese lineage is known as the Bamboo Forest School.

"Thay is in its eighth or ninth generation and he's
very much embedded in the fullness of these traditions. During the 1960's, when his Vietnam Peace
activism was at its height, he also founded a lay order
called Tiep Hien, or 'Interbeing.' It's in this mindfulness tradition that he's empowered fifty of his students
to teach."

This helps explain the formidable group of teachers,
writers and activists who in various capacities are affil-
iated with the growing "engaged Buddhism" movement
Thich Nhat Hanh has inspired—Joan Halifax, Joanna
Macy, Deena Metzger, bell hooks, Wendy Johnson,
Maxine Hong Kingston and others. The San Francisco
leg of Thich Nhat Hanh's recent U.S. visit brought out
distinguished teachers such as Jack Kornfield, Sylvia
Boorstein and Ram Dass.

At Spirit Rock, the Marin County dharma centre
inspired by Jack Kornfeld and other teachers, Thich
Nhat Hanh led a "Day of Mindfulness" that drew more
than two thousand people to the former nature con-
servancy's natural amphitheater.

Happily, a mindful carpool shuttle introduced me
to new friends en route, so I was not alone in the large
crowd. The landscape was beautiful—flowing ridges,

woodland and moor. The event was an example of North American Buddhism par excellence. The day-long outdoor program included meditation, mindful walking, music and song, silent eating, an offbeat organic "apple" meditation by Ed Brown and a lengthy, absorbing dharma talk by Master Hanh that became a Sermon in the Vale.

"Today, communication has expanded greatly throughout the world," Master Hanh remarked. "E-mail, fax, voice pager—you can contact New York from Tokyo in half a minute so easily. Yet in families and in neighborhoods, between husbands and wives, between friends and each other, real communication is still difficult. Suffering continues, pain increases.

"In our time, many young people also do not feel connected with anything, so they look for something to get relief—alcohol, drugs, money—or they turn on the TV set, absorbing violence and insecurity. How then can the dharma help dysfunctional, emotionally hurt individuals?" he asked.

"Bodhisattva Avalokitesvara is a very good listener, a compassionate listener," he offered. "We need to rediscover a way to talk and listen to each other as in a loving family. But what technology can help with this? I feel the need is for practice, for mindful listening. A heart free to listen is a flower that blooms on the tree of practice."

Listening to Thich Nhat Hanh one gradually attunes to the meditation bell which is much a part of his practice path. The mindfulness bell is the voice of our spiritual ancestors, he instructs: "Its sounds call us back to our true home in the present moment—to emptiness. When we inter-are, we find peace, stability, freedom—the root of our happiness. With non-self we discover the nature of emptiness." Thich Nhat Hanh recommends study and chanting of the Heart Sutra as a means of understanding how everything can be empty of separate self, while at the same time being full of everything else in the cosmos. In this dharma realm, he says, "Birth, death, being and non-being do not truly exist." They are simply notions, he observes, and the practice of the Heart Sutra is the practice of removing all ideas.

What becomes clear is that what Thich Nhat Hanh teaches is not so much "Buddhism" as steady perseverance in meditative practice. "Deep listening," "deep touching," "deep seeing"—his interpretations of Vipashyana meditation are as applicable to Christian, Jewish, Taoist or other spiritual traditions as they are to Buddhism, whatever sect you fancy. In looking at my notes on the nine days in which I had the opportunity to follow, listen and sit in his presence, I realized how seldom he discourses on Buddhist theology—a point known to raise eyebrows among purists.

"That's correct; Thay doesn't talk about Buddhism much," agrees Arnie Kotler. "He talks about practice. As Trungpa Rinpoche informed us in his first book, *Meditation in Action*, meditation is Buddhism's core practice. That's very much what Thich Nhat Hanh is offering: meditation in activity."

"Is he charismatic?" an old friend grown wise, but in weakened health, inquired one afternoon in Golden Gate Park.

"No," I answered her, surprised a little by my response. "Not in the usual sense. But he's the real thing. And he's a poet. My Vietnamese friends call him a Living Buddha."

As a martial artist of long years I share a taste for masters like Diogenes the Dog and Chuang-tzu, who on meeting emperors brought notice to the world in their own unique fashion. So it was when Thich Nhat Hanh spoke again at the State of the World Forum, this time to Mr. Gorbachev and the eminences arrayed.

"Intellect alone is not enough to guide us," Master Hanh declared to them humbly. "To shape the future of the twenty-first century we need something else. Without peace and happiness we cannot take care of ourselves; we cannot take care of other species and we cannot take care of the world.

"That is why it is important for us to live in such a way that every moment we are there deeply with our true presence, always alive and nourishing the insight of Interbeing."

Interspersed in his talk were observations from Living Buddha, Living Christ. A brilliant articulation of his belief in a Living Holiness shared by both East and West, this new book establishes a basis for the "New World Dharma" pointed to in such landmark texts of recent years as William Irwin Thompson's *Pacific Shift*, Gary Snyder's *Practice of the Wild* and Alan Hunt Badiner's eco-Buddhist compendium *Dharma Gaia*.

"To me, mindfulness is very much like the Holy Spirit," he explained to the assembly of the powerful. "All of us have the seed of the Holy Spirit in us; the capacity of healing, transforming and loving. Where there is suffering, mindfulness responds with the energy of compassion and understanding. Compassion is where the rivers of Christianity and Buddhism meet.

"In the Christian and Jewish traditions, we learn to live in the presence of God," he affirmed. "Our

Buddhist equivalent is the practice of cultivating mindfulness, of living deeply every moment with the energy of the Holy Spirit. If we change our daily lives—the way we think, speak and act—we begin to change the world.

"This is what I discussed with Dr. Martin Luther King many years ago; that the practice of mindfulness is not just for hours of silent meditation, but for every moment of the day. Other teachers, like St. Basil, have said it is possible to pray as we work, and in Vietnam, we invented 'Engaged Buddhism' so we could continue our contemplative life in the midst of helping the victims of war. We worked to relieve the suffering while trying to maintain our own mindfulness.

"So to conclude, the practice of looking deeply does not mean being inactive. We become very active with our understanding. Non-violence does not mean non-action. It means we act with love and compassion, living in such a way that a future will be possible for our children and their children. Thank you."

It happened then. The temporality of language and power was reduced for a prolonged still moment to reverberant silence, to presentness. There was nothing left to say. The monk gathered himself, rose and departed as anonymously as he'd arrived. I'd remember this.

Sometime during the visit I'd asked him about the mystery of death: what happens when we die? Thich Nhat Hanh knows how to laugh. "Nothing is born. Nothing dies. That is a statement made by Lavoisier—not a Buddhist," he responded with something like a smile. "But as we know, Buddhists too are made up only of non-Buddhist elements."

At the Forum, the sound of women singing, nuns in his Order, drifted up from a place nearby. "Breathing in Breathing out," they sang, "Breathing in . . . Breathing out." Then an echo up the halls of the noble old hotel: "I am free, I am free, I am free."

I thought for a moment of St. Francis of Assisi, then looking about the room at my speechless companions, I could have sworn I saw the universe smile.

from Be Free Where You Are

by *Thich Nhat Hanh*

Thich Nhat Hanh, during a 1999 visit to the Maryland
Correctional Institution, urged inmates to use the
energy of mindfulness to "take care of" the energy of
anger. He maintained that this energy could help them
to discover freedom even in prison.

For Warmth

Dear Friends, I wrote the following poem during the
war in Vietnam after the town of Ben Tre was bombed
by the United States Air Force. Ben Tre is the home-
town of my colleague, Sister Chân Không. The U.S.
forces destroyed the entire town because there were five
or six guerrillas there. Later on, one officer declared
that he had to bomb and destroy Ben Tre to save it from
Communism. This poem is about anger.

> I hold my face in my two hands.
> No, I am not crying.

I hold my face in my two hands
to keep my loneliness warm—
two hands protecting,
two hands nourishing,
two hands preventing
my soul from leaving me
in anger.*

I was very angry. It was not just my anger, but the anger
of a whole nation. Anger is a kind of energy that makes
us and the people around us suffer. As a monk, when I
get angry, I practice caring for my anger. I don't allow
it to cause suffering or to destroy me. If you take care of
your anger and are able to find relief, you will be able to
live happily with much joy.

The Energy of Liberation
To take care of my anger I bring my attention to my
breathing and look deeply inside myself. Right away I
notice an energy there called anger. Then I recognize
that I need another kind of energy to take care of this
anger, and I invite that energy to come up to do that
job. This second energy is called mindfulness. Every
one of us has the seed of mindfulness within us. If we
know how to touch that seed, we can begin to generate
the energy of mindfulness, and with that energy, we can
take good care of the energy of anger.

Mindfulness is a kind of energy that helps us to be
aware of what is going on. Everyone is capable of being
mindful. Those of us who practice daily have a greater

---

* See Thich Nhat Hanh, "For Warmth," in *Call Me By My True Names*
(Berkeley: Parallax Press, 1999).

capacity for being mindful than those who do not. Those who do not practice still have the seed of mindfulness, but its energy is very weak. By practicing just three days, the energy of mindfulness will already increase.

There can be mindfulness in anything you do. While you are drinking a cup of water, if you know that you are drinking water in that moment and you are not thinking of anything else, you are drinking mindfully. If you focus your whole being, body and mind, on the water, there is mindfulness and concentration, and the act of drinking may be described as mindful drinking. You drink not only with your mouth, but with your body and your consciousness, too. Everyone is capable of drinking his or her water mindfully. This is the way I was trained as a novice.

Walking mindfully is possible anywhere you are. When you walk, focus all your attention on the act of walking. Become aware of every step you take and don't think of anything else. This is called mindful walking. It is wonderfully effective. By doing this, you will begin to walk in such a way that every step brings you solidity, freedom, and dignity. You are the master of your own self.

Anytime I have to go from one place to another, I practice walking meditation— even if the distance is only five or six feet. Climbing up the stairs, I practice walking meditation. Going down the stairs, I practice walking meditation. Boarding an airplane, I practice walking meditation. Going from my room to the toilet, I practice walking meditation. Going to the kitchen, I practice walking meditation. I do not have any other style of walking—just mindful walking. It helps me very much. It brings me transformation, healing, and joy.

When you eat, you can practice mindfulness. Mindful eating can bring you a lot of joy and happiness. In my tradition, eating is a deep practice. First, we sit in a stable position and look at the food. Then, mindfully, we smile at it. We see the food as an ambassador that has come to us from the sky and from the Earth. Looking at a string bean, I can see a cloud floating in it. I can see the rain and the sunshine. I realize that this string bean is a part of the Earth and the sky.

When I bite into the string bean, I am aware that this is a string bean that I have put into my mouth. There is nothing else in my mouth—not my sorrow or my fear. When I chew the string bean, I am just chewing a string bean—not my worries or my anger. I chew very carefully, with one hundred percent of myself. I feel a connection to the sky, the Earth, the farmers who grow the food, and the people who cook it. Eating like this, I feel that solidity, freedom, and joy are possible. The meal not only nourishes my body, but also my soul, my consciousness, and my spirit.

Cultivating Freedom
For me, there is no happiness without freedom, and freedom is not given to us by anyone; we have to cultivate it ourselves. I will share with you how we get greater freedom for ourselves. During the time that we sit, walk, eat, or work outside, we cultivate our freedom. Freedom is what we practice every day.

No matter how or where you find yourself, if you have freedom, you are happy. I have many friends who spent time in forced labor camps and because they knew how to practice, they did not suffer as greatly. In fact, they grew in their spiritual lives, for which I am very proud of them.

By freedom I mean freedom from afflictions, from anger, and from despair. If you have anger in you, you have to transform anger in order to get your freedom back. If there is despair in you, you need to recognize that energy and not allow it to overwhelm you. You have to practice in such a way that you transform the energy of despair and attain the freedom you deserve—the freedom from despair.

You can practice freedom every moment of your daily life. Every step you take can help you reclaim your freedom. Every breath you take can help you develop and cultivate your freedom. When you eat, eat as a free person. When you walk, walk as a free person. When you breathe, breathe as a free person. This is possible anywhere.

By cultivating freedom for yourself, you will be able to help the people you live with. Even though you live in the same place, with the same physical and material conditions, if you practice, you will be a much freer person, a more solid person. Watching the way you walk, the way you sit, and the way you eat, people will be impressed. They will see that joy and happiness are possible for you, and will want to be like you because you are your own master, no longer a victim of anger, frustration, and despair. The practice that I have taken up as a Buddhist monk is the practice of freedom. When I became a novice, my teacher gave me a little book entitled *Stepping into Freedom: A Manual for a Novice Monk.*

To be able to breathe in and out is a miracle. A person on his or her deathbed cannot breathe freely, and he or she will soon stop breathing altogether. But

I am alive. I can breathe in and become aware of my in-breath; I can breathe out and become aware of my out-breath. I smile at my out-breath and am aware that I am alive. So when you breathe in, be aware of your in-breath. "Breathing in, I know this is my in-breath." No one can prevent you from enjoying your in-breath. When you breathe out, be aware that this is your out-breath. Breathe as a free person.

For me, to be alive is a miracle. It is the greatest of all miracles. To feel that you are alive and are breathing in is to perform a miracle—one that you can perform at any time. Feeling that you are alive and that you are taking a step is a miracle. Master Linchi, a well-known meditation teacher who lived in the ninth century, said that the miracle is not walking on water but walking on the Earth.

Everyone walks on the Earth, but there are those who walk like slaves, with no freedom at all. They are sucked in by the future or by the past, and they are not capable of dwelling in the here and now, where life is available. If we get caught up in our worries, our despair, our regrets about the past, and our fears of the future in our everyday lives, we are not free people. We are not capable of establishing ourselves in the here and now.

Touching Miracles
According to the Buddha, my teacher, life is only available in the here and now. The past is already gone, and the future is yet to come. There is only one moment for me to live—the present moment. So the first thing I do is to go back to the present moment. By doing so, I touch life deeply. My in-breath is life, my out-breath is life. Each step I take is life. The air I breathe is life. I can

touch the blue sky and the vegetation. I can hear the sound of the birds and the sound of another human being. If we can return to the here and now, we will be able to touch the many wonders of life that are available.

Many of us think that happiness is not possible in the present moment. Most of us believe that there are a few more conditions that need to be met before we can be happy. This is why we are sucked into the future and are not capable of being present in the here and now. This is why we step over many of the wonders of life. If we keep running away into the future, we cannot be in touch with the many wonders of life—we cannot be in the present moment where there is healing, transformation, and joy.

You Are a Miracle

When I eat an orange, I can eat the orange as an act of meditation. Holding the orange in the palm of my hand, I look at it mindfully. I take a long time to look at the orange with mindfulness. "Breathing in, there is an orange in my hand. Breathing out, I smile at the orange." For me, an orange is nothing less than a miracle. When I look at an orange in the here and now, I can see it with my spiritual eyes—the orange blossom, the sunshine and the rain going through the blossoms, the tiny green orange, and then the tree working over time to bring the orange to its full size. I look at the orange in my hand and I smile. It is nothing short of a miracle. Breathing in and out mindfully, I become fully present and fully alive, and now I see myself as a miracle.

Dear friends, you are nothing less than a miracle. There may be times when you feel that you are worthless. But you are nothing less than a miracle. The fact that you are here—alive and capable of breathing in and out—is ample proof that you are a miracle. One string bean contains the whole cosmos in it: sunshine, rain, the whole Earth, time, space, and consciousness. You also contain the whole cosmos.

We contain the Kingdom of God, the Pure Land of the Buddha, in every cell of our bodies. If we know how to live, the Kingdom of God will manifest for us in the here and now; with one step, we can penetrate it. We don't have to die to enter the Kingdom of God; in fact, we have to be very much alive. Hell, too, is in every cell of our body. It is up to us to choose. If we keep watering the seed of Hell in us each day, then Hell will be the reality we live in twenty-four hours a day. But if we know how to water the seed of the Kingdom of God in us each day, then the Kingdom of God will become the reality we live in every moment of our daily lives. This is my experience.

There is not a day I do not walk in the Kingdom of God. Whether I am in this place or somewhere else, I am always capable of walking mindfully, and the ground beneath my feet is always the Pure Land of the Buddha. No one can take that away from me. For me, the Kingdom of God is now or never. It is not situated in time or space; it is in our hearts. You have to develop mindful walking and touch the Earth as if it were a miracle. If you know how to go back to the here and now, if you know how to touch the Kingdom of God in every cell of your body, it will manifest to you right away in the here and now.

Freedom Is Possible Now

To touch the Kingdom of God, you need a little bit of

training and a friend—a brother or a sister whose own practice can help you. When we see someone walking mindfully and enjoying every step he or she takes, we are motivated to go back to ourselves and do the same. A prisoner wrote to me in France saying that he had read my books and learned how to practice walking meditation in prison. He said he always walks up and down the stairs mindfully, and he enjoys every step he takes. Ever since he began this practice, his life has become pleasant. When he sees other inmates rushing up and down the stairs—with no stability or solidity, no calm or joy—he wishes they could learn to do walking meditation like him because every step he takes nourishes and transforms him.

Walk as a free person. Walk in such a way that every step brings you more dignity, freedom, and stability. Then joy and compassion will be born in your heart. You will realize that most other people do not walk like this, that they are possessed by their anger, their fear, and their despair. This may motivate you to help them learn how to live in the present moment, how to sit and walk as a free person does. One person sitting, walking, eating, and breathing as a free person can make an impact on the whole environment around him.

When I first came to the West, I was already practicing mindfulness. My purpose in coming here was to try to stop the destruction of human life in my country. I was just one person at that time. Everywhere I went, I practiced mindful walking and breathing, embodying the practice. As I made friends here, more and more people joined with me to call for an end to the atrocities being committed in Vietnam. Now I have tens of thousands of friends who practice mindfulness

all over the world. Those who practice daily have been
able to transform their lives and nourish their compassion and forgiveness. By doing this, they have been able
to lessen the suffering of the people around them.

Walk as a Free Person

This morning when I stepped into the prison com-
pound, I walked very mindfully. I noticed that the
quality of the air was exactly like the quality of the air
outside. When I looked at the sky, I saw that it was exactly
the same as the sky outside. When I looked at the grass
and the flowers, they too looked the same as the grass
and flowers outside. Each step I took brought me the
same kind of solidity and freedom that I experienced
outside. So there is nothing that can prevent us from
practicing successfully and bringing freedom and
solidity to ourselves.

When you walk, breathe in; as you take two or three
steps, call the name of someone you love, someone who
can bring you a feeling of freshness, compassion, and
love. With every step, call his or her name. Suppose I
call the name of David. When I breathe in, I take two
steps and quietly call, "David, David." When I call his
name, David will be with me. I walk with peace and
freedom so that David can walk with peace and freedom
at the same time with me. When I breathe out, I take
another two steps and say, "Here I am, here I am." So
not only is David there for me, but I am there for him
at the same time. "David, David. Here I am, here I
am." I am entirely concentrated on the acts of
walking and breathing. My mind is not thinking
about anything else.

You can call to the Earth, "Earth, Earth. Here I am,

here I am." The Earth is our mother and is always there for us. She has produced us, brought us to life; and she will receive us and bring us back again and again, countless times. So when I call, "Earth," I call to my awareness that is the ground of my being. "Here I am, here I am." If you practice like this for a few weeks or months, you will begin to feel much better.

The practice is to get in touch with elements inside ourselves that are wonderful, that refresh and heal us. Without mindfulness in our daily life, we tend to allow in many elements that are harmful to our bodies and our consciousnesses. The Buddha said that nothing can survive without food. Our joy cannot survive without food; neither can our sorrow or our despair.

If we have despair, it is because we have fed our despair the kind of food it thrives on. If we are depressed, the Buddha advises that we look deeply into the nature of our depression to identify the source of food that we use to nourish it. Once the source of the nutriments has been identified, cut it off. The depression will fade away after a week or two.

Without mindfulness in our daily lives, we feed our anger and despair by looking at or listening to things around us that are highly toxic. We consume many toxins each day, what we see on television or read in magazines can nourish our anger and despair. But if we breathe in and out mindfully and realize that these are not the kinds of things we want to consume, then we will stop consuming them. To live mindfully means to stop ingesting these kinds of poisons. Instead, choose to be in touch with what is wonderful, refreshing, and healing within yourself and around you.

On Building a Community of Love

by *bell hooks*

Author, feminist, scholar and teacher bell hooks considered Thich Nhat Hanh a teacher and guide for more than twenty years before she met him, believing that when the time was right their paths would cross. Eventually they did. One result was this interview for *Shambhala Sun*'s January 2000 issue.

*A*s teacher and guide Thich Nhat Hanh has been a presence in my life for more than twenty years. In the last few years I began to doubt the heart connection I felt with him because we had never met or spoken to one another, yet his work was ever-present in my work. I began to feel the need to meet him face to face, even as my intuitive self kept saying that it would happen when the time was right. My work in love has been to trust that intuitive self that kept saying that it would happen when the time was right. My work in love has been to trust that intuition knowledge.

Those who know me intimately know that I have been contemplating the place and meaning of love in our lives and culture for years. They know that when a subject attracts my intellectual and emotional imagination, I am long to observe it from all angles, to know it inside and out.

In keeping with the way my mind works, when I began to think deeply about the metaphysics of love I talked with everyone around me about it. I talked to large audiences and even had wee one-on-one conversations with children about the way they think about love. I talked about love in every state. Indeed, I encouraged the publishers of my new book *all about love: new visions* to launch it with postcards, T-shirts, and maybe even a calendar with the logo "Love in Every State." I talked about love everywhere I traveled.

To me, all the work I do is built on a foundation of loving-kindness. Love illuminates matters. And when I write provocative social and cultural criticism that causes readers to stretch their minds, to think beyond set paradigms, I think of that work as love in action. While it may challenge, disturb, and at times even frighten or enrage readers, love is always the place where I begin and end.

A central theme of *all about love* is that from childhood into adulthood we are often taught misguided and false assumptions about the nature of love. Perhaps the most common false assumption about love is that love means we will not be challenged or changed. No doubt this is why people who read writing about racism, sexism, homophobia, religion, etc. that challenges their set assumptions tend to see that work as harsh rather than loving.

Of all the definitions of love that abound in our universe, a special favorite of mine is the one offered in *The Road Less Traveled* by psychoanalyst H. Scott Peck. Defining love as "the will to extend one's self for the purpose of nurturing one's own or another's spiritual growth," he draws on the work of Erich Fromm to emphasize again and again that love is first and foremost exemplified by action—by practice—not solely by feeling.

Fromm's *The Art of Loving* was published when I was four years old. It was the book I turned to in my late teens when I felt confused about the nature of love. His insistence that "love is the active concern for the life and growth of that which we love" made sense to me then and it still does. Peck expands this definition. Knowing that the world would be a paradise of peace and justice if global citizens shared a common definition of love which would guide our thoughts and action, I call for the embrace of such a common understanding in *all about love: new visions*. That common understanding might be articulated in different words carrying a shared meaning for diverse experiences and cultures.

Throughout the more than twenty years that I have written on the subject of ending domination in whatever form it appears (racism, sexism, homophobia, classism), I have continually sought those paths that would lead to the end of violence and injustice. Since so much of my thinking about love in my late teens revolved around familial and romantic love, it was not until I was in my early twenties writing feminist theory that I began to think deeply about love in relation to domination.

During my first years in college Martin Luther King's message of love as the path to ending racism and healing the wounds of racial domination had been replaced by a black power movement stressing militant resistance. While King had called for non-violence and compassion, this new movement called on us to harden our hearts, to wage war against our enemies. Loving our enemies, militant leaders told us, made us weak and easy to subjugate, and many turned their backs on King's message.

Just as the energy of a racially-based civil rights liberation struggle was moving away from a call for love, the women's movement also launched a critique of love, calling on females to forget about love so that we might seize power. When I was nineteen, participating in feminist consciousness-raising groups, love was dismissed as irrelevant. It was our "addiction to love" that kept us sleeping with the enemy (men). To be free, our militant feminist leaders told us, we needed to stop making love the center of our imaginations and yearnings. Love could be a good woman's downfall.

These two movements for social justice that had captured the hearts and imagination of our nation— movements that began with a love ethic—were changed by leaders who were much more interested in questions of power. By the late seventies it was no longer necessary to silence discussions of love; the topic was no longer on any progressive agenda.

Those of us who still longed to hold on to love looked to religions as the site of redemption. We searched everywhere, all around the world, for the spiritual teachers who could help us return to love. My seeking led me to Buddhism, guided there by the Beat poets, by personal interaction with Gary Snyder. At his mountain home I would meet my first Buddhist nun and walk mindfully with her, all the while wondering if my heart could ever know the sweet peace emanating from her like a perfume mist.

My seeking led me to the work of a Buddhist monk Martin Luther King had met and been touched by— Thich Nhat Hanh. The first work I read by this new teacher in my life was a conversation book between him and Daniel Berrigan, *The Raft Is Not the Shore.*

At last I had found a world where spirituality and politics could meet, where there was no separation. Indeed, in this world all efforts to end domination, to bring peace and justice, were spiritual practice. I was no longer torn between political struggle and spiritual practice. And here was the radical teacher—a Vietnamese monk living in exile—courageously declaring that "if you have to choose between Buddhism and peace, then you must choose peace."

Unlike white friends and comrades who were often contemptuous of me because I had not traveled to the East or studied with important teachers, Thich Nhat Hanh was calmly stating: "Buddhism is in your heart. Even if you don't have any temple or any ranks, you can still be a Buddhist in your heart and life." Reading his words I felt an inner rapture and could only repeat, "Be still my heart." Like one wandering in the desert overcome by thirst, I had found water. My thirst was quenched and my spiritual hunger intensified.

For a period of more than ten years since leaving home for college I had felt pulled in all directions by anti-racist struggle, by the feminist movement, sexual liberation, by the fundamentalist Christianity of my upbringing. I wanted to embrace radical politics and still know god. I wanted to resist and be redeemed. *The Raft Is Not the Shore* helped strengthen my spiritual journey. Even though I had not met with Thich Nhat Hanh he was the teacher, along with Chögyan Trungpa Rinpoche, who were my chosen guides. Mixing the two was a fiery combination.

As all became well with my soul, I began to talk about the work of Thich Nhat Hanh in my books, quoting from his work. He helped me bring together theories of political recovery and spiritual recovery. For years I did not want to meet him face to face for fear I would be disappointed. Time and time again I planned to be where he was and the plan would be disrupted. Our paths were crossing but we were never meeting face to face.

Then suddenly, in a marvelous serendipitous way, we were meeting. In his presence at last, I felt overwhelmed with gratitude that not only was I given the blessing of meeting him, but that a pure spirit of love connected us. I felt ecstatic. My heart jumped for joy— such union and reunion to be in the presence of one who has tutored your heart, who has been with you in spirit on your journey.

The journey is also to the teacher and beyond. It is always a path to the heart. And the heart of the matter is always our oneness with divine spirit—our union with all life. As early as 1975, Thich Nhat Hanh was sharing: "The way must be in you; the destination also must be in you and not somewhere else in space or time. If that kind of self-transformation is being realized in you, you will arrive."

Walking on love's path on a sunny day on my way to meet my teacher, I meet Sister Chan Khong. She too

has taught me. She felt my heart's readiness. Together
we remembered the teacher who is everywhere awakening the heart. As she writes at the end of *Learning True
Love*, "I am with you just as you have been with me, and
we encourage each other to realize our deepest love,
caring and generosity . . . together on the path of love."

BELL HOOKS: *I began writing a book on love because I felt that the
United States is moving away from love. The civil rights movement was
such a wonderful movement for social justice because the heart of it was
love—loving everyone. It was believing, as you taught us yesterday, that
we can always start anew; we can always practice forgiveness. I don't
have to hate any person because I can always start anew, I can always
reconcile. What I'm trying to understand is why are we moving away
from this idea of a community of love. What is your thinking about why
people are moving away from love, and how we can be part of moving
our society towards love.*

THICH NHAT HANH: In our own Buddhist sangha,
community is the core of everything. The sangha is a
community where there should be harmony and peace
and understanding. That is something created by our
daily life together. If love is there in the community, if
we've been nourished by the harmony in the community, then we will never move away from love.

The reason we might lose this is because we are
always looking outside of us, thinking that the object or
action of love is out there. That is why we allow the
love, the harmony, the mature understanding, to slip
away from ourselves. This is, I think, the basic thing.
That is why we have to go back to our community and
renew it. Then love will grow back. Understanding and
harmony will grow back. That's the first thing.

The second thing is that we ourselves need love; it's not only society, the world outside, that needs love. But we can't expect that love to come from outside of us. We should ask the question whether we are capable of loving ourselves as well as others. Are we treating our body kindly—by the way we eat, by the way we drink, by the way we work? Are we treating ourselves with enough joy and tenderness and peace? Or are we feeding ourselves with toxins that we get from the market—the spiritual, intellectual, entertainment market?

So the question is whether we are practicing loving ourselves. Because loving ourselves means loving our community. When we are capable of loving ourselves, nourishing ourselves properly, not intoxicating ourselves, we are already protecting and nourishing society. Because in the moment when we are able to smile, to look at ourselves with compassion, our world begins to change. We may not have done anything but when we are relaxed, when we are peaceful, when we are able to smile and not to be violent in the way we look at the system, at that moment there is a change already in the world.

So the second help, the second insight, is that between self or no-self there is no real separation. Anything you do for yourself you do for the society at the same time, and anything you do for society you do for yourself also. That insight is very powerfully made in the practice of no-self.

BELL HOOKS: *I think one of the most wonderful books that Martin Luther King rote was* Strength to Love. *I always liked it because of the word "strength," which counters the Western notion of love as easy. Instead, Martin Luther King said that you must have courage to love,* *that you have to have a profound will to do what is right to love, that it does not come easy.*

THICH NHAT HANH: Martin Luther King was among us as a brother, as a friend, as a leader. He was able to maintain that love alive. When you touch him, you touch a bodhisattva, for his understanding and love was enough to hold everything to him. He tried to transmit his insight and his love to the community, but maybe we have not received it enough. He was trying to transmit the best things to us—his goodness, his love, his nonduality. But because we had clung so much to him as a person, we did not bring the essence of what he was teaching into our community. So now that he's no longer here, we are at a loss, we have to be aware that crucial transmission he was making was not the transmission of power, of authority, of position, but the transmission of the dharma. It means love.

BELL HOOKS: *Exactly. It was not a transmission of personality. Part of why I have started writing about love is feeling, as you say, that our culture is forgetting what he taught. We name more and more streets and schools after him but that's almost irrelevant, because what is to be remembered is that strength to love.*

That's what we have to draw courage from—the spirit of love, not the image of Martin Luther King. This is so hard in the West because we are such an image and personality driven culture. For instance, because I have learned so much from you for so many years of my life, people kept asking me whether I had met you in person.

THICH NHAT HANH: (laughs) Yes, I understand.

BELL HOOKS: *And I said yes, I have met him, because he has given*

*his love to me through his teachings, through mindfulness practice. I
kept trying to share with people that, yes, I would like to meet you some
day, but the point is that I am living and learning from his teaching.*

THICH NHAT HANH: Yes, that's right. And that is the
essence of interbeing. We had met already in the very
non-beginning (laughs). Beginning with longing,
beginning with blessings.

BELL HOOKS: *Except that you have also taught that to be in the
presence of your teacher can also be a moment of transformation. So
people say, is it enough that you've learned from books by him, or must
you meet him, must there be an encounter?*

THICH NHAT HANH: In fact, the true teacher is within
us. A good teacher is someone who can help you to go
back and touch the true teacher within, because you
already have the insight within you. In Buddhism we call
it buddhanature. You don't need someone to transfer
buddhanature to you, but maybe you need a friend who
can help you touch that nature of awakening and
understanding working in you. So a good teacher is
someone who can help you to get back to a teacher
within. The teacher can do that in many different ways;
she or he does not have to meet you physically. I feel that
I have many real students whom I have not met. Many
are in cloisters and they never get out. Others are in
prison. But in many cases they practice the teachings
much better than those who meet me every day. That is
true. When they read a book by me or hear a tape and
they touch the insight within them, then they have met
me in a real way. That is the real meeting.

BELL HOOKS: *I want to know your thoughts on how we learn to love a world full of justice, more than coming together with someone just because they share the same skin or the same language as we do. I ask this question of you because I first learned about you through Martin Luther King's homage to your compassion towards those who had hurt your country.*

THICH NHAT HANH: This is a very interesting topic. It was a very important issue for the Buddha. How we view justice depends on our practice of looking deeply. We may think that justice is everyone being equal, having the same rights, sharing the same kind of advantages, but maybe we have not had the chance to look at the nature of justice in terms of no-self. That kind of justice is based on the idea of self, but it may be very interesting to explore justice in terms of no-self.

BELL HOOKS: *I think that's exactly the kind of justice Martin Luther King spoke about—a justice that was for everyone whether they're equal or not. Sometimes in life all things are not equal, so what does it mean to have justice when there is no equality? A parent can be just towards a child, even though they're not equal. I think this is often misunderstood in the West, where people feel that there can be no justice unless everything is the same. This is part of why I feel we have to relearn how we think about love, because we think about love so much in terms of the self.*

THICH NHAT HANH: Is justice possible without equality?

BELL HOOKS: *Justice is possible without equality, I believe, because of compassion and understanding. If I have compassion, then if I have more than you, which is unequal, I will still do the just thing by you.*

THICH NHAT HANH: Right. And who has created inequality?

BELL HOOKS: *Well, I think inequality is in our minds. I think this is what we learn through practice. One of the concepts that you and Daniel Berrigan spoke about in* The Raft Is Not the Shore *is that the bridge of illusion must be shattered in order for a real bridge to be constructed. One of the things we learn is that inequality is an illusion.*

THICH NHAT HANH: Makes sense (laughs).

BELL HOOKS: *Before I came here I had been struggling with the question of anger toward my ex-boyfriend. I have taken my vows as a bodhisattva, and so I always feel very depressed when I have anger. I had come to a point of despair because I had so much difficulty with my anger in relation to this man. So yesterday's dharma talk about embracing our anger, and using it, and letting it go, was very essential for me at this moment.*

THICH NHAT HANH: You want to be human. Be angry, it's okay. But not to practice is not okay. To be angry, that is very human. And to learn how to smile at your anger and make peace with your anger is very nice. That is the whole thing—the meaning of the practice, of the learning. By taking a look at your anger it can be transformed into the kind of energy that you need— understanding and compassion. It is with negative energy that you can make the positive energy. A flower, although beautiful, will become compost someday, but if you know how to transform the compost back into the flower, then you don't have to worry. You don't have to worry about your anger because you know how

to handle it—to embrace, to recognize, and to transform it. So this is what is possible.

BELL HOOKS: *I think this is what people misunderstand about
Martin Luther King saying to love your enemies. They think he was
just using this silly little phrase, but what he meant was that as Black
Americans we need to let our anger go, because holding on to it we
hold ourselves down. We oppress ourselves by holding on to anger.
My students tell me, we don't want to love! We're tired of being
loving! And I say to them, if you're tired of being loving, then you
haven't really been loving, because when you are loving you have
more strength. As you were telling us yesterday, we grow stronger in
the act of loving. This has been, I think, a very hurting thing for
Black Americans—to feel that we can't love our enemies. People
forget what a great tradition we have as African-Americans in the
practice of forgiveness and compassion. And if we neglect that tradition, we suffer.*

THICH NHAT HANH: When we have anger in us, we suffer.
When we have discrimination in us, we suffer. When we
have the complex of superiority, we suffer. When we
have the complex of inferiority, we suffer also. So
when we are capable of transforming these negative
things in us, we are free and happiness is possible.

If the people who hurt us have that kind of energy
within them, like anger or desperation, then they
suffer. When you see that someone suffers, you might
be motivated by a desire to help him not to suffer anymore. That is love also, and love doesn't have any
color. Other people may discriminate against us, but
what is more important is whether we discriminate
against them. If we don't do that, we are a happier

person, and as a happier person, we are in a position to help. And anger, this is not a help.

BELL HOOKS: *And lastly, what about fear? Because I think that many white people approach black people or Asian people not with hatred or anger but with fear. What can love do for that fear?*

THICH NHAT HANH: Fear is born from ignorance. We think that the other person is trying to take away something from us. But if we look deeply, we see that the desire of the other person is exactly our own desire—to have peace, to be able to have a chance to live. So if you realize that the other person is a human being too, and you have exactly the same kind of spiritual path, and then the two can become good practitioners. This appears to be practical for both.

The only answer to fear is more understanding. And there is no understanding if there is no effort to look more deeply to see what is there in our heart and in the heart of the other person. The Buddha always reminds us that our afflictions, including our fear and our desiring, are born from our ignorance. That is why in order to dissipate fear, we have to remove wrong perception.

BELL HOOKS: *And what if people perceive rightly and still act unjustly?*

THICH NHAT HANH: They are not able yet to apply their insight in their daily life. They need community to remind then. Sometimes you have a flash of insight, but it's not strong enough to survive. Therefore in the

practice of Buddhism, samadhi is the power to maintain insight alive in every moment, so that every
speech, every word, every act will bear the nature of that
insight. It is a question of cleaning. And you clean
better if you are surrounded by sangha—those who are
practicing exactly the same.

BELL HOOKS: *I think that we best realize love in community. This is*
something I have had to work with myself, because the intellectual tra-
dition of the West is very individualistic. It's not community-based. The
intellectual is often thought of as a person who is alone and cut off from
the world. So I have had to practice being willing to leave the space of
my study to be in community, to work in community, and to be changed
by community.

THICH NHAT HANH: Right, and then we learn to
operate as a community and not as individuals. In
Plum Village, that is exactly what we try to do. We are
brothers and sisters living together. We try to operate
like cells in one body.

BELL HOOKS: *I think this is the love that we seek in the new millen-*
nium, which is the love experienced in community, beyond self.

THICH NHAT HANH: So please, live that truth and dis-
seminate that truth with your writing, with your
speaking. It will be helpful to maintain that kind of
view and action.

BELL HOOKS: *Thank you for your open-hearted example.*

THICH NHAT HANH: You're welcome. Thank you.

from Anger:

Wisdom for Cooling the Flames

by *Thich Nhat Hanh*

Buddhist theology holds that the body and mind are not separate. Here Thich Nhat Hanh discusses the relationship between our anger and the food we eat.

*W*e all need to know how to handle and take care of our anger. To do this, we must pay more attention to the biochemical aspect of anger, because anger has its roots in our body as well as our mind. When we analyze our anger, we can see its physiological elements. We have to look deeply at how we eat, how we drink, how we consume, and how we handle our body in our daily life.

Anger Is Not Strictly a Psychological Reality
In the teaching of the Buddha, we learn that our body and mind are not separate. Our body is our mind, and,

at the same time, our mind is also our body. Anger is not only a mental reality because the physical and the mental are linked to each other, and we cannot separate them. In Buddhism we call the body/mind formation *namarupa*. Namarupa is the psyche-soma, the mind-body as one entity. The same reality sometimes appears as mind, and sometimes appears as body.

Looking deeply into the nature of an elementary particle, scientists have discovered that sometimes it manifests as a wave, and sometimes as a particle. A wave is quite different from a particle. A wave can be only a wave. It cannot be a particle. A particle can be only a particle, it cannot be a wave. But the wave and the particle are the same thing. So instead of calling it a wave or a particle, they call it a "wavicle," combining the words *wave* and *particle*. This is the name scientists have given the elementary particle.

The same thing is true with mind and body. Our dualistic view tells us that mind cannot be body, and body cannot be mind. But looking deeply, we see that body is mind, mind is body. If we can overcome the duality that sees the mind and body as entirely separate, we come very close to the truth.

Many people are beginning to realize that what happens to the body also happens to the mind, and vice versa. Modern medicine is aware that the sickness of the body may be a result of sickness in the mind. And sickness in our minds may be connected to sickness in our bodies. Body and mind are not two separate entities— they are one. We have to take very good care of our body if we want to master our anger. The way we eat, the way we consume, is very important.

. . .

We Are What We Eat

Our anger, our frustration, our despair, have much to do with our body and the food we eat. We must work out a strategy of eating, of consuming to protect ourselves from anger and violence. Eating is an aspect of civilization. The way we grow our food, the kind of food we eat, and the way we eat it have much to do with civilization because the choices we make can bring about peace and relieve suffering.

The food that we eat can play a very important role in our anger. Our food may contain anger. When we eat the flesh of an animal with mad cow disease, anger is there in the meat. But we must also look at the other kinds of food that we eat. When we eat an egg or a chicken, we know that the egg or chicken can also contain a lot of anger. We are eating anger, and therefore we express anger.

Nowadays, chickens are raised in large-scale modern farms where they cannot walk, run, or seek food in the soil. They are fed solely by humans. They are kept in small cages and cannot move at all. Day and night they have to stand. Imagine that you have no right to walk or to run. Imagine that you have to stay day and night in just one place. You would become mad. So the chickens become mad.

In order for the chickens to produce more eggs, the farmers create artificial days and nights. They use indoor lighting to create a shorter day and a shorter night so that the chickens believe that twenty-four hours have passed, and then they produce more eggs. There is a lot of anger, a lot of frustration, and much suffering in the chickens. They express their anger and frustration by attacking the chickens next to them.

They use their beaks to peck and wound each other. They cause each other to bleed, to suffer, and to die. That is why farmers now cut the beaks off all the chickens, to prevent them from attacking each other out of frustration.

So when you eat the flesh or egg of such a chicken, you are eating anger and frustration. So be aware. Be careful what you eat. If you eat anger, you will become and express anger. If you eat despair, you will express despair. If you eat frustration, you will express frustration.

We have to eat happy eggs from happy chickens. We have to drink milk that does not come from angry cows. We should drink organic milk that comes from cows that are raised naturally. We have to make an effort to support farmers to raise these animals in a more humane way. We also have to buy vegetables that are grown organically. It is more expensive, but, to compensate, we can eat less. We can learn to eat less.

Consuming Anger Through Other Senses

Not only do we nourish our anger with edible food, but also through what we consume with our eyes, ears, and consciousness. The consumption of cultural items is also linked to anger. Therefore, developing a strategy for consuming is very important.

What we read in magazines, what we view on television, can also be toxic. It may also contain anger and frustration. A film is like a piece of beefsteak. It can contain anger. If you consume it, you are eating anger, you are eating frustration. Newspaper articles, and even conversations, can contain a lot of anger.

You may feel lonely sometimes and want to talk to someone. In one hour of conversation, the other person's words may poison you with a lot of toxins. You may ingest a lot of anger, which you will express later on. That is why mindful consumption is very important. When you listen to the news, when you read a newspaper article, when you discuss something with others, are you ingesting the same kind of toxins that you ingest when you eat unmindfully?

Eating Well, Eating Less

There are those who take refuge in eating to forget their sorrow and their depression. Overeating can create difficulties for the digestive system, contributing to the arising of anger. It can also produce too much energy. If you do not know how to handle this energy, it can become the energy of anger, of sex, and of violence.

When we eat well, we can eat less. We need only half the amount of food that we eat every day. To eat well, we should chew our food about fifty times before we swallow. When we eat very slowly, and make the food in our mouth into a kind of liquid, we will absorb much more nutrition through our intestines. If we eat well, and chew our food carefully, we get more nutrition than if we eat a lot but don't digest it well.

Eating is a deep practice. When I eat, I enjoy every morsel of my food. I am aware of the food, aware that I am eating. We can practice mindfulness of eating—we know what we are chewing. We chew our food very carefully and with a lot of joy. From time to time, we stop chewing and get in touch with the friends, family, or sangha—community of practitioners—around us. We appreciate that it is wonderful to be sitting here chewing like this, not worrying about anything. When we eat mindfully, we are not eating or chewing our anger, our anxiety, or our projects. We are chewing the food, prepared lovingly by others. It is very pleasant.

When the food in your mouth becomes almost liquefied, you experience its flavor more intensely and the food tastes very, very good. You may want to try chewing like this today. Be aware of each movement of your mouth. You will discover that the food tastes so delicious. It may only be bread. Without any butter or jelly at all. But it's wonderful. Perhaps you will also have some milk. I never drink milk. I chew milk. When I put a piece of bread into my mouth, I chew for a while in mindfulness, and then I take a spoonful of milk. I put it in my mouth, and I continue to chew with awareness. You don't know how delicious it can be just chewing some milk and some bread.

When the food has become liquid, mixed with your saliva, it is half digested already. So when it arrives in your stomach and intestines, the digestion becomes extremely easy. Much of the nutrients in the bread and milk will be absorbed into our body. You get a lot of joy and freedom during the time you chew. When you eat like this, you will naturally eat less.

When you serve yourself, be aware of your eyes. Don't trust them. It is your eyes that push you to take too much food. You don't need so much. If you know how to eat mindfully and joyfully, you become aware that you need only half the amount that your eyes tell you to take. Please try. Just chewing something very simple like zucchini, carrots, bread, and milk may turn out to be the best meal of your life. It's wonderful.

Many of us in Plum Village, our practice center in France, have experienced this kind of eating, chewing very mindfully, very slowly. Try eating like this. It can help you to feel much better in your body and, therefore, in your spirit, in your consciousness.

Our eyes are bigger than our stomach. We have to empower our eyes with the energy of mindfulness so that we know exactly what amount of food we really need. The Chinese term for the alms bowl used by a monk or nun means "the instrument for appropriate measure." We use this kind of bowl to protect us from being deceived by our eyes. If the food comes to the top of the bowl, we know that it is largely sufficient. We take only that amount of food. If you can eat like that, you can afford to buy less. When you buy less food, you can afford to buy organically grown food. This is something that we can do, alone or in our families. It will be a tremendous support for farmers who want to make a living growing organic food.

The Fifth Mindfulness Training

All of us need a diet based on our willingness to love and to serve. A diet based on our intelligence. The Five Mindfulness Trainings are the way out of suffering, for the world and for each of us as individuals. Looking deeply at the way we consume is the practice of the Fifth Mindfulness Training.

This mindfulness training concerns the practice of mindful consumption, of following a diet that can liberate us and liberate our society. Because we are aware of the suffering caused by unmindful consumption, we make the commitment:

> . . . to cultivate good health, both physical and
> mental, for myself, my family, and my society
> by practicing mindful eating, drinking, and

consuming. I vow to ingest only items that
preserve peace, well-being, and joy in my
body, in my consciousness, and in the collective body and consciousness of my family and
society. I am determined not to use alcohol or
any other intoxicant or to ingest food or other
items that contain toxins, such as certain
TV programs, magazines, books, films, and
conversations. . . ."

If you want to take care of your anger, your frustration, and your despair, you might consider living
according to this mindfulness training. If you drink
alcohol mindfully, you can see that it creates suffering.
The intake of alcohol causes disease to the body and the
mind, and deaths on the road. The making of alcohol
also involves creating suffering. The use of the grains
in its production is linked to the lack of food in the
world. Mindfulness of eating and drinking can bring
us this liberating insight.

Discuss a strategy of mindful consumption with the
people you love, with members of your family, even if
they are still young. Children can understand this, so
they should participate in such discussions. Together
you can make decisions about what to eat, what to
drink, what television programs to watch, what to read,
and what kind of conversations to have. This strategy is
for your own protection.

We cannot speak about anger, and how to handle
our anger, without paying attention to all the things
that we consume, because anger is not separate from
these things. Talk to your community about a strategy

of mindful consuming. In Plum Village, we try our best to protect ourselves. We try not to consume things that nurture our anger, frustration, and fear. To consume more mindfully, we need to regularly discuss what we eat, how we eat, how to buy less, and how to have higher-quality food, both edible and the food we consume through our senses.

What I Would Say to Osama bin Laden:

AN INTERVIEW WITH THICH NHAT HANH

by *Thich Nhat Hanh and Anne A. Simpkinson*

During the war in Vietnam Americans devastated his homeland and caused the deaths of many close friends and fellow Buddhists, but Thich Nhat Hanh retained compassion for people on all sides of the conflict. He urges Americans to use a "drop of compassion" for their supposed enemies to extinguish the fire of hatred on both sides.

If you could speak to Osama bin Laden, what would you say to him? Likewise, if you were to speak to the American people, what would you suggest we do at this point, individually and as a nation?

If I were given the opportunity to be face to face with Osama bin Laden, the first thing I would do is listen. I would try to understand why he had acted in that cruel way. I would try to understand all of the suffering that had led him to violence. It might not be easy to listen in that way, so I would have to remain calm and lucid. I would need several friends with me, who are strong in the practice of deep listening, listening without reacting, without judging and blaming. In this way, an atmosphere of support would be created for this person and those connected so that they could share completely, trust that they are really being heard.

After listening for some time, we might need to take a break to allow what has been said to enter into our consciousness. Only when we felt calm and lucid would we respond. We would respond point by point to what had been said. We would respond gently but firmly in such a way to help them to discover their own misunderstandings so that they will stop violent acts from their own will.

For the American people, I would suggest that we do everything we can to restore our calm and our lucidity before responding to the situation. To respond too quickly before we have much understanding of the situation may be very dangerous. The first thing we can do is to cool the flames of anger and hatred that are so strong in us. As mentioned before, it is crucial to look at the way we feed the hatred and violence within us and to take immediate steps to cut off the nourishment for our hatred and violence.

When we react out of fear and hatred, we do not yet have a deep understanding of the situation. Our action will only be a very quick and superficial way of responding to the situation and not much true benefit and healing will occur. Yet if we wait and follow the process of calming our anger, looking deeply into the situation, and listening with great will to understand the roots of suffering that are the cause of the violent actions, only then will we have sufficient insight to respond in such a way that healing and reconciliation can be realized for everyone involved.

In South Africa, the Truth and Reconciliation Commission has made attempts to realize this. All the parties involved in violence and injustice agreed to listen to each other in a calm and supportive environment, to look together deeply at the roots of violent acts and to find agreeable arrangements to respond to the situations. The presence of strong spiritual leaders is very helpful to support and maintain such an environment. We can look at this model for resolving conflicts that are arising right in the present moment; we do not have to wait many years to realize this.

You personally experienced the devastation caused by the war fought in Vietnam and worked to end the hostilities there. What do you say to people who are grief-stricken and enraged because they have lost loved ones in the terrorist attack?

I did lose my spiritual sons and daughters during the war when they were entering the fighting zone trying to save those under the bombs. Some were killed by war and some by murder due to the misunderstanding that they were supporting the other side. When I looked at the four slain corpses of my spiritual sons murdered in such a violent way, I suffered deeply. I understand the suffering of those who have lost beloved ones in this tragedy. In situations of great loss and grief, I had to find my calm in order to restore my lucidity and my heart of understanding and compassion. With the practice of deep looking, I realized that if we respond to cruelty with cruelty, injustice and suffering will only increase.

When we learned of the bombing of Ben Tre village in Vietnam, where the pilots told the journalists that they had destroyed the village in order to save it, I was shocked, and [racked] with anger and grief. We practiced walking calmly and gently on the earth to bring back our calm mind and peaceful heart.

Although it is very challenging to maintain our openness in that moment, it is crucial that we not respond in any way until we have calmness and clarity with which to see the reality of the situation. We knew that to respond with violence and hatred would only damage ourselves and those around us. We practiced [so that we might] look deeply into the suffering of the people inflicting violence on us, to understand them more deeply and to understand ourselves more deeply. With this understanding we were able to produce compassion and to relieve our own suffering and that of the other side.

What is the "right action" to take with regard to responding to terrorist attacks? Should we seek justice through military action? Through judicial processes? Is military action and/or retaliation justified if it can prevent future innocents from being killed?

All violence is injustice. The fire of hatred and violence cannot be extinguished by adding more hatred and violence to the fire. The only antidote to violence is compassion. And what is compassion made of? It is made of understanding. When there is no understanding, how can we feel compassion, how can we begin to relieve the great suffering that is there? So understanding is the very real foundation upon which we build our compassion.

How do we gain the understanding and insight to guide us through such incredibly challenging

moments that we now face in America? To understand, we must find paths of communication so that
we can listen to those who desperately are calling out
for our understanding—because such an act of violence is a desperate call for attention and for help.

How can we listen in a calm and clear way so that we
don't immediately kill the chance for understanding to
develop? As a nation we need to look into this: how to
create the situations for deep listening to occur so that
our response to the situation may arise out of our calm
and clear mind. Clarity is a great offering that we can
make at this time.

There are people who want one thing only: revenge.
In the Buddhist scriptures, the Buddha said that by
using hatred to answer hatred, there will only be an
escalation of hatred. But if we use compassion to
embrace those who have harmed us, it will greatly dif-
fuse the bomb in our hearts and in theirs.

So how can we bring about a drop of compassion
that can put out the fire of hatred? You know, they do
not sell compassion in the supermarket. If they sold
compassion, we would only need to bring it home and
we could solve the problem of hatred and violence in
the world very easily. But compassion can only be produced in our own heart by our own practice.

America is burning with hatred. That is why we have
to tell our Christian friends, "You are children of
Christ." You have to return to yourselves and look
deeply and find out why this violence happened. Why is
there so much hatred? What lies under all this violence? Why do they hate so much that they would sacrifice their own lives and bring about so much
suffering to other people? Why would these young

people, full of vitality and strength, have chosen to lose their lives, to commit such violence? That is what we have to understand.

We have to find a way to stop violence, of course. If need be, we have to put the men responsible in prison. But the important thing is to look deeply and ask, "Why did that happen? What responsibility do we have in that happening?" Maybe they misunderstood us. But what has made them misunderstand us so much to make them hate so much?

The method of the Buddha is to look deeply to see the source of suffering; the source of the violence. If we have violence within ourselves, any action can make that violence explode. This energy of hatred and violence can be very great and when we see that in the other person then we feel sorry for them. When we feel sorry for them, the drop of compassion is born in our hearts and we feel so much happier and so much more at peace in ourselves. That [empathy] produces the nectar of compassion within ourselves.

If you come to the monastery, it is in order to learn to do that, so that whenever you suffer and feel angry, you know how to look deeply, so that the drop of compassion in your heart can come out of your heart and can put out the fever of anger. Only the drop of compassion can put out the flames of hatred.

We must look deeply and honestly at our present situation. If we are able to see the sources for the suffering within ourselves and within the other person, we can begin to unravel the cycle of hatred and violence. When our house is on fire, we must first put out the fire before investigating its cause. Likewise, if we first extinguish the anger and hatred in our own heart, we will have a chance to deeply investigate the situation with clarity and insight in order to determine all the causes and conditions that have contributed to the hatred and violence we are experiencing within ourselves and within our world.

The "right action" is the action that results in the fires of hatred and violence being extinguished.

Do you believe that evil exists? And, if so, would you consider terrorists as evil persons?

Evil exists. God exists also. Evil and God are two sides of ourselves. God is that great understanding, that great love within us. That is what we call Buddha also, the enlightened mind that is able to see through all ignorance.

What is evil? It is when the face of God, the face of the Buddha within us has become hidden. It is up to us to choose whether the evil side becomes more important, or whether the side of God and the Buddha shines out. Although the side of great ignorance, of evil, may be manifesting so strongly at one time that does not mean that God is not there.

It is said clearly in the Bible, "Forgive them for they know not what they do." This means that an act of evil is an act of great ignorance and misunderstanding. Perhaps many wrong perceptions are behind an act of evil; we have to see that ignorance and misunderstanding is the root of the evil. Every human being contains within him or herself all the elements of great understanding, great compassion, and also ignorance, hatred, and violence.

In your new book Anger, *you give an example of "compassionate listening" as a tool to heal families. Can that tool be used at a national level, and if so, how would that work?*

This past summer a group of Palestinians and Israelis came to Plum Village, the practice center where I live in southern France, to learn and practice the arts of deep listening and loving speech. (Around 1,600 people come to Plum Village each summer from over a dozen countries to listen and to learn how to bring peace and understanding to their daily lives.) The group of Palestinians and Israelis participated in the daily schedule of walking meditation, sitting meditation, and silent meals, and they also received training on how to listen and speak to each other in such a way that more understanding and peace could be possible between them as individuals and as nations.

With the guidance and support of the monks and nuns, they sat down and listened to each other. When one person spoke no one interrupted him or her. Everyone practiced mindfulness of their breathing and listening in such a way that the other person felt heard and understood.

When a person spoke, they refrained from using words of blame, hatred, and condemnation. They spoke in an atmosphere of trust and respect. Out of these dialogues the participating Palestinians and Israelis were very moved to realize that both sides suffer from fear. They appreciated the practice of deep listening and made arrangements to share what they had learned with others upon returning to their home countries.

We recommended that the Palestinians and Israelis

talk about their suffering, fears, and despair in a public forum that all the world could hear. We could all listen without judging, without condemning in order to understand the experience of both sides. This would prepare the ground of understanding for peace talks to occur.

The same situation now exists between the American people and people of Islamic and Arabic nations. There is much misunderstanding and lack of the kind of communication that hinders our ability to resolve our difficulties peacefully.

Compassion is a very large part of Buddhism and Buddhist practice. But at this point in time, compassion towards terrorists seems impossible to muster. Is it realistic to think people can feel true compassion now?

Without understanding, compassion is impossible. When you understand the suffering of others, you do not have to force yourself to feel compassion, the door of your heart will just naturally open. All of the hijackers were so young and yet they sacrificed their lives for what? Why did they do that? What kind of deep suffering is there? It will require deep listening and deep looking to understand that.

To have compassion in this situation is to perform a great act of forgiveness. We can first embrace the suffering, both outside of America and within America. We need to look after the victims here within our country and also to have compassion for the hijackers and their families because they are also victims of ignorance and hatred. In this way we can truly practice non-discrimination. We do not need to wait many years or decades to realize reconciliation and forgiveness. We need a wake up call now in order not to allow hatred to overwhelm our hearts.

Do you believe things happen for a reason? If so, what was the reason for the attacks on the U.S.A.?

The deep reason for our current situation is our patterns of consumption. U.S.A. citizens consume 60% of the world's energy resources yet they account for only 6% of the total world's population. Children in America have witnessed 100,000 acts of violence on television by the time they finish elementary school. Another reason for our current situation is our foreign policy and the lack of deep listening within our relationships. We do not use deep listening to understand the suffering and the real needs of people in other nations.

What do you think would be the most effective spiritual response to this tragedy?

We can begin right now to practice calming our anger, looking deeply at the roots of the hatred and violence in our society and in our world, and listening with compassion in order to hear and understand what we have not yet had the capacity to hear and to understand. When the drop of compassion begins to form in our hearts and minds, we begin to develop concrete responses to our situation. When we have listened and looked deeply, we may begin to develop the energy of brotherhood and sisterhood between all nations, which is the deepest spiritual heritage of all religious and cultural traditions. In this way the peace and understanding within the whole world is increased day by day.

To develop the drop of compassion in our own heart is the only effective spiritual response to hatred and violence. That drop of compassion will be the result of calming our anger, looking deeply at the roots of our violence, deep listening, and understanding the suffering of everyone involved in the acts of hatred and violence.

from Friends on the Path:

LIVING SPIRITUAL COMMUNITIES

by *Thich Nhat Hanh*

"A Sangha is a community of friends practicing the
Dharma together in order to bring about and to maintain awareness," writes Thich Nhat Hanh. He believes
that the Sangha alleviates suffering by providing support and a sense of belonging so that love can take
root and flower, creating the only basis for lasting
world peace.

*P*ersonally, I want the twenty-first century to be
called the "century of love," because we desperately need love, the kind of love that will not
produce suffering. Unless we have enough loving kindness and compassion, we will not be able to survive as a
planet. Our problems in the twenty-first century are
not the same as the problems the Buddha and his friends
and disciples encountered during their lifetimes. Today
meditation has to be practiced collectively—as a family,
a city, a nation, and a community of nations.

There is a Buddha that is supposed to be born to us
named Maitreya or Loving Kindness, the Buddha of

Love—Mr. Love, Ms. Love. A Sangha that practices loving kindness and compassion is the Buddha that we need for the twenty-first century. Each of us is a cell in the body of the Buddha of Love. Each cell has its own role to play, and we cannot afford to miss one of our cells. We have to stay together. We have the power to bring Sanghakaya, the Sangha body, and Maitreya Buddha into existence just by sitting together and practicing deeply.

So the next Buddha may not take the form of an individual. In the twenty-first century the Sangha may be the body of the Buddha. We have the power to bring the next Buddha into existence in this century. If we sit together and practice looking deeply, we can bring the Sanghakaya and the Buddha into existence. All of us have the duty to bring that Buddha into being, not only for our sake, but for the sake of our children and the planet Earth. This is not wishful thinking, this is a real determination.

What Is a Sangha?

A Sangha is a community of friends practicing the Dharma together in order to bring about and to maintain awareness. The essence of a Sangha is awareness, understanding, acceptance, harmony, and love. When you do not see these in a community, it is not a true Sangha, and you should have the courage to say so. But when you find these elements are present in a community, you know that you have the happiness and fortune of being in a real Sangha.

In Matthew 5:13 in the New Testament of the Christian Bible, we find this statement: "Ye are the salt of the earth; but if the salt hath lost its savor, wherewith shall it be salted? It is thenceforth good for nothing but to be cast out and to be trodden underfoot of men." In this passage, Jesus describes his followers as salt. Food needs salt in order to be tasty. Life needs understanding, compassion, and harmony in order to be livable. This is the most important contribution to life that the followers of Jesus can bring to the world. It means that the Kingdom of Heaven has to be realized here, not somewhere else, and that Christians need to practice in a way that they are the salt of life and a true community of Christians.

Salt is also an important image in the Buddhist canon, and this Christian teaching is equivalent to the Buddha's teaching about Sangha. The Buddha said that the water in the four oceans has only one taste, the taste of salt, just as his teaching has only one taste, the taste of liberation. Therefore the elements of Sangha are the taste of life, the taste of liberation, and we have to practice in order to become the salt. When we say, "I take refuge in the Sangha," it is not a statement, it is a practice.

In the Buddhist scriptures it is said that there are four communities: monks, nuns, laymen, and laywomen. But I also include elements that are not human in the Sangha. The trees, water, air, birds, and so on, can all be members of our Sangha. A beautiful walking path may be part of our Sangha. A good cushion can be also. We can make many things into supportive elements of our Sangha. This idea is not entirely new; it can be found throughout the sutras and in the *Abhidharma,* too. A pebble, a leaf, and a dahlia are mentioned in the *Saddharmapundarika Sutra* in this respect. It is said in the *Pure Land Sutra* that if you are

mindful, then when the wind blows through the trees,
you will hear the teaching of the Four Establishments
of Mindfulness, the Eightfold Path, and so on. The
whole cosmos is preaching the Buddhadharma and
practicing the Buddhadharma. If you are attentive, you
will get in touch with that Sangha.

Sangha As Our Roots

I don't think the Buddha wanted us to abandon our
society, our culture, or our roots in order to practice.
The practice of Buddhism should help people go back to
their families. It should help people reenter society in
order to rediscover and accept the good things that are
there in their culture and to rebuild those that are not.

Our modern society creates so many young people
without roots. They are uprooted from their families
and their society; they wander around, not quite
human beings, because they do not have roots. Quite a
number of them come from broken families and feel
rejected by society. They live on the margins, looking
for a home, for something to belong to. They are like
trees without roots. For these people, it's very difficult to practice. A tree without roots cannot absorb
anything; it cannot survive. Even if they practice
intensively for ten years, it's very hard for them to be
transformed if they remain an island, if they cannot
establish a link with other people.

A community of practice, a Sangha, can provide a
second chance to a young person who comes from a
broken family or is alienated from his or her society. If
the community of practice is organized as a family with
a friendly, warm atmosphere, young people can succeed in their practice.

Suffering (*dukkha*) is one of the biggest problems of our times. First we have to recognize this suffering and acknowledge it. Then we need to look deeply into its nature in order to find a way out. If we look into the present situation in ourselves and our society, we can see much suffering. We need to call it by its true names—loneliness, the feeling of being cut off, alienation, division, the disintegration of the family, the disintegration of society. Our civilization, our culture has been characterized by individualism. The individual wants to be free from the society, from the family. The individual does not think he or she needs to take refuge in the family or in the society and thinks that he or she can be happy without a Sangha. That is why we do not have solidity, we do not have harmony, we do not have the communication that we so need.

The practice is, therefore, to grow some roots. The Sangha is not a place to hide in order to avoid your responsibilities. The Sangha is a place to practice for the transformation and the healing of self and society. When you are strong, you can be there in order to help society. If your society is in trouble, if your family is broken, if your church is no longer capable of providing you with spiritual life, then you work to take refuge in the Sangha so that you can restore your strength, your understanding, your compassion, your confidence. And then in turn you can use that strength, understanding, and compassion to rebuild your family and society, to renew your church, to restore communication and harmony. This can only be done as a community—not as an individual, but as a Sangha.

In order for us to develop some roots, we need the kind of environment that can help us become rooted.

A Sangha is not a community of practice in which each
person is an island, unable to communicate with each
other—this is not a true Sangha. No healing or transformation will result from such a Sangha. A true
Sangha should be like a family in which there is a spirit
of brotherhood and sisterhood.

There is a lot of suffering, yes, and we have to
embrace all this suffering. But to get strong, we also
need to touch the positive elements, and when we are
strong, we can embrace the suffering in us and all
around us. If we see a group of people living mindfully,
capable of smiling, of loving, we gain confidence in
our future. When we practice mindful breathing,
smiling, resting, walking, and working, then we
become a positive element in society, and we will
inspire confidence all around us. This is the way to
avoid letting despair overwhelm us. It is also the way to
help the younger generation so they do not lose hope.
It is very important that we live our daily life in such a
way that demonstrates that a future is possible.

We Need a Sangha

In my tradition we learn that as individuals we cannot
do much. That is why taking refuge in the Sangha, taking
refuge in the community, is a very strong and important practice. When I say, "I take refuge in the Sangha,"
it does not mean that I want to express my devotion.
No. It's not a question of devotion; it's a question of
practice. Without being in a Sangha, without being supported by a group of friends who are motivated by the
same ideal and practice, we cannot go far.

If we do not have a supportive Sangha, we may not be
getting the kind of support we need for our practice,

that we need to nourish our bodhicitta (the strong desire to cultivate love and understanding in ourselves). Sometimes we call it "beginner's mind." The mind of a beginner is always very beautiful, very strong. In a good and healthy Sangha, there is encouragement for our beginner's mind, for our bodhicitta. So the Sangha is the soil, and we are the seed. No matter how beautiful, how vigorous our seed is, if the soil does not provide us with vitality, our seed will die.

One of the brothers from Plum Village, Brother Phap Dung, went to Vietnam some years ago with a few members of the Sangha. It was a very important experience for him. He had been in the West since he was a small child. Then when he went to northern Vietnam, he got in touch with some of the most ancient elements in Vietnamese culture and with the mountains and the rivers of northern Vietnam. He wrote to me and said: "Our land of Vietnam is so beautiful, it is as beautiful as a dream. I don't dare take heavy steps on this earth of Vietnam." By this he meant that he had right mindfulness when he walked. His right mindfulness was due to the practice and support he had in the Sangha before he went to Vietnam. That is beginner's mind, the mind you have in the beginning when you undertake the practice. It's very beautiful and very precious, but that beginner's mind can be broken, can be destroyed, can be lost if it is not nourished or supported by a Sangha.

Although he had his little Sangha near him in Vietnam, the environment was very distracting, and he saw that if he stayed too long without the larger Sangha, he would be swept away by that environment, by his forgetfulness—not only his own forgetfulness, but the forgetfulness of everybody around him. This is because right mindfulness for someone who has only just started the practice is still weak, and the forgetfulness of the people around us is very great and capable of dragging us away in the direction of the five cravings. Because most people around us are being drowned in the five cravings, it is this environment that drags us away and stops us from practicing right mindfulness.

To practice right mindfulness we need the right environment, and that environment is our Sangha. Without a Sangha we are very weak. In a society where everyone is rushing, everyone is being carried away by their habit energies, practice is very difficult. That is why the Sangha is our salvation. The Sangha where everyone is practicing mindful walking, mindful speaking, mindful eating seems to be the only chance for us to succeed in ending the vicious cycle.

And what is the Sangha? The Sangha is a community of people who agree with each other that if we do not practice right mindfulness, we will lose all the beautiful things in our soul and all around us. People in the Sangha standing near us, practicing with us, support us so that we are not pulled away from the present moment. Whenever we find ourselves in a difficult situation, two or three friends in the Sangha who are there for us, understanding and helping us, will get us through it. Even in our silent practice we help each other.

In my tradition they say that when a tiger leaves the mountain and goes to the lowland, it will be caught by humans and killed. When a practitioner leaves his or her Sangha, he or she will abandon her practice after a few months. In order to continue our practice of transformation and healing, we need a Sangha. With a Sangha it's much easier to practice, and that is why I always take refuge in my Sangha.

How a Sangha Helps Us

The presence of a Sangha is a wonderful opportunity to allow the collective energy of the Sangha to penetrate into our body and consciousness. We profit a lot from that collective energy. We can entrust ourselves to the Sangha because the Sangha is practicing, and the collective energy of mindfulness is strong. Although we can rely on the energy of mindfulness that is generated by our personal practice, sometimes it is not enough. But if you know how to use that energy of mindfulness in order to receive the collective energy of the Sangha, you will have a powerful source of energy for your transformation and healing.

Your body, your consciousness, and your environment are like a garden. There may be a few trees and bushes that are dying, and you may feel overwhelmed by anguish and suffering at the sight of that. You may be unaware that there are still many trees in your garden that are solid, vigorous, and beautiful. When members of your Sangha come into your garden, they can help you see that you still have a lot of beautiful trees and that you can enjoy the things that have not gone wrong within your landscape. That is the role that the Sangha can play. Many people in the Sangha are capable of enjoying a beautiful sunset or a cup of tea. They dwell firmly in the present moment, not allowing worries or regrets to spoil the present moment. Sitting close to these people, walking close to these people, you can profit from their energy and restore your balance.

When their energy of mindfulness is combined with yours, you will be able to touch beauty and happiness.

Nothing is more important than your peace and happiness in the here and now. One day you will lie like a dead body and no longer be able to touch the beauty of a flower. Make good use of your time; practice touching the positive aspects of life in you and around you.

Don't lock yourself behind your door and fight alone. If you think that by yourself you cannot go back to embrace strong feelings, you can ask one, two, or three friends to sit next to you and to help you with their support. They can give you mindfulness energy so that you can go back home with strength. They can say, "My brother, I know that the pain in you is very deep, and I am here for you."

Taking refuge in the Sangha is a very important practice. Abandoned, alone, you get lost, you get carried away. So taking refuge in the Sangha is a very deep practice, especially for those of us who feel vulnerable, shaky, agitated, and unstable. That is why you come to a practice center, to take refuge in the Sangha. You allow the Sangha to transport you like a boat so that you can cross the ocean of sorrow.

When we throw a rock into a river the rock will sink. But if we have a boat, the boat can carry hundreds of pounds of rocks, and it will not sink. The same thing is true with our sorrow and pain. If we have a boat, we can carry our pain and sorrow, and we will not sink into the river of suffering. And what is that boat? That boat is, first of all, the energy of mindfulness that you generate by your practice. That boat is also the Sangha—the community of practice consisting of brothers and sisters in the Dharma.

We don't have to bring just joy when we come to the Sangha; we can also bring our suffering with us. But we have to walk on the path of joy with our suffering, we have to share joy with our brothers and sisters. Then we will be in touch with the seeds of happiness in ourselves, and the suffering will grow weaker and be transformed. Allow yourself to be supported, to be held by the Sangha. When you allow yourself to be in a Sangha the way a drop of water allows itself to be in a river, the energy of the Sangha can penetrate into you, and transformation and healing will become possible.

Practice Is Easier with a Sangha

The only way to support the Buddha, to support our Sangha, to support the Earth, to support our children and future generations, is to really be here for them. "Darling, I am here for you" is a statement of love. You need to be here. If you are not here, how can you love? That is why the practice of meditation is the practice of being here for the ones we love.

To be present sounds like an easy thing to do. For many of us, it is easy because we have made it a habit. We are in the habit of dwelling in the present moment, of touching the morning sunshine deeply, of drinking our morning tea deeply, of sitting and being present with the person we love. But for some of us it may not be so easy, because we have not cultivated the habit of being in the here and the now. We are always running, and it is hard for us to stop and be here in the present moment, to encounter life. For those of us who have not learned to be present, we need to be supported in that kind of learning. It's not difficult when you are supported by the Sangha. Then you will be able to learn the art of stopping.

The Sangha is a wonderful home. Every time you go back to the Sangha, you feel that you can breathe more easily, you can walk more mindfully, you can better enjoy the blue sky, the white clouds, and the cypress tree in your yard. Why? Because the Sangha members practice going home many times a day—through walking, breathing, cooking, and doing their daily activities mindfully. Everyone in the Sangha is practicing in the same way, walking mindfully, sitting mindfully, eating mindfully, smiling, enjoying each moment of life.

When I practice walking I make mindful and beautiful steps. I do that not only for myself but also for all of my friends who are here; because everyone who sees me taking a step like that has confidence and is reminded to do the same. And when they make a step in the present moment, smiling and making peace with themselves, they inspire all of us. You breathe for me, I walk for you, we do things together, and this is practicing as a Sangha. You don't need to make much effort, and you enjoy doing it a lot. When you have a good Sangha, your practice is easy, because you feel that you are supported by the Sangha.

When we sit together as a Sangha, we enjoy the collective energy of mindfulness, and each of us allows the mindful energy of the Sangha to penetrate us. Even if you don't do anything, if you just stop thinking and allow yourself to absorb the collective energy of the Sangha, it's very healing. Don't struggle, don't try to do something, just allow yourself to be with the Sangha. Allow yourself to rest, and the energy of the Sangha will help you, will carry and support you. The Sangha is there to make the training easy. When we are surrounded by brothers and sisters doing exactly the same thing, it is easy to flow in the stream of the Sangha.

As individuals we have problems, and we also have problems in our families, our societies, and our nations. Meditation in the twenty-first century should become a collective practice; without a Sangha we cannot achieve much. When we begin to focus our attention on the suffering on a larger scale, we begin to connect with and to relate to other people, who are also ourselves, and the little problems that we have within our individual circle will vanish. In this way our loneliness or our feeling of being cut off will no longer be there, and we will be able to do things together.

If we work on our problems alone, it becomes more difficult. When you have a strong emotion come up, you may feel that you cannot stand it. You may have a breakdown or want to die. But if you have someone, a good friend sitting with you, you feel much better. You feel supported, and you have more strength in order to deal with your strong emotion. If you are taking something into your body that is toxic and realize it will make you sick, even with this insight you may not be able to change your habit. But if you are surrounded by people who do not have the same problem, it becomes easier to change. That is why it is very important to practice in the context of a Sangha.

It is fortunate when we have a friend who is strong in the practice, a Dharma brother or sister. Without a

Sangha, without co-practitioners, the practice will be difficult. You can always ask your brothers and sisters to practice looking deeply with you every time you need support. Because you feel supported there, the Sangha is the most appropriate setting and environment for the practice of looking deeply. If you have a Sangha of two, three, maybe even fifty people who are practicing correctly—getting joy, peace, and happiness from the practice—then you are the luckiest person on Earth.

So practice in the setting of the Sangha is much easier. We don't have to practice so intensely. Our practice becomes the practice of "non-practice." That means a lot We don't have to force ourselves to practice. We can give up all the struggle and allow ourselves to be, to rest. For this, however, we need a little bit of training, and the Sangha is there to make the training easy. Being aware that we are in a Sangha where people are happy with being mindful, where people are living deeply the moments of their days, that is enough. I always feel happy in the presence of a happy Sangha. If you put yourself in such an environment, then transformation will happen without much effort. This is my experience.

I Take Refuge in the Sangha

The reason we take refuge in anything is because we need protection. But very often we take refuge in people or things that are not at all solid. We may feel that we are not strong enough to be on our own, so we are tempted to look for someone to take refuge in. We are inclined to think that if we have someone who is strong and can be our refuge, then our life will be easier. We need to be very careful, because if we take refuge in a person who has no stability at all, then the little bit of solidity we have ourselves will be entirely lost. Many people have done that, and they have lost the little solidity and freedom they once had.

When a situation is dangerous, you need to escape, you need to take refuge in a place that is safe, that is solid. Earth is something we can take refuge in because it is solid. We can build houses on earth, but we cannot build on sand. The Sangha is the same. Mindfulness, concentration, and insight have built up Sanghas and individuals that are solid, so when you take refuge in the Sangha, you take refuge in the most solid elements.

When you are angry, if you know how to go back to your mindful breathing and take refuge in your mindfulness, you become strong. You can dwell peacefully in that moment and you are capable of dealing with the situation in a much more lucid way. You know that within you there are the elements of mindfulness, concentration, and insight. Those seeds are always there. If you have a friend, a teacher, a Sangha that can help you to touch those seeds and help them to grow, then you have the best kind of protection.

This is the role Sangha plays in supporting, protecting, and nourishing us. In the Sangha there is stability and joy. The Sangha is devoted to the practice of mindfulness, concentration, and insight, and while everyone in the Sangha profits from his or her own mindfulness, they can also take refuge in the collective energy of mindfulness, concentration, and insight of the Sangha. That is why there is a sense of solidity and security in the Sangha. We are not afraid because the Sangha is there to protect us.

It is like the flocks of wild geese that travel together

from the north to the south in huge numbers. If one bird goes off on its own, it will be easily caught, but if they stay together, they are much safer. Near Plum Village there are hunters who use a bird cry to lure the geese down. If a wild goose leaves the flock and comes down alone, he will easily be shot by the hunters.

It's the same with the Sangha. If we think we can live alone, apart from the Sangha, we don't know our own strength or our own weakness. Thanks to the Sangha we do not enter paths of darkness and suffering. Even when the Sangha doesn't seem to be doing anything at all, it in fact is doing a lot, because in the Sangha there is protection.

Without the Sangha we easily fall into the traps of the five cravings. Once in those traps, we will be burnt by the flames of the afflictions and suffering. Keeping the mindfulness trainings and taking refuge in the Sangha's protection is a very good way to avoid being caught in the traps of the five cravings. We keep the mindfulness trainings so that they protect us. The rest of the Sangha will also be keeping the same mindfulness trainings and helping us.

Some people have told me that they have never felt secure before coming to a retreat. Then after sitting, eating, and walking mindfully with the Sangha, for the first time they get a feeling of security. Even small creatures living nearby feel safer, because we are mindful and do our best not to harm them. That feeling of security can lead to joy. We can practice like this:

> Breathing in, I see that I am part of a Sangha, and I am
> being protected by my Sangha.
> Breathing out, I feel joy.

The Dharma can protect you—Dharma not in the sense of a Dharma talk or a book—but Dharma as the practice embodied by people like yourself. When you practice mindful breathing, mindful walking, mindful listening to the bell, you bring into yourself the elements of peace and stability, and you are protected during that time. You begin to radiate the energy of stability and peace all around you. This will help to protect your children and your loved ones. Although you may not give a Dharma talk with your words, you are giving a Dharma talk with your body, with your in-breath, with your out-breath, with your life. That is the living Dharma. We need that very much, just as we need the living Sangha.

Practicing in the Sangha
If you are a beginner in the practice, you should not worry about what is the correct thing to do. When surrounded by many people, we might be caught by the idea, "I don't know what is the right thing to do." That idea may make us very uncomfortable. We may think, "I feel embarrassed that I'm not doing the right thing. There are people who are bowing, and I am not bowing. People are walking slowly, and I am walking a little bit too fast." So the idea that we may not be doing the right thing can embarrass us.

I would like to tell you what is really the right thing. The right thing is to do whatever you are doing in mindfulness. Mindfulness is keeping one's consciousness alive to the present reality. To bow may not be the right thing to do if you don't bow in mindfulness. If you don't bow but are mindful, not bowing is the right thing. Even if people are walking slowly and you run, you are doing the right thing if you run mindfully. The wrong thing is whatever you do without mindfulness. If we understand this, we will not be embarrassed anymore. Everything we do is right provided we do it in mindfulness. To bow or not to bow, that is not the question. The question is whether to bow in mindfulness or not, or not to bow in mindfulness or not.

If you take a step and you feel peaceful and happy, you know that is the correct practice. You are the only one who knows whether you are doing it correctly or not. No one else can judge. When you practice breathing in and out, if you feel peaceful, if you enjoy your in-breath and out-breath, you know you are doing it correctly. You are the best one to know. Have confidence in yourself. Wherever you find yourself, if you feel you are at ease and peaceful, that you are not under pressure, then you know you are doing it right.

The function of the bell in a Sangha is to bring us back to ourselves. When we hear the bell we come back to ourselves and breathe, and at that point we improve the quality of the Sangha energy. We know that our brother and our sister, wherever they are, will be stopping, breathing, and coming back to themselves. They will be generating the energy of right mindfulness, the Sangha energy. When we look at each other, we feel confident, because everyone is practicing together in the same way and contributing to the quality of the Sangha. So we are friends on the path of practice.

The Sangha is made out of the work of individuals, so we have the duty to help create the energy of the Sangha. Our presence, when it is a mindful presence, contributes to that energy. When we are absent during the activities of the Sangha, we are not contributing to

Sangha energy. If we don't go to a sitting meditation, we are not feeding our Sangha. We are also letting ourselves go hungry, because we are not benefiting from the Sangha. We don't profit from the Sangha, and the Sangha doesn't profit from us.

Don't think that we sit for ourselves. You don't sit for yourself alone, you sit for the whole Sangha—not only the Sangha, but also for the people in your city, because when one person in the city is less angry, is smiling more, the whole city profits. If we practice looking deeply, our understanding of interfacing will grow, and we will see that every smile, every step, every breath is for everybody. It is for our country, for the future, for our ancestors.

The best thing we can do is to transform ourselves into a positive element of the Sangha. If members of the Sangha see us practicing well, they will have confidence and do better. If there are two, three, four, five, six, seven of you like that in the Sangha, I'm sure the Sangha will be a happy Sangha and will be the refuge of many people in the world.

The Sangha Isn't Perfect
Our transformation and healing depend on the quality of the Sangha. If there are enough people smiling and happy in the Sangha, the Sangha has more power to heal and transform. So you have to invest in your Sangha. Every member of the Sangha has his or her weaknesses and strengths, and you have to recognize them in order to make good use of the positive elements for the sake of the whole Sangha. You also have to recognize the negative elements so that you and the whole Sangha can help embrace them. You don't leave

that negative element to the person alone, because he may not be able to hold and transform it by himself.

You don't need a perfect Sangha—a family or a community doesn't have to be perfect in order to be helpful. In fact, the Sangha at the time of the Buddha was not perfect. But it was enough for people to take refuge in, because in the Sangha there were people who had enough compassion, solidity, and insight to embrace others who did not have as much compassion, solidity, and insight. I also have some difficulties with my Sangha, but I'm very happy because everyone tries to practice in my Sangha.

If we lived in a Sangha where everyone was perfect, everyone was a bodhisattva or a Buddha, that would be very difficult for us. Weakness in the other person is very important, and weakness within yourself is also very important. Anger is in us, jealousy is in us, arrogance is in us. These kinds of things are very human. It is thanks to the presence of weakness in you and weakness in a brother or a sister that you learn how to practice. To practice is to have an opportunity to transform. So it is through our shortcomings that we learn to practice.

There are some people who think of leaving the Sangha when they encounter difficulties with other Sangha members. They cannot bear little injustices inflicted on them because their hearts are small. To help your heart grow bigger and bigger, understanding and love are necessary. Your heart can grow as big as the cosmos; the growth of your heart is infinite. If your heart is like a big river, you can receive any amount of dirt. It will not affect you, and you can transform the dirt very easily.

The Buddha used this image. If you put a little dirt in a pitcher of water, then that water has to be thrown away. People cannot drink it. But if you put the same amount of dirt into a huge river, people can continue to drink from the river, because the river is so immense. Overnight that dirt will be transformed within the heart of the river. So if your heart is as big as a river, you can receive any amount of injustice and still live with happiness. You can transform overnight the injustices inflicted on you. If you still suffer, your heart is still not large enough. That is the teaching of forbearance and inclusiveness in Buddhism. You don't practice to suppress your suffering; you practice in order for your heart to expand as big as a river.

One time the Buddha said to his disciples: "There are people among us who do not have the same capacity as we do. They do not have the capacity to act rightly or to speak rightly. But if we look deeply, we see in their hearts that there are good seeds, and therefore we have to treat those people in such a way that those good seeds will not be lost." Among us there are people who we may think do not have the capacity to practice as well as we do. But we should know that those people also have good seeds, and we have to cultivate those good seeds in such a way that these good seeds have a chance to be watered and to sprout.

The Buddha saw all his disciples as his children, and I think of mine in the same way. Any disciple of mine is my child that I have given birth to. In my heart I feel at ease, I feel light and happy, even though that child may still have a problem. You can use that method, too. If there is a person in the Sangha who troubles you, don't give up hope. Remember, "My teacher has given birth to that child. How can I practice in order to see that person as my sister? Then my heart will feel more at ease and I will be able to accept her. That person is still my sister, whether I want her to be or not." That feeling and those words can help dissolve the irritation that you are having with that person.

If we have harmony in the Sangha, we can give confidence to many people. We don't need to be perfect. I myself am not perfect, and you don't need to be perfect either. But if in your own way you can express your harmony in the Sangha, this is your gift.

Man Is Not Our Enemy

by *Thich Nhat Hanh*

Thich Nhat Hanh says the essential tenet of his Buddhist practice is "Interbeing": the state of mutual
dependency between all things. He believes we must
understand Interbeing to overcome suffering and
violence.

I still remember the time when in my work for the
peace movement (around 1963–1973) I was often
accused of not being able to tell friends from enemies. At that time I and my friends based our struggle
for peace on the realisation that *"man is not our enemy"* but
fanaticism, hatred, ambition and violence. Because of
this standpoint we were condemned by both warring
parties. Our greatest crime was that we saw people of
both sides as our brothers whether they were on the
Communist or the anti-Communist side. The collection of poems called *With Joined Palms We Pray for the
White Dove to Appear* published underground in Saigon

in the year 1964 was opposed by both warring parties. It was confiscated by one of them and condemned on the radio by the other.

The Green Sun

I still adhere to my standpoint of those times but now I have gone farther. Before I used to say our enemy is ambition, hatred, discrimination and violence but for the past twenty years or more I have no longer wanted to call these negative mental formations enemies which need to be destroyed. I have seen that they can be transformed into positive energies such as under-standing and love, just like a gardener can transform rubbish into green manure which can be used to grow flowers and vegetables. For the last thirty years I have been practising and teaching Buddhism in the West from this perspective called the insight of Interbeing which is explained in the Avatamsaka Sutra. Interbeing can be translated into French as inter-être and into German as intersein. My friends in the West who have been able to learn and practice according to this insight have been able to transform greatly and have found much happiness.

If you wish to have the insight of Interbeing you only need to look at a basket of fresh green vegetables which you have just picked. Looking deeply you will see the sunshine, clouds, compost, gardener and hundreds of thousands of elements more. Vegetables cannot arise on their own, they can only arise when there is sun, clouds, earth, etc. If you take the sun out of the basket of vegetables the vegetables will no longer be there. If you take the clouds away it is the same.

Let us take another example. Let us look at the only

legal Buddhist organisation in Vietnam which people jokingly call the Government Congregation. If we look at it we shall see the elements which have created it, both positive and negative. Among these elements we see the Unified Buddhist Church of Vietnam represented by monks such as Huyen Quang, Quang Do, Duc Nhuan, Tue Sy, Khong Tanh, etc. Because these monks have struggled keenly, the monks in the Government Congregation such as Thien Sieu, Minh Chau, Tri Tinh, Tri Quang—have been allowed by the government to translate and publish Buddhist works and to organise a Groundwork for Buddhist Studies, etc. The more the monks of the Unified Buddhist Church put up a struggle, are imprisoned, the more space the monks of the Government Congregation have to work. Thus the monks of the Unified Buddhist Church are those who have and who are supporting the Government Congregation in the most positive way. If you say they oppose the Government Congregation you have not yet seen the deep truth from the inside and have not understood Interbeing. The monks Huyen Quang, Quang Do, Duc Nhuan, if they were to look into the Institute of Buddhist Studies, Institute of Buddhist Research, the work of translating the Vietnamese Canon, etc., could smile and say: *"Do not think that this is your work alone. We have been helping you realise these things. We have been working together."* Monks such as Thich Thien Sieu and Minh Chau, when they look into the struggles of the Unified Buddhist Church, could also smile, feel gratitude and say: *"Thanks to your struggles the government has eased up and allowed us to do some work on behalf of the Buddha. We are not so naive as to say: 'What have you managed to achieve in all those years of opposition? Only we who do not oppose the government have been able to do this work.' "* With the Insight of interbeing monks of both congregations could look with love and understanding at each other, without needing to blame anyone, because they are all able to see that the monks of both congregations are the manifestations of bodhisattvas, all of them working for their ideal and for the people and both sides can be happy because neither side feels hatred or discrimination. If we continue to blame each other and be angry with each other we are still the victims of people outside who want to divide. If we have the insight into Interfacing that person will not be able to divide us, bring about the situation of hens in the same coop fighting each other. One side wears the colours of the Unified Buddhist Church and the other side wears the colours of the government. To fight each other because of the colours we are wearing is not intelligent, it is to lack the wisdom of Interfacing. For the last thirty years there has not been a moment when I have not looked at all Buddhist monks as my brothers, whether they are part of the Government Congregation or the Unified Congregation.

The King of the Land of So Loses His Bow

For the last thirty years a number of people in Vietnam and elsewhere continue to blame me for being too close to Christians and Communists. They just want me to be close to Buddhists and anti-communists. I have tried to remind them that my actions are always based on the perception that Man is not our enemy. I want everyone to have the chance to live and the right to live happily. However not everyone has been able to accept this attitude of mine easily. My practice is to be able to embrace both Communists and Christians because I cannot just embrace Buddhists and anti-Communists. Narrowness, fanaticism and prejudice are not just found among Christians and Communists. Among Buddhists there is a fair share of narrowness, fanaticism and prejudice which has brought about no small amount of suffering for families and the individuals who have prejudice or against whom the prejudice is directed. Many, including monks and nuns, who claim to be Buddhists have reached such a level of corruption, cruelty and prejudice that their children or disciples have not been able to bear it, let alone other people. They break the precepts of killing, wrong speech, sexual misconduct, wounding themselves and their society in no small measure. There are Protestants, Catholics and Communists who are far better than these Buddhists, far more wholesome and much closer to the Buddha's teachings. Thus to practise in the spirit of Buddhism I wish to embrace and love everyone without exception, including all those who have made me and my people suffer. To embrace people does not mean to agree with their narrowness, prejudice and fanaticism. When they lack tolerance, compassion and the ability to look deeply human beings become narrow, prejudiced and fanatical. The responsibility of Buddhist practitioners is to help people untie (release) that narrowness, prejudice and fanaticism, to help people become understanding, tolerant and compassionate, and it is not to pick up a gun and destroy them.

In Buddhism we are taught to love according to the principles of loving-kindness, compassion, joy and equanimity. Equanimity means not discriminating against. True love is the love which includes and can embrace all people and all species which are suffering. Whenever we see someone suffering we love that person, we do not have to know whether they are Buddhist, Communist or Christian. Practising in this spirit I have written dialogues with Christians and Communists in words of joy, equanimity and compassion. Books which are aimed at dialoguing with Christians such as *Living Buddha Living Christ* and *Going Home, Jesus and Buddha as Brothers* have been written by me, using the kind of language which Buddhism calls loving speech. They have helped hundreds of thousands of Christians understand Buddhism, to see the true spirit of Christianity and to let go of a narrow and prejudiced attitude. Christians, including priests and nuns, have written letters thanking me deeply. As far as Catholics in Vietnam are concerned I have also used this loving speech. In the book *Lotus in a Sea of Fire* (1966) I said clearly that if our Catholic friends in Vietnam go in a direction of people's Catholicism and are determined to live in harmony with all other segments of the people there is no reason for Vietnam not opening its arms to welcome them into the heart of the nation. I have also used loving speech towards Vietnamese Communists, especially in the book *Dialogue, the Door to Peace* (1967). At that time not many Communists wanted to listen to me but now I think there are many Communists who read my books and hear my message. I know that there are many cadres and security police who have had the opportunity to read my books and hear my cassettes and thanks to that have transformed a great deal of their suffering. Sometimes I have seen the mentality of the cadres and security police, especially the security police in the cultural and religious sectors. From the highest places to the lowest in the government the policy is that Thay Nhat Hanh's books and cassettes should not be published. For that reason whenever my books and cassettes are brought into Saigon or Hanoi they are confiscated, either at the airport or by the post office. I tell my friends over here: *"Do not be upset, because the people who confiscate books and tapes have a chance to listen to and read those books and tapes."* That is thinking in the spirit of the King of the Land of So who lost his bow. But the people of the land got back the bow so nothing was lost.

From time to time the security police go on a raid and confiscate my books and tapes which have been printed and copied underground in every part of the country. The truth is that there are security police who after confiscating or censoring my books and tapes (without returning them to the person who properly has the right to receive them) have sat and read or listened to them all night. They have realised how interesting and beneficial these books and tapes are and have been able to transform much of their suffering through them. Nevertheless, after censoring the books and tapes they do not return them to the people who by right should receive them. Sometimes they do return them, but first of all they erase all the images and sounds on the tape. Before that they have copied the tapes, sending one copy to the Ministry of the Interior and keeping another copy for themselves to listen to from time to time. I understand and love them, because they are afraid of being reprimanded by their superiors and losing their job. There are security police who, when they have read my books or heard my tapes, are asked: *"Why are those books and tapes not allowed to be circulated? Can you see in the books and tapes ways of thought which are harmful for the country, the people or the government?"* They have replied: *"Everything taught by Thay Nhat Hanh in these books and tapes is very interesting, wonderful, in accord with the spiritual path and very beneficial for the spiritual life and the human heart. The reason why we do not allow the books and tapes to be circulated is that we do not know whether behind the teachings and practice of Thay is hidden a political conspiracy or not."* They have spoken out what they really feel—their fear and suspicion. This fear and suspicion is not theirs alone, it is also that of their superiors.

These cadres and security police also from time to time manifest their awakened understanding and compassion. They turn a blind eye to the underground publication of some of my books and tapes. They do this because they know that the books and tapes have a good effect on the people at this point in the life of the country and the people. They know only too well that social evils abound: corruption, drug abuse, prostitution, hatred, children running away, marriages breaking up, divorce, families broken, pornographic films and books. While politicians and educators have almost given up trying to clear away these huge mountains of garbage, the tapes and books of Thay Nhat Hanh which encourage people to practice being awake, reconcile with each other and return to a pure way of life are prohibited and confiscated. The security police are forced to censor and confiscate them but in their heart of hearts they have qualms about it. They do not feel one bit at ease about this policy and that is why they have sometimes turned a blind eye to the underground publication and copying of some cultural and moral works. Monks, nuns and laypeople, whenever they conduct relief operations for the victims of flooding or poverty often slip into the gift packages a chant or short sutra in the belief that this gift will help relieve their material distress only for a couple of weeks but the sutra will relieve their suffering and sorrow for much longer. There are security police who are narrow, prejudiced and determined not to give permission saying that these chants are political handbills. However, there are security police who are happy about, give secret approval to and even like the teachings. We have wholesome roots in our hearts. If we are accepted and dealt with in a wholesome way the seeds of compassion and tolerance in us will be watered. If we are always despised, hated and opposed we shall lose that opportunity. Therefore however severe and unpleasant the security police in the cultural and religious sectors are, the monks, nuns and lay people who know how to practise are still sweet and patient with them. One day or another with this kind of treatment they will also have a chance to transform. A security policeman in Hue was heard to say: *"Thay Nhat Hanh lives far away, I cannot do anything about him. But you are here right in our hands. I can crush you into little pieces whenever I want."* When I heard that I felt much compassion for that security policeman. Someone who just wanted to perform some social service for his fellow countrymen, why should we crush them into small pieces?

A True Change for the Better

My children and brothers, whether you are descendants of Buddha, of Jesus Christ, of Communism or Anti-Communism, you are all children of Vietnam and all my children and brothers. Whenever someone is suffering and needs help I have to come and help

them. It is only in this way that we can love in the spirit
Buddha taught.

All of us have made mistakes—whether we are Buddhist, Catholic, Communist, the Party or the Government. Because we are so sure of our perceptions,
because we are fanatic and prejudiced we could have
wounded painfully our people, but if we can wake up
and know how truly to begin anew we could learn from
the painful lessons of the past. There are security police
and cadres who have made us miserable but with
Buddha's love we continue to want them to have a chance
to change for the better, to make rubbish into compost
and flowers, to produce understanding and love so that
their life will be relieved of suffering and we can have
more space to live in. If we are too trusting in ideologies we can bring about great distress for our people
and our country where millions have already died in
conflict. In the past (in 1964 when the collection of
poems *With Joined Palms We Pray for the White Dove to Appear* was
published) I said: *"Ideologies are the fetters of the results of wrong
action used to bind the body of our people."* Tran Manh Hao puts
it better than I do: *"The paths which are like rods of history which
whip our country."* When we wake up and see our mistakes
the determination to follow the path of love and compassion is always the thing we want most.

Since I have been in exile it has given me great happiness to be able to continue to write books for my
countrymen to read. From 1966, although some of my
books have been published in South Vietnam, it has
had to be under a pen name because I have committed
the crime of calling for peace. From 1975, my books
have only been copied by hand, and then printed and
circulated underground. I myself do not know who has

organised the printing and publishing. Because of my countrymen's need to learn and to practise there are people or groups of people who without regard for their own safety made possible the printing and publishing of those books. The same applies to audio and videocassette tapes. The former Prime Minister Pham Van Dong has read the three volumes of the *History of Vietnamese Buddhism* which I wrote and expressed his admiration of it. In the Ministries of Home and Foreign Affairs many have read my books, especially in the Ministry of Home Affairs. All the Vietnamese ambassadors in the West have also read my books. I am certain that many Communists have read and greatly liked my books. There are elderly Party officers and members who have read books such as *Old Path White Clouds, Going Back Home, Peace is Every Step* . . . . . and liked them so much. They have felt they have rediscovered the clear ideal of their youth. I have the feeling that nearly everyone who was once infatuated by Marxist ideology but no longer has any faith in it are those who are happiest when reading my books. Countless people have taken up following a religion or the Party with all the purity and zeal of youth. However, after thirty years of their religious practice or following the Party they have felt they have lost a great deal because they have suffered from their religion or the Party. Such people can more easily accept the Buddhist practice of loving kindness, compassion, joy and equanimity than anyone else. They are the people who gain most happiness from reading my books and hearing my tapes. They are very silent and very content whenever they meet someone who is truly practising. However, they are also very unhappy when they see monks and nuns who are corrupt going in search of honours or sensual pleasure without knowing they are betraying their ideal of monkhood. Among the young, children and grand-children of the politicians and cadres living in Vietnam or outside of Vietnam, many read my books eagerly. In the Vatican there are many bishops who have read my books. To me it is not important whether people agree or do not agree with what I write. What is important is whether they are ready or not to read what I have written. Some people start reading in order to examine and censor but as they read they enjoy what they are reading because they feel it is benefitting them, making them feel well and light.

The Path of Loving Kindness

Having learnt and practised the teachings of Interbeing I no longer see anyone as my enemy and in my heart is a feeling of lightness and immense space. I do not even feel hatred towards people who have made me or my people suffer because I know how to look at them with the eyes of understanding and love. You may ask: *"Then are you going to give that band of mad, cruel, fanatical thieves and murderers freedom to continue to destroy and make misery without doing anything to stop them?"* No! We have to do everything we can to stop them, we cannot allow them to continue to kill, plunder, oppress and destroy, but our actions will never be motivated by hatred. We have to stop them, not allowing them to cause misery. If necessary we can bind them, put them in prison, but this action has to be directed by our bodhisattva's heart and while we act like this we continue to maintain our loving-kindness, wanting them to be able to have a chance to wake up, and change. Acting from a basis of loving-kindness, compassion, joy and equanimity we automatically choose the path of nonviolence whereon we make an effort to protect the life of all species as much as we possibly can. Obviously we cannot be absolutely non-violent, just as my plate of steamed greens cannot be 100% vegetarian, because when we boil vegetables so many bacteria die. However, going in the direction of non-violence we can spare bloodshed and protect the life of all species to the greatest possible extent.

In a struggle against a foreign invasion, all activities in the fields of information, culture and education aimed at purposefully creating trust, unification of the whole people, carrying out a policy of non-co-operation with the invaders can be directed wholly in the spirit of openness, tolerance and non-violence. If we succeed in these fields the military only need play a very small role. Even if we are forced to use military strength, we can still act in the spirit of non-violence, sparing bloodshed as much as is possible; the bloodshed of our people and of the invaders. So, the military can also practise loving-kindness and compassion as can moral leaders, statesmen and humanists. The great military victory of the Iran era (14th C.) against the invasions of the Mongols was largely possible because of the work of moral leadership, statesmanship and culture of the Tran era. The military factor is not the only factor which leads to success. The movement for democratic rights in the time of Mr. Diem was the same, the army only played a concluding role which, though necessary, was very minor. Whether our country and people, having come out of this difficult period, make progress or not depends on whether or not we know how to practise in order to give up discrimination and hatred. If we call for unification but continue to discriminate against each other, hate and eliminate each other, when can there be true unification? To be able to look well in order to see that the other person is also our brother or sister and not to try and find ways to remove that person from our daily life is the learning and practice we all have to undertake, whether we are Buddhist or not. Some people are amiable, some are difficult and some are very difficult. However if we are a descendant of the Buddha we have to try to love everyone according to the principle "Man is not our enemy." Our enemy is not our enemy or, in other words, the person who hates us is not the person we hate. We do not have enemies. If we can see that and act according to that, when at last we lie down and close our eyes we shall be able to smile.

from No Death, No Fear:

COMFORTING WISDOM FOR LIFE

by *Thich Nhat Hanh*

Thich Nhat Hanh in this passage from his 2002 book argues that concepts such as life and death or being and non-being do not represent reality. He explains that moving beyond these notions frees us from the fear that clouds our existence.

We are afraid of death, we are afraid of separation, and we are afraid of nothingness. In the West, people are very afraid of nothingness. When they hear about emptiness, people are also very afraid, but emptiness just means the extinction of ideas. Emptiness is not the opposite of existence. It is not nothingness or annihilation. The idea of existence has to be removed and so does the idea of nonexistence. Emptiness is a tool to help us.

Reality has nothing to do with existence and nonexistence. When Shakespeare says: "To be, or not to be—that is the question," the Buddha answers: "To be or not to be is not the question." To be and not to be are just two ideas opposing each other. But they are not reality, and they do not describe reality.

Not only does awakened insight remove the notion of permanence, but it also removes the notion of impermanence. The notion of emptiness is the same. Emptiness is an instrument, and if you are caught in the notion of emptiness you are lost. The Buddha said in the Ratnakuta Sutra: "If you are caught by the notion of being and non-being, then the notion of emptiness can help you to get free. But if you are caught by the notion of emptiness, there's no hope." The teaching on emptiness is a tool helping you to get the real insight of emptiness, but if you consider the tool as the insight, you just get caught in an idea.

If you have a notion about nirvana, that notion should be removed. Nirvana is empty of all notions, including the notion of nirvana. If you are caught in the notion of nirvana, you have not touched nirvana yet. This deep insight and discovery of the Buddha took him beyond fear, beyond anxiety and suffering and beyond birth and death.

Burning Our Notions
When you have a match, you have the condition to make a fire. If the flame you make with the match lasts long enough, it will also burn up the match. The match gives rise to the fire, but the fire itself burns up the match; the teaching of impermanence is the same. It helps us to have the awakened understanding of impermanence, and the insight of impermanence is what will burn up our idea of impermanence.

We have to go beyond the idea of permanence, but

we also have to go beyond the idea of impermanence. Then we can be in touch with nirvana. The same is true of no self. No self is the match; it helps to give rise to the fire of the insight of no self. It is the awakened understanding of no self that will burn up the match of no self.

To practice is not to store up a lot of ideas about no self, impermanence, nirvana or anything else; that is just the work of a cassette recorder. To speak about and distribute ideas is not the study or practice of Buddhism. We can go to a university to study Buddhism, but we will learn only theories and ideas. We want to go beyond ideas to have real insight, which will burn up all our ideas and help us to be free.

Where Is Nirvana?

Look at a quarter. One side of it is called heads, the other side is called tails; they cannot exist without each other. The metal from which they are made contains them both. Without the metal the two sides would not exist. The three elements, heads, tails and metal, inter-are. The metal we could describe as something like nirvana, and the heads and tails as something like the manifestation of impermanence and no self. Through the appearance of either the tails or the heads, you can touch and recognize the presence of the metal. Similarly by looking deeply into the nature of impermanence and no self, you can also touch the nature of nirvana.

The ultimate dimension of nirvana cannot be separated from the historical dimension. When you touch deeply the historical dimension, you also touch the ultimate dimension. The ultimate dimension is always in you. For a practitioner it's very important to touch his or her own nature of impermanence and non-self. If he is successful he will touch the nature of nirvana and attain non-fear. Now he can ride on the waves of birth and death, smiling serenely.

The Historical and Ultimate Dimensions

We look upon reality in our daily lives through the historical dimension, but we can also look upon the same reality in the ultimate dimension. Reality can be manifested in the historical dimension, or it can be manifested in the ultimate dimension. We are similar. We have our daily and historical concerns, but each of us also has our ultimate concerns.

When we look for God or nirvana or the deepest kind of peace, we are concerned about the ultimate. We are not only concerned with the facts of daily life—fame, profit, or our position in society and our projects—but we are also concerned about our true nature. To meditate deeply is to begin to fulfill our ultimate concern.

Waves Are Water

When you look at the surface of the ocean, you can see waves coming up and going down. You can describe these waves in terms of high or low, big or small, more vigorous or less vigorous, more beautiful or less beautiful. You can describe a wave in terms of beginning and end, birth and death. That can be compared to the historical dimension. In the historical dimension, we are concerned with birth and death, more powerful, less powerful, more beautiful, less beautiful, beginning and end and so on.

Looking deeply, we can also see that the waves are at the same time water. A wave may like to seek its own true nature. The wave might suffer from fear, from complexes. A wave may say, "I am not as big as the other waves," "I am oppressed," "I am not as beautiful as the other waves," "I have been born and I have to die." The wave may suffer from these things, these ideas. But if the wave bends down and touches her true nature she will realize that she is water. Then her fear and complexes will disappear.

Water is free from the birth and death of a wave. Water is free from high and low, more beautiful and less beautiful. You can talk in terms of more beautiful or less beautiful, high or low, only in terms of waves. As far as water is concerned, all these concepts are invalid.

Our true nature is the nature of no birth and no death. We do not have to go anywhere in order to touch our true nature. The wave does not have to look for water because she is water. We do not have to look for God, we do not have to look for our ultimate dimension or nirvana, because we are nirvana, we are God.

You are what you are looking for. You are already what you want to become. You can say to the wave, "My dearest wave, you are water. You don't have to go and seek water. Your nature is the nature of nondiscrimination, of no birth, of no death, of no being and of no non-being."

Practice like a wave. Take the time to look deeply into yourself and recognize that your nature is the nature of no-birth and no-death. You can break through to freedom and fearlessness this way. This method of practice will help us to live without fear, and it will help us to die peacefully without regret.

If you carry within yourself deep grief, if you have lost a loved one, if you are inhabited by fear of death, oblivion and annihilation, please take up this teaching and begin to practice it. If you practice well, you will be capable of looking at the cloud, the rose, the pebble or your child with the kind of eyes the Buddha has transmitted to us. You will touch the no-birth, no-death, no-coming, no-going nature of reality. This can liberate you from your fear, from your anxiety and your sorrow. Then you can truly have the kind of peace that will make you strong and stable, smiling as events happen. Living this way will allow you to help many people around you.

Where Were You Before You Were Born?
Sometimes people ask you: "When is your birthday?" But you might ask yourself a more interesting question: "Before that day which is called my birthday, where was I?"

Ask a cloud: "What is your date of birth? Before you were born, where were you?"

If you ask the cloud, "How old are you? Can you give me your date of birth?" you can listen deeply and you may hear a reply. You can imagine the cloud being born. Before being born it was the water on the ocean's surface. Or it was in the river and then it became vapor. It was also the sun because the sun makes the vapor. The wind is there too, helping the water to become a cloud. The cloud does not come from nothing; there has been only a change in form. It is not a birth of something out of nothing.

Sooner or later the cloud will change into rain or snow or ice. If you look deeply into the rain, you can see the cloud. The cloud is not lost; it is transformed into rain, and the rain is transformed into grass and the grass into cows and then to milk and then into the ice cream you eat. Today if you eat an ice cream, give yourself time to look at the ice cream and say: "Hello, cloud! I recognize you." By doing that, you have insight and understanding into the real nature of the ice cream and the cloud. You can also see the ocean, the river, the heat, the sun, the grass and the cow in the ice cream.

Looking deeply, you do not see a real date of birth and you do not see a real date of death for the cloud. All that happens is that the cloud transforms into rain or snow. There is no real death because there is always a continuation. A cloud continues the ocean, the river and the heat of the sun, and the rain continues the cloud.

Before it was born, the cloud was already there, so today, when you drink a glass of milk or a cup of tea or eat an ice cream, please follow your breathing. Look into the tea or the ice cream and say hello to the cloud.

The Buddha took the time to look deeply and so can we. The Buddha was not a God; he was a human being like us. He suffered, but he practiced, and that is why he overcame his suffering. He had deep understanding, wisdom and compassion. That is why we say he is our teacher and our brother.

If we are afraid of death it is because we have not understood that things do not really die. People say that the Buddha is dead, but it is not true. The Buddha is still alive. If we look around us we can see the Buddha in many forms. The Buddha is in you because you have been able to look deeply and see that things are not really born and that they do not die. We can say that you are a new form of the Buddha, a continuation of the Buddha. Do not underestimate yourself. Look around you a little bit and you will see continuations of the Buddha everywhere.

Am I Yesterday's Me?

I have a photograph of myself when I was a boy of sixteen. Is it a photograph of me? I am not really sure. Who is this boy in the photograph? Is it the same person as me or is it another person? Look deeply before you reply.

There are many people who say that the boy in the photograph and I are the same. If that boy is the same as I am, why does he look so different? Is that boy still alive or has he died? He is not the same as I am and he is also not different. Some people look at that photograph and think the young boy there is no longer around.

A person is made of body, feelings, perceptions, mental formations and consciousness, and all of these have changed in me since that photograph was taken. The body of the boy in the photograph is not the same as my body, now that I am in my seventies. The feelings are different, and the perceptions are very different. It is just as if I am a completely different person from that boy, but if the boy in the photograph did not exist, then I would not exist either.

I am a continuation like the rain is the continuation of the cloud. When you look deeply into the photograph, you can see me already as an old man. You do not have to wait fifty-five years. When the lemon tree is in flower, you may not see any fruit, but if you look deeply you can see that the fruit is already there. You just need one more condition to bring forth the lemons: time. Lemons are already there in the lemon tree. Look at the tree and you only see branches, leaves and flowers. But if the lemon tree has time it will express itself in lemons.

Sunflowers in April

If you come to France in April, you will not see any sunflowers. But in July the area around Plum Village has so many sunflowers. Where are the sunflowers in April? If you come to Plum Village in April and look deeply, you will see sunflowers. The farmers have ploughed the land and sown the seed, and the flowers are just waiting for one more condition to show themselves. They are waiting for the warmth of May and June. The sunflowers are there, but they have not fully manifested.

Look deeply at a box of matches. Do you see a flame in it? If you do, you are already enlightened. When we look deeply at a box of matches, we see that the flame is there. It needs only the movement of someone's fingers to manifest. We say: "Dear flame, I know you are there. Now I shall help you express yourself."

The flame has always been in the box of matches and also in the air. If there were no oxygen, the flame could not express itself. If you lit a candle and then covered the flame with something, the flame would go out for lack of oxygen. The survival of the flame depends on oxygen. We cannot say that the flame is inside the box of matches or that the flame is outside the box of matches. The flame is everywhere in space, time and consciousness. The flame is everywhere, waiting to manifest itself, and we are one of the conditions that will help the flame to manifest. However, if we blow on the flame we shall help the flame stop showing itself. Our breath, when we blow on the flame, is a condition that stops the manifestation of the flame in its flame form.

We can light two candles from the match and then blow out the flame on the match. Do you think the flame from the match has died? The flame is not of the nature to be born or to die. The question is, is the flame on the two candles the same flame or two different flames? It is not the same and it is not different. Now another question: is the flame of the match dead? It is both dead and not dead. Its nature is not to die and not to be born. If we leave the candle burning for an hour, will the flame remain the same or become another flame? The wick, the wax and the oxygen are always changing. The part of the wick and the wax that is burning is always transforming. If these things transform, the flame must change too. So the flame is not the same, but it also is not different.

Being Is Not the Opposite of Annihilation
We have an idea of being that it is the opposite of not being. These ideas are no more solid than ideas of right and left. Look at a pen. Can we remove totally its right-hand side? If we use a knife and cut away half of the pen, the part that remains still has a right-hand side. Political parties of the right and the left are immortal—they cannot be removed. As long as there is a right wing, there will be a left wing.

Therefore those on the left of the political spectrum should desire the eternal presence of those on the right. If we remove the right, we have to remove the left at the same time. The Buddha said: "This is because

that is. This manifests because that has manifested."
This is the Buddha's teaching concerning the creation
of the world. It is called the teaching on co-arising.
The flame is there because the matches are there. If the
matches were not there, the flame would not be there.

The Answer Lies Within

Where does the flame come from? What is its origin?
We should look deeply into this question. Do you need
to sit in the lotus position to find the answer? I am sure
that the answer is already in you. It is just waiting for
one more condition to manifest itself. The Buddha
said that everyone has Buddha nature in them. Buddha
nature is the ability to understand and touch our real
nature. The answer is already in you. A teacher cannot
give you the answer. A teacher can help you be in touch
with the awakened nature, the great understanding and
compassion in you. The Buddha invites you to be in
touch with the wisdom that is already in you.

Many of us ask: "Where do you go when you die?
What happens when you die?" We have friends who
have lost someone they love and they ask: "Where is my
beloved one now? Where has she gone now?" Philosophers ask: "Where does man come from? Where does
the cosmos or the world come from?"

When we look deeply, we see that when all the conditions are sufficient something will manifest. What
manifests does not come from anywhere. And when a
manifestation ceases, it does not go anywhere.

Creation

"To create" seems to mean that from nothing you suddenly have something. I prefer the use of the expression

"manifestation" to the word "creation." Look deeply, and you can understand creation in terms of manifestation. Just as we can understand a cloud as a manifestation of something that has always been there, and rain as the end of the cloud manifestation, we can understand human beings, and even everything around us, as a manifestation that has come from somewhere and will go nowhere. Manifestation is not the opposite of destruction. It simply changes form. Understanding our lives and the cosmos as a manifestation can bring us tremendous peace. If you are grieving over the loss of a loved one, this is an invitation to look deeply and to heal your pain.

There are theologians who have said that God is the ground of being, but what being? It is not the being that is opposed to non-being. If it is the notion of being as opposed to non-being, then that is not God. God transcends all notions, including the notions of creation and destruction. If you look deeply at the notion of creation with the insight of manifestation in mind, you will discover the depth of the teaching on creation. You will discover that nothing is born and nothing dies. There is only manifestation.

Finding Relief

We come to spiritual practice, to a church, a synagogue, a mosque or a meditation center, to find relief from pain and sorrow. But the greatest relief can only be obtained when we are capable of touching the ultimate dimension. In Judaism and in Christianity you may call that dimension God. God is our true nature, the true nature of no birth, no death. That is why if you know how to trust God, to trust your true nature, you will lose your fear and sorrow.

In the beginning you might think of God as a person, but a person is the opposite of a non-person. If you think of God in terms of notions and concepts, you have not yet discovered the reality of God. God transcends all our notions. God is neither a person nor a non-person. A wave in her ignorance is subject to the fear of birth, death, high, low, more or less beautiful, and the jealousy of others. But if a wave is able to touch her true nature, the nature of water, and know that she is water, then all her fear and jealousy will vanish. Water doesn't undergo birth and death, high and low.

Causes

When we look at things like a flower, a table or a house, we think that a house has to be made by someone and a table has to be made by someone in order to be there. Our tendency is to look for a cause that has given birth to the house, a cause that has given birth to the table. We come to the conclusion that the cause of the house must be the house builder: the mason or the carpenter. What is the cause of the table? Who created the table? A carpenter. Who is the creator of the flower? Is it the earth or the farmer or the gardener?

In our minds we think very simply in terms of cause. We think that one cause is enough to bring about what is there. With the practice of looking deeply we find out that one cause can never be enough in order to bring about an effect. The carpenter is not the only cause of the table. If the carpenter does not have things

like nails, saw, wood, time and space, food to eat, a
ther and mother who brought him to life and a multitude of conditions, he would not be able to bring the
table into being. The causes are actually infinite.

When we look at the flower we see the same thing.
The gardener is only one of the causes. There must be
the soil, the sunshine, the cloud, the compost, the seed
and many, many other things. If you look deeply, you
will see that the whole cosmos has come together in
order to help the flower to manifest. If you look deeply
into a piece of carrot that you eat at lunch, you will see
that the whole cosmos has come together in order to
help manifest that piece of carrot.

If we continue to look deeply, we see that a cause is at
the same time an effect. The gardener is one of the
causes that has helped to manifest the flower, but the
gardener is also an effect. The gardener has manifested
because of other causes: ancestors, father, mother,
teacher, job, society, food, medicine and shelter. Like
the carpenter, he is not only a cause, he is also an effect.

Looking deeply, we find that every cause is at the
same time an effect. There cannot be something that
we can call "pure cause." There are many things we can
discover with the practice of looking deeply, and if we
are not bound to any dogma or concept we will be free
to make our discoveries.

No Pure Cause

When the Buddha was asked, "What is the cause of everything?" he answered with very simple words. He said,
"This is, because that is." It means that everything relies
on everything else in order to manifest. A flower has to
rely on non-flower elements in order to manifest. If

you look deeply into the flower, you can recognize non-flower elements. Looking into the flower, you recognize the element sunshine; that is a non-flower element. Without sunshine, a flower cannot manifest. Looking at the flower, you recognize the element cloud; that is a non-flower element. Without clouds, the flower cannot manifest. Other elements are essential, such as minerals, soil, the farmer and so on; a multitude of non-flower elements has come together in order to help the flower manifest.

This is why I prefer the expression "manifestation" to the word "creation." This does not mean that we should not use the word "creation." Of course we can do so, but we should understand that creation does not mean making something out of nothing. Creation is not something that is destroyed and can become nothing. I very much like the term "Wonderful Becoming." It is close to the true meaning of creation.

Acknowledgments

Many people made this anthology.

At Marlowe & Company and Avalon Publishing Group:
Thanks to Will Balliett, Linda Kosarin, Matthew Lore, Shona McCarthy,
Sue McCloskey, Dan O'Connor, Neil Ortenberg, Paul Paddock, Susan
Reich, David Reidy, Simon Sullivan and Mike Walters for their support,
dedication and hard work.

At The Writing Company:
Nat May worked hard to secure the necessary permissions.

At the Portland Public Library in Portland, Maine:
Thanks to the librarians for their assistance in finding and borrowing
books and other publications from around the country.

Thanks to Maria Fernandez for overseeing production with graceful
efficiency.

Finally, I am grateful to Thich Nhat Hanh and the other writers whose
work appears in this book.

326

We gratefully acknowledge everyone who gave permission for written material to appear in this book. We have made every effort to trace and contact copyright holders. If an error or omission is brought to our notice we will be pleased to correct the situation in future editions of this book. For further information, please contact the publisher.

Bibliography

The selections used in this anthology were taken from the editions listed below. In some cases, other editions may be easier to find. Hard-to-find or out-of-print titles often are available through inter-library loan services or through Internet booksellers.

"Interbeing: An Interview with Thich Nhat Hanh." Originally appeared in *Tricycle: The Buddhist Review*, Summer 1995.

Carolan, Trevor. "Mindfulness Bell: A Profile of Thich Nhat Hanh." Originally appeared in *Shambhala Sun*, January 1996.

hooks, bell. "On Building a Community of Love." Originally appeared in *Shambhala Sun*, January 2000.

Nhat Hanh, Thich, and Daniel Berrigan. *The Raft Is Not the Shore: Conversations Toward a Buddhist Christian Awareness*. Boston: Beacon Press, 1975. (For "Religion in the World" and "Self-Immolation.")

Nhat Hanh, Thich, and Anne. E. Simpkinson. "What I Would Say to Osama bin Laden." http://www.beliefnet.com/story/88/story_8872.html.

Nhat Hanh, Thich. "Man Is Not Our Enemy." http://www.plumvillage. org/vietnam/man_is_not_our_enemy.htm.

Nhat Hanh, Thich. *Anger: Wisdom for Cooling the Flames*. New York: Riverhead Books, 2001.

Nhat Hanh, Thich. *Be Free Where You Are*. Berkeley, CA: Parallax Press, 2002.

Nhat Hanh, Thich. *Being Peace*. Berkeley, CA: Parallax Press, 1987.

Nhat Hanh, Thich. *Call Me By My True Names: The Collected Poems of Thich Nhat Hanh*. Berkeley, CA: Parallax Press, 1993.

Nhat Hanh, Thich. *For a Future to Be Possible: Commentaries on the Five Wonderful Precepts*. Berkeley, CA: Parallax Press, 1993.

Nhat Hanh, Thich. *Fragrant Palm Leaves: Journals 1962-1966*. Berkeley, CA: Parallax Press, 1998.

Nhat Hanh, Thich. *Friends on the Path: Living Spiritual Communities*. Berkeley, CA: Parallax Press, 2002.

Nhat Hanh, Thich. *Living Buddha, Living Christ*. New York: Riverhead Books, 1995.

Nhat Hanh, Thich. *Love in Action*. Berkeley, CA: Parallax Press, 1993. (For "To Veterans.")

Nhat Hanh, Thich. *The Miracle of Mindfulness: An Introduction to the Practice of Meditation*. Boston: Beacon Press, 1987.

Nhat Hanh, Thich. *No Death, No Fear: Comforting Wisdom for Life*. New York: Riverhead Books, 2002.

Nhat Hanh, Thich. *Present Moment Wonderful Moment*. Berkeley, CA: Parallax Press, 1990.

Nhat Hanh, Thich. *A Rose for Your Pocket*. Berkeley, CA: Parallax Press, 1987.

Nhat Hanh, Thich. *Touching Peace: Practicing the Art of Mindful Living*. Berkeley, CA: Parallax Press, 1992.

About the Editor

JENNIFER SCHWAMM WILLIS HAS PRACTICED YOGA AND MEDITATION
FOR MANY YEARS. SHE IS THE EDITOR OF SEVERAL ANTHOLOGIES
INCLUDING *WHY WE STAY TOGETHER: 20 WRITERS ON MARRIAGE
AND ITS REWARDS* AND *THE JOY OF YOGA*. SHE LIVES IN MAINE WITH
HER HUSBAND AND TWO SONS.

CPSIA information can be obtained at www.ICGtesting.com
Printed in the USA
LVOW11s1845041115

461096LV00004B/300/P